LUCKY FROM VIRGIN

LUCKY FROM VIRGIN
An Unlikely Story

Lucky Severson
October 2017

ISBN10: 1718869487
Library of Congress Control Number: 978198399997

To the fabulous
Michael "S."

For Queenie and Dad

Thanks

To Rini Cobbey for editing the manuscript. To Barbara 'Sam'McDuffie and Steve Davis for badgering me into writing it. To my buddy Michael Graham for helping me through the publishing process and to Lenny Brinkerhoff for historical information on Virgin. To my daughter Brandi for old photos, and to Roy Gibson my first journalism professor for starting me off on a fine adventure.

Colleague Comments

"Lucky Severson is a gifted, talented, scrupulous journalist and writer who for twenty years reported numerous excellent stories for PBS's Religion and Ethics NewsWeekly. His pieces were wide-ranging and received many awards. They included profiles of a former Hollywood executive now a Good Samaritan operating orphanages in the third world to a charismatic tattooed Lutheran pastor and author in Denver, Colorado as well as so many segments on criminal justice issues that he may have spent more time in prisons than many of the inmates he interviewed. He could always be depended on to deliver a wise, thoughtful, fair and very well written and delivered segment that enriched the program."
Arnie Labaton
Executive Producer, PBS's Religion & Ethics Newsweekly

"Lucky is a natural communicator, a consummate storyteller and one of the best listeners I've ever met. His inexhaustible curiosity about the world's characters and cultures is infectious and makes him a one of a kind journalist."
Jeanie Vink
Senior Executive Producer, Discovery

"Lucky Severson is one of the best. A television feature correspondent who excels in what is a surprisingly difficult art form to master. Putting together a long-form story or mini-documentary has been compared to assembling a jigsaw puzzle in in which some pieces will be mismatched, some blank and some will require a hammer to fit. All this while striving to create a seamless final picture that tells a compelling story and does justice to the original subject. I was most fortunate to work on many adventures with

Lucky for over 30 years, traveling through all fifty states, the Mid-East, Asia, even (once) to the North Pole!"
Ned Judge
Emmy-Award winning producer/director

"Lucky Severson has long been a master storyteller but in Lucky from Virgin, An Unlikely Story he outdoes even himself. From his bittersweet, sometimes hilarious Mormon adventures, to his exotic far-flung travels, to his trenchant behind-the-scenes look at television network news when it really mattered, the pages of this book literally crackle with humor and astute insights. In Lucky from Virgin you never quite know what's coming next so strap yourself in for one rollicking ride; tour guides don't get any better than Severson."
Bob Faw
Former CBS & NBC correspondent

"Lucky Severson has a passion for journalism and thoughtful reporting. He started one of the best local magazine shows in the history of television: KUTV's EXTRA. He hired me, and we've been in touch on stories ever since. I've fought with Lucky; I've had drinks with Lucky. What I always enjoyed in any discussion with Lucky Severson is thoughtful, insightful, meaningful conversation. Lucky does what all journalists should do: he produces stories that matter instead of blather that doesn't. This is a man who's reported on stories around the world and has demonstrated a lifetime of journalistic excellence in every reporting job he's ever had."
Karl Idsvoog
Associate Professor
School of Journalism & Mass Communication
Kent State University

"Oh the places you'll go and the people you'll meet if you read Lucky Severson's new book. I was lucky enough to work with my

wise funny friend at NBC News in the most exotic little corners of America you'll ever find. From Tonopah, Nevada on the edge of Area 51 where even the school children guard our military's top secrets, to the fishermen of Everglades City, Florida who became drug-running millionaires when the feds took their legal livelihoods away. We ate middle-eastern food in Dearborn, Michigan as the bombs started falling on Baghdad in the first Gulf War. If you want to savor some of America's most colorful places without spending years on the road do yourself a favor and read this book."
Michele Dumont
Former producer, NBC & CBS News

"So, you are stuck next to someone on an eleven-hour international flight. Pray to God it is Lucky. He is polite and speaks quietly. You listen and say, "and then what happened?" And you really want to know! He has been everywhere and done things you won't believe. He is a raconteur, a conversationalist in the best sense. He knows how to tell a great story and so he does."
Trent Harris
Film director

CONTENTS

ISSUES THAT DRIVE ME CRAZY

STORYTELLING

SCRIPTS

INTRODUCTION

I am Lucky, although I didn't think so when I was growing up in the tiny Mormon town of Virgin. I never dreamed I would travel the globe, interviewing extraordinary people in places far away. Back then I wasn't much of a dreamer. This book is about my improbable journey from Virgin, where I was a misfit, to a 47-year career in journalism as a correspondent for NBC News, the Discovery Channel and PBS doing stories I never could have imagined.

I've been to the inner cities, the housing projects, to prisons and holy places. I've interviewed serial killers, heads of state, heads of churches and mono-maniacs.

I've met church people who inspired me and some who should go to hell. I've met preachers who care almost as much about saving the environment as saving souls. I've met God-fearing people who seem more afraid of the NRA. I've met some black-hearted people but have found far more good in humankind than bad.

There are almost always parts left out of stories for one reason or another. I remember standing on the North Pole watching people— who spent a small fortune to get there—watching my camera crew at work as much as the unworldly world that surrounded them. I snorted Kava with the prime minister of Vanuatu. My producer did, too, and almost drove us into a tree. She later became the Pentagon spokesperson. Those things never made it in my stories.

As a journalist I'm not supposed to have my own views, but of course I do. We all do. This book gives me the opportunity to put them out there. I'm uneasy about it. It's much safer to tell other people's stories than get too deep into mine, but here goes.

Lucky is my real name. My dad was a serious gambler and I know my name was his idea. I wasn't as certain where Virgin got its name. Maybe the town was full of virgins, I never knew.

I adored my mom and idolized my dad but my relationship with Virgin was troubled. It still is. Virgin was not Norman Rockwell's America. It wasn't friendly or nurturing. I felt I was in the wrong place, the wrong skin, that I was becoming them and not me.

I grew up looking over my shoulder, always self-conscious, which is not a desirable condition if you're a television reporter. It's a reason, I think, why I've never overcome stage fright.

I've always liked people. It's almost impossible to shut me up in an elevator. Of course we had no elevators in Virgin. My first experience at talking with people from the outside was when I dispensed gas at my dad's two-pump station near the entrance of Zion National Park. Tourists wanted to know the "real" name of the town and where I got my "Southern" accent. It's actually just a lazy way of speaking I got from my mom's side.

The most important characteristic I acquired from my parents was to relate to the underdog and I got that from my mom in particular. She was a fierce protector of those who couldn't defend or care for themselves. We had several such people in Virgin and God help anyone who treated them badly. I think her fierce defense of the downtrodden influenced my outlook more than any other thing.

It's why I spent so much time in hard scrabble places, in prisons from Folsom to Sing Sing to Angola with many in between. You would be hard pressed to find a correspondent who has done more stories about race and, after 9/11, bigotry. I've done my share of features, but they're not my favorite.

I like stories with a beginning, middle, and end, where the good guys are not as good as I thought going in and the bad ones not as bad. I like stories with nuances. I like to let them unravel as they did in real life. I've learned from almost every story I've ever done.

I grew up a Mormon even though my dad was not one and my mom rarely attended church. My mom saw to it that I took piano lessons from when I was four, so I became the pianist in our one-room church. Even though Virgin was ninety-nine percent Mormon, it wasn't a very religious town.

Most of the menfolk drank alcohol (at my dad and mom's bar), which is frowned on by the Church. My uncle was reportedly inebriated when the brethren dropped by to ask him to become bishop.

When I was 18, I lost my driver's license for drunken driving and entered the Salt Lake City mission home drunk after I requested a mission assignment to a foreign country where they drove on the right side of the road. By the time I arrived in New Zealand, I had earned a reputation as a troublemaker. The mission president assigned me a companion who had a reputation as the strictest missionary in the field.

For two years I took being a missionary very seriously, and ended up baptizing more converts than any other missionary in New Zealand. I've lost sleep wondering whether what I did was a good thing or a bad thing. I do know that the experience of knocking on doors and greeting people who wanted nothing to do with me gave me a leg up in my career.

When I returned home I alienated church elders when I suggested it was a mistake to teach kids to say they knew the Church was true without giving them a chance to find out what they actually knew. My speech was not well-received. It was my first break with the brethren but I would have left the Church anyway.

I could never accept that there is only one true church and that I was one of the chosen. I've always felt that too many members put their politics over their religion. I'm sure some of my missionary companions are convinced I'll go to hell.

I started out by flunking out of BYU. Then I got married and blew through three jobs in three years. One job where I was in charge of keeping track of train shipments, I lost a whole train. Another one, when I called to quit, my boss refused to listen. He said he wanted the pleasure of firing me. After I drowned my ulcer in half-gallons of wine I finally sobered up and decided I had to have a job where I was beholden to no one but myself. I was going to be a TV journalist.

When I knocked on the doors of Salt Lake's television stations, only one news director agreed to talk to me. He let me hang around for a few weeks and when one reporter left town on a family emergency, I got his job. It turned out I was pretty good at it. I had a natural skepticism of the establishment and of all things sacred. Issues like African Americans being denied the Mormon priesthood, or the second class status of women, and the Church's views toward gay people.

I also ended up defending some (not all) who practiced polygamy in the shadows. Salt Lake City had more than its share of sacred cows.

I hosted and produced an excellent news magazine show called *Extra* where nothing was sacred. By the time NBC offered me a job I had a bachelor's degree in journalism from the University of Utah and a master's in law from Yale.

NBC News was very good to me, assigning me several primetime hour specials as well as the campaigns of Vice President Bush and Jesse Jackson. I was even allowed to host a program for the Discovery Channel called *Invention.* For two years I traveled around the country doing stories for the *Today* show in an old green pickup that I grew to hate. Then I became NBC's man in Asia, where I did lots of stories about the coming-out of China and the bizarre culture of North Korea.

But Asia was a career ender. I was hired without the executive producer's involvement and we ended up bitter enemies. General Electric had just purchased NBC and the bottom line became the deciding factor on what stories we covered, or often didn't. I got no satisfaction out of a-minute-thirty spots and wasn't very good at it.

The acting news president met with me and said my days were numbered if I didn't join the team and get with the program. Of course all that was moot when I was arrested for possession of marijuana back in Utah. I knew my career was over when I couldn't find my name on the NBC's employee roster the very next day. I was never there.

Within a couple of weeks I was working again, for a PBS program called *Religion and Ethics Newsweekly*. Who would have thought? I had worked at NBC for the new program's executive producer, Gerry Solomon, and he apparently wasn't ready to throw me overboard because of my "dope problem." I loved working for *R & E*. I met inspiring religious and social justice leaders like the Aga Khan, who heads about 15 million Muslim Ismalis. I spent time with the Dalai Lama at his home in India. He would argue that he is not a religious leader.

One of the biggest men I ever interviewed in stature and persona was Terry Waite, the hostage negotiator who was himself held hostage under extreme conditions for five years.

Then there were the pastors you never hear about who hold families and communities together and those who drive them apart. Some of the most inspirational individuals I ever met were pastors; so were some of the biggest crooks. Before the show went off air I did more than 300 stories for *R & E* and will always be grateful for the ride.

I know my views of issues and life have been shaped by my travels and the people I've met. The best part of writing this book is recalling things and folks that had become lost in the caverns of my mind. It's been a hoot, but it's much more fun to write about others.

I've had far more experiences and adventures than I could put in a single book. More fun than I deserve. I've met extraordinary people, mostly good, some bad, traveled five million miles, but I'm not sure I ever left Virgin. I don't think it ever left me.

PITCAIRN

I've been to some faraway places, but none as far as Pitcairn. It's a tiny island, a rock really, about two miles in diameter in the middle of the South Central Pacific Ocean. Pitcairn is approximately 3,600 miles west of Santiago, Chile, and about the same distance east of Auckland, New Zealand. It was a perfect hideaway for Fletcher Christian and his crew after their infamous mutiny on the *Bounty*.

That was in 1789. After taking everything of value off the ship, the mutineers and their Tahitian women then burned it in what is now Bounty Bay. It was twenty years before a passing ship stopped by Pitcairn and discovered its occupants. That's how far out of the way this place is.

For over 200 years, the mutineers' descendants have been populating Pitcairn with no outside help. In other words, they have been inbreeding generation after generation. For anthropologists it is the mother lode. I'm only aware of one comprehensive study by Oxford and it didn't find any serious side effects from inbreeding. I had always wanted to go there, but it's so far away that NBC News was never willing to foot the bill. I know because I tried when I was reporting for the *Today* show.

Getting there would have required airfare to Tahiti, and from there a private jet to the Gambier Islands, and then a charter boat the last several hundred miles to Pitcairn. For a crew of four, the trip and production would cost more than a hundred thousand dollars for an eight-minute story. I couldn't argue with NBC vetoing the expense.

So, when my son Jak said he could get us to Pitcairn for practically nothing, we were skeptical but intrigued. We were: myself, Chris Koch, and a cameraman I had worked with for years, O.C. Budge. The two couldn't be more opposite. Chris is cerebral. He was the executive producer of NPR's *All Things Considered*, along with other PBS and Discovery Channel programs including the one I hosted, *Invention*. Chris knows how to make television.

O.C., on the other hand, is glib, a very good bull-shitter, and a good cameraman. He had a very good eye. I hired and fired O.C. more than once when we worked together in Salt Lake City, but the firings never had anything to do with his shooting. He simply couldn't stand for things to go along too smoothly for too long. The first time I fired him, he had fallen in love and pretended to be sick so he could get back to his girlfriend. I can't remember why I fired him the second time. One of the things I liked about OC was that he actually listened to the interviews so he knew when to push in and pull out. We became very good friends.

And then of course we would be traveling with my son Jak. He was the one who said he could put our trip together. When I have worked with crews who have also worked with my son, they always ask me if I'm his real father. I have found myself asking the same question. Jak is a hustler but he usually delivers. He was reporting stories for CNN when he was only eighteen. I remember him calling me from the South Island of New Zealand when he was about to do an on-camera bungee jump from a very high bridge. He was scared to death but had no intention of backing out. A few days later I saw him do the jump on CNN.

In his teens, Jak was jetting around the world doing travelogues. He and his cameraman, who was O.C. for a few years, and whatever girlfriend he had at the time would usually ride in the front of the

2

plane. I think he would offer the airline a credit in exchange for his airfare.

I remember one time he stayed with me in Washington while he pitched a story to the networks. He wasn't yet twenty. I told him it would never happen. By the time he left for home he had sold the story to ABC News. When I took him to the airport I did something I normally wouldn't do: I parked the car and went inside with him. He got in the first class line. The agent told him he was in the wrong line and his ticket was for the next day. Jak said, "Do you have empty seats on the plane?" The agent said, "Yes, but you're not getting it." I wanted to say the same thing. Jak said, "Could I talk to a manager?"

The manager started to lecture him but eventually gave him a seat. Then I heard Jak say, "Do you have any seats in first class?" The manager looked like he wanted to kill the kid. By then I had distanced myself so that no one would think I was with this brash young man. When I left the airport, he was flying out of National in first class. I'm sure Delta just wanted to get rid of him.

Jak told us that on one of his visits to Tahiti he had dinner with the president of the country, who said he would arrange travel for us free of charge to the Gambier Islands. I had grown accustomed to Jak's dinner dates with important people. I remember a dinner he had with Charles Bebe Rebozo, Richard Nixon's confidant in Key West.

If Jak thought someone was interesting, he called them and they usually agreed to see him, I'm sure out of curiosity. I still have no idea what Jak promised the president of Tahiti. I imagine he told Air France we would give the airline a credit at the end of the show in exchange for our first class flight to Tahiti.

In Tahiti we settled in a nice hotel on the beach to wait for our next journey. We waited, one, two, three days. The wait wasn't dreadful because the hotel was on a nude beach populated with beautiful French sunbathers. The days flew by and it was apparent things weren't coming together the way Jak planned. There was a part of me that enjoyed his angst. He was always so sure of himself. After a few days Chris couldn't wait any longer and took off for home.

I was getting ready to head home myself when Jak announced that a friend of the president, a rich businessman, would have us flown to the Gambier Islands in his private jet. It was stunning the day we flew out of Papeete through sunny blues skies and pure white cumulous clouds. I was thinking of the song from the WWII movie called "Comin' in on a Wing and a Prayer," only we were going out on a wing and a prayer.

Our only refueling stop was on an island in the middle of the French Polynesian atomic testing site. They apparently don't get many civilian visitors and they did not act pleased to see us. While our plane was getting gassed up, we were escorted one by one, each with our own personal armed escort, to the toilet. No small talk, no smiles. No invitation to stick around for lunch.

Our last stop was in Gambier Islands, a group of nine small islands I had never heard of before, about a thousand miles south of Tahiti. A couple of things hit me as I stepped off the plane. The first was the almost instant high from the ganja fragrance floating through the air. Apparently one of the islands has only the one crop and it was harvest season.

The second, even more overwhelming sensation was the sudden knowledge that we were a long, long way from home or from any kind of rescue if we needed one. When our jet took off, it took my better judgment with it. What if the plane wasn't there to pick us up on our return? Why would they come back to get us? We weren't paying a damn cent for the plane. And if they didn't come, how on earth were we going to get home? These were not idle thoughts.

Eventually a small boat pulled up to the dock and a native who did not speak English motioned us to get in. Half an hour later we pulled into the harbor of the main island and there our very own immigration and customs agent greeted us. He seemed surprised yet pleased to see us. Apparently he doesn't get much business. And then we met the man who was going to take us the rest of the way, about 300 miles, to Pitcairn. He was a New Zealander biologist named Graham Wragg who had spent several months on Pitcairn and spoke of it almost reverently as a place trapped in time. He said he had never experienced any place like it.

Wragg's boat did not instill confidence. It was a rustic and rusty thirty-six-foot fishing boat called *Temanu* that looked as if it had made one journey too many. It was a really big ocean out there and the boat was, well, tiny. Graham was one of those irrepressible types who refused to recognize reality. He assured us that *Temanu* was a workhorse that could get us to Pitcairn without sinking along the way.

What Graham did not tell us was that we would be sailing on the tail end of a typhoon, which is to say the sailing would be very rough and "a little dangerous," as he eventually admitted. In reality, it was hell. If we were not wearing seasickness patches behind our ears, we would have been real sick puppies.

The waves were so ferocious we were each tethered to the boat with a rope in case we were washed overboard. When we would go down below to get some sleep, it was painful. The waves would hit the bow with such force that it felt as though our ribs would crack. Sleep was impossible.

Captain Wragg assigned each of us four hours of watch duty during the dark night—watching out for what? If we saw something, what could we do about it? This was one of the least traveled routes on any ocean in the world. If the *Temanu* were to sink, the chances of another boat close enough to rescue us were about one in a zillion.

I think Captain Wragg was trying to divert our attention from our personal reality and misery. In the middle of the night I realized the ridiculousness of the situation. You know how dark things can be when you wake in the middle of the night. Boy they were dark that night. I promised myself that if I ever got home alive I would never again do anything so foolish.

Mealtime was the worst. Captain Wragg was from New Zealand and New Zealand had never been known for good cuisine unless it was a variation of lamb. That's because there are more sheep in New Zealand than humans. Fortunately there was no lamb on board the *Temanu* but Wragg managed to come up with another New Zealand specialty - a soggy spaghetti sandwich: white bread with red sauce spaghetti stuffed in between. Makes me nauseous even to think about it but on that lurching boat, I actually threw up. I hated Wragg.

There was no letup in the rough seas the whole way, constant gut-wrenching, until we finally spotted Pitcairn. It was like finding a treasure at the end of the rainbow, only it was a rock about two miles in diameter in a vast, empty sea.

Nowhere is there a sandy beach, a tiny cove, or even a coral reef. The surf surrounding the island is so dangerous, it is virtually impossible for a boat as small as ours to make it through without smashing against the cliffs. At least three sailboats had sunk trying.

Aside from natural death, falling off cliffs is the leading cause of death on Pitcairn.

Captain Wragg had radioed ahead that we were coming and so two of the island's longboats sailed out to meet us, filled by about a quarter of the island's population. They don't get much company in Pitcairn. The longboats were designed especially to make it through the treacherous surf. The folks onboard spoke English but didn't look "English."

They resembled Polynesians except with much lighter skin. They were very friendly. So were we. We were so relieved to get off that boat we would have been friendly even if they were hostile. O.C. and Jak swore they'd never leave the island unless they could do it on a plane. That was problematic because there was no way and nowhere to build a landing strip on a volcanic rock.

As we pulled into the island's protected dock, the remainder of the population was there to greet us, including Tom Christian, the great-great-great-grandson of Fletcher Christian. He was our host. Tom was tallish and soft-spoken with a strong New Zealand-like accent. He was the sort who blended into the background, but he was the titular head of Pitcairn.

He drove us home in a four-wheeler, which was the most popular mode of transportation on Pitcairn. When the islanders discovered four-wheelers it was as if God had answered their prayers. There were some off-road motorcycles but you can't transport a family on a motorcycle. Cars were simply too big to negotiate the paths. The island is too hilly for bicycles.

We did not see many Pitcairners who were overweight. There were only two directions to walk on Pitcairn: uphill and downhill. The island's small historic cemetery was on one of the only pieces of flat land available.

We counted sixty-six inhabitants of Pitcairn. It was actually smaller and less populated than Virgin. Forty years before, there were as many as 150. In the mid-1800s the population peaked at 237 but many left to find a more normal life and a mate who wasn't so closely related. The males outnumbered females by almost two to one because the young girls usually moved away, often to New Zealand.

Pitcairn was the first Pacific island claimed by the British and remains the only island in the Pacific under British control. Actually it's a protectorate of New Zealand, which means if there is any crime on Pitcairn it will be New Zealand authorities who investigate. At the time, there didn't appear to be crime of any sort. Years later we learned that appearance was not reality.

Tom Christian lived in a clapboard house with several bedrooms. He and his wife Betty had three girls that we knew of, but two had moved away. Eighteen-year-old Raelene remained and she intended to leave.

Over the years islanders generally, though not always, obeyed an unwritten rule not to marry anyone closer than a second cousin. It was only a rule, not a law. Tom was sensitive about the perception of inbreeding on Pitcairn and told me several times there didn't seem to be any mental or physical defects resulting from such a close-knit population.

Tom told me he was not necessarily proud to be a direct descendent of Fletcher Christian but grateful that they were able to descend from the mutineers before the mutineers all died. Who can argue with that reasoning? Actually, all but one mutineer died violent deaths within three years of landing at Pitcairn. Popular legend has it that all died because of greed, grog, and women. Alcohol has long been forbidden on the island, although it could be found.

The Pitcairn version of a supermarket is open two afternoons a week; the proprietor was a stout woman named Royal Warren. She said when she was a kid there were 300 people on the island. Her kids all moved away. Her husband died and she was lonely. Royal could talk your head off. We had no problem getting anybody to talk to us. It was actually difficult to get them to stop talking. I kept thinking about what they could talk about with each other day after day after day.

All the kids we spoke with at their tiny school, and all the grownups, were convinced that Pitcairn was an island of safety in a sea of violence and crime. Some were actually afraid to leave the island. It's no wonder. Even though Pitcairn had no television reception, every house had at least one television set and a large library of videos.

While we were there one of the most popular videos was *Home Alone*. To those of us in most of the world, *Home Alone* was a heart-warming Christmas comedy. To Pitcairners it portrayed the world as a very violent place. Remember how the kid beat the hell out of the bungling burglars. How we all laughed. That was scary to the kids there. Imagine the response if they saw an actual scary movie.

Tom's mom and dad lived with him. Both were quite ancient. The dad, Ray, was a gentle soul who spent most of his time carving replicas of the *Bounty*. His mom terrified me. If there was something on her mind she said it. I remember the morning at the breakfast table after my first night in the family's house.

I knew the walls were thin but I had no idea they were paper thin. She looked across the table at me and started snorting. She kept it up. Snort, snort, snort. I couldn't figure out what she meant, and then it struck me. Apparently I had snored the night away and kept her awake. So the next night I slept fitfully, trying to make certain that I didn't snore. In fact I barely slept at all because I could hear her loud and clear. She was in the next room farting all night long. I didn't have the guts to feign a fart at the breakfast table the next morning. Thought about it but couldn't figure a way to put it in words. I didn't sleep well the whole time I was on Pitcairn.

There was one church on the island that belonged to the Seventh Day Adventists. Apparently missionaries discovered the place many years ago and succeeded in converting the entire population. But it was not a zealous religious community, maybe because there was no one to proselytize. It reminded me in ways of my little hometown of Virgin. An outsider could never really learn any of the Island's secrets.

Seafood was obviously a specialty on Pitcairn but there were no professional fishermen. There was no need. It was easy enough for each family to catch all the fish they needed. I saw some of the most spectacular fish in a variety of brilliant colors—on the end of a homemade fishing pole with a young kid at the other end.

The waters surrounding Pitcairn are teaming with lobster. Unfortunately, Seventh Day Adventists aren't allowed to eat shellfish. I guess that's why there were so many lobsters.

Nearly everyone on the island was a carver or a basket weaver. It was how they made their living, how they earned the money to buy television sets, four-wheelers, and motor scooters. I was interviewing a fellow who made wooden sharks fitted with real shark teeth. When I asked the carver where he got the shark teeth he said they used to get them from the sharks but they depleted the shark population so now they were running out.

For many years whenever a ship passed close to Pitcairn, islanders would take long boats out to meet it and sell their carvings. But in recent years a dwindling number of ships traveled near Pitcairn and the islanders were desperate for business.

A few months before we arrived, a British freighter passed by and even though the seas were especially rough the islanders took their longboat out to meet it. The boat nearly capsized which would have decimated half the population.

While we were there, a tugboat traveling from New Zealand to Chile stopped by to drop off the mail. It was a very festive day, but even in relatively calm waters, keeping two boats side by side without crashing into each other is no small feat. The islanders sold souvenirs for the first time in a long time. More importantly, they got their mail. Some letters were postmarked more than a year earlier. I can't imagine how they would react to texting and instant messaging.

After a week on the rock, I was sleep-deprived and Jak and O.C. were bored. They were ready to get off even if it meant getting back on the damn *Temanu*. Captain Wragg assured us the trip home would be much more pleasant and it was.

It took only about forty-eight hours to make it back to the Gambier Islands. We arrived fairly late one night and when we were fifty yards from the dock we hit a sandbar and had to wade to shore. We didn't look at it as bad luck. We could actually touch bottom.

Pitcairn has been in the news twice since our visit and after our documentary aired on *Dateline*. First, when a British expedition discovered an abundance of precious minerals like copper, gold, ore, and zinc offshore, inside Pitcairn territorial waters. If or when international companies choose to excavate, Pitcairners will earn enough from royalties to alleviate most of their money worries.

The other news is not so good. After a criminal investigation uncovered dozens of allegations of sex abuse, six Pitcairn men have been convicted and now reside inside Pitcairn's new jail. The one-roomer when we were there was seldom occupied. Several of the victims were teenage girls. Islanders say it's been a tradition on the island for generations, that twelve years is the age of consent for girls on Pitcairn. They say it's a tradition that stems from their Polynesian ancestry.

At the same time there was another sex abuse investigation on Norfolk Island, about 900 miles off the Queensland coast. In the nineteenth century a shipload of Pitcairners immigrated to Norfolk. Today there are about 600 *Bounty* descendants residing there. The investigation led to the conviction of a prominent businessman of pedophilia offenses going back twenty years. The lenient sentence of jail every weekend for forty-eight weeks angered many islanders who complained that sex abuse was rampant.

A Seventh Day Adventists pastor, Neville Tosen, who spent two years in Pitcairn says he thinks the abuse can be traced back to the island's original settlers. Thirteen were murdered, many in fights over women. He thinks the mentality lives on. We never saw any of this. I must be a helluva reporter. The thought never occurred to me. Now I wonder why.

One last note: We had two young men on board the boat from the Gambier Islands. They were both black pearl farmers, and did not appear to be low on cash. They both carried with them a stash of hash, which they had traded canned goods for on Pitcairn.

One of them admired my yellow weatherproof Minolta camera. It was allegedly weatherproof but not waterproof and by then it was a few years old. When we got back to Gambier, the young man wanted to show us his pearls. So the next morning we got up early and he rowed us out to what appeared to be lobster buoys. He pulled up a string of oysters and started opening them up with a big hunting knife. The first one held a black pearl about the size of the end of a pinky finger. He offered it to O.C., the cameraman. O.C. gave him his still camera in return. He sliced open another oyster and handed an even bigger pearl to O.C. In return O.C. offered him a pair of binoculars. I was afraid O.C. was going to offer his movie camera.

Then he pulled up another string, slit open the oyster and handed me the most beautiful black pearl I've ever seen. Actually a good black pearl is a very dark green. He said he would trade the pearl for my camera. I gave it to him as well as another pair of binoculars. He was happy and so was I, although I felt a tinge of guilt about it. I did tell him it was a used camera. Anyhow, when we got back to Tahiti, I took the pearl to a major jeweler on the island. He appraised the black pearl at $3,500. Turned out my wife doesn't particularly favor pearls, even after knowing the hell I went through to get them.

In the Gambier Islands with cameraman OC Budge, my son Jak, myself and our captain Graham Wragg. We were about to embark on a very rough ride to Pitcairn Island.

Jak at the wheel while OC catches some shut eye. They both swore they'd never get back on the boat again. Of course, they had no choice.

FORWARD TO THE PAST

Pitcairn is about 4400 miles from Virgin. It's actually about the same size physically as my hometown, but I managed to find a place with an even smaller population. To my knowledge there was no inbreeding in Virgin, although most everyone seems to be related in one way or the other. On my mom's side, I was a cousin to about a third of the town. I'm not sure that the views of the world outside were that much different. Pitcairn is about as isolated as you can get geographically, but isolation is also a state of mind.

VIRGIN

I grew up in Virgin, Utah. The sign on the lonely highway passing through town read population 104; elevation 2,200 feet. Tourists always seemed to get confused about which was which. They would stop at my Dad's store and ask where the 2,200 people lived.

Sometimes I would feel embarrassed that I lived in "nowheresville," and I'd tell them that most of the town lived across the river, the part you couldn't see from the highway. Some cruel cynics even questioned the 104 figure, saying the number included dogs and cats. They may have been right. I was never able to count 104 humans residing in Virgin. Most motorists just zipped through town without knowing we were there. It didn't help that the road signs that announced Virgin kept disappearing. I think people would steal them to put in their bedrooms.

Virgin was settled by Mormon pioneers in 1857, under the direction of Brigham Young. I always thought it was named after the Virgin River and that whoever named the river had a good sense of humor. I cannot remember when it looked pure and wasn't the color of the red dirt that sets Southern Utah apart. Actually it was named after an early settler Thomas Virgin, who was later killed by Mohave Indians.

Virgin is on the only highway into the West entrance of Zion National Park, which is sixteen miles away but close enough to command the horizon above the town. It is in a pocket at the bottom of magnificent and rugged red and white mountains. At sunset, Virgin disappears in the shadow of the Hurricane Mesa. My Mom and Dad are buried in the Virgin cemetery, which can best be described as a boot hill with a million dollar view.

Virtually everyone in Virgin was a Mormon, although more than half would fall in the category of "Jack" Mormons, which means they were baptized Mormon but spent a lot more time at my Mom and Dad's bar and café than they did at church. The town had a tiny one-room church with a hand-rung bell that announced services. It wasn't quaint, but it was small. My sister and I went to church regularly at Mom's insistence, even though she hardly ever attended. Dad wasn't a Mormon.

Virgin may have been a Mormon town, but it was not a religious town. Mormonism was the culture and the social hub. The times the community came together were for Sunday church, weekend dances, and then there were the parties up at Delmar's pond, where it was not uncommon for folks to get quite inebriated. It was almost necessary to be inebriated to go water skiing on Delmar's pond. It was only about 200 yards long and half as wide. Skiers regularly crashed into the bank making the turn.

It was easy enough to identify the good Mormons from the bad by whether they kept the Word of Wisdom; those who drank alcohol and caffeine and smoked cigarettes were the bad Mormons. There were a number of secret smokers. I caught them from time to time and they caught me.

Religion, it seemed to me, was a wedge that divided Virgin more than uniting it. There were three or four cliques that made up rumors about each other. One faction was always angry with the Bishop, my uncle, accusing him of showing favoritism to someone they didn't like. Maybe that's the way all small towns are. When I visited a friend's house, I would usually hear some gossip about one of the neighbors. Probably when I moved on, they gossiped about me.

There was one woman who was the epicenter for town gossip. I liked her, but she drove me crazy. One time when I found out she had tattled on me to my parents, I started yelling at her. I walked backward away from her house toward mine, yelling unkind things. When I turned around, I saw my Dad standing there. That was awkward. He made me go back and apologize, and then sat me down and we had a talk.

I don't mean to say that I didn't like the people of Virgin. I liked them fine, but they didn't seem interested in my life, and I wasn't very interested in theirs. Mom always cautioned me to avoid talking about our family. My interactions with the people of Virgin were usually pleasant and brief.

Up the road about a mile from my Dad's place there was another bar and café called the 101 Rancho. It was more bar than café. The 101 was owned by Evan Lee who reminded me of Judge Roy Bean, the Texas saloonkeeper and justice of the peace who referred to himself as "the law west of the Pecos." He held court in his saloon, and it wasn't always by the book.

Evan was a direct descendant of John D. Lee, the Mormon who led a massacre of over one hundred Arkansans on a wagon train passing through Southern Utah in the 1850s. Lee hid out in the mountains overlooking Virgin and was eventually executed sitting on his casket. Evan, and Lee's descendants who lived in Virgin, felt that Brigham Young ordered the massacre and then threw John D. Lee to the wolves.

My Mom spent part of her childhood in a log cabin on a small farm amid monolithic red rock formations in the mountains above Virgin called Lower Kolob, which in Mormon doctrine is a very special place.

Her name was Odessa Matthews and she was a beauty. We called her Queenie. Queenie was quite shy until she had a couple of Coors beers, then she was the life of the party, and she loved to party—in secret, of course, because everyone in Virgin was *some* sort of Mormon.

Queenie dropped out of school in the eighth grade and forever felt inferior to anyone who graduated from high school. But she was street smart and knew me better than anyone, which is probably why we fought like cats and dogs. Whenever I did something wrong, which was at least once a day, she would be there to catch me. She never punished me physically, although on more than one occasion she lobbed pots and pans and knives in my direction. But God help anyone who said something bad about me or my younger sister Jackie. Our Mom morphed into Barbara Bush whenever anyone threatened her family.

Odessa could be fierce but she had a very tender heart, especially for the 'lesser' among us, who knew that their protector and best friend was my Mom.

There was Orville who had extremely crossed eyes and knew more about cars and Elvis than anyone. Colleen had Down Syndrome. Virgil lived in a one-room, eight-by-twelve shack. Robert always lit up when my Mom called him Roy Rogers. There were others. Mom gave them money, fed them and helped clothe them. Should anyone be foolhardy enough to insult or mistreat any of her people, they would feel the wrath of Odessa up close and it wasn't pleasant. She'd get so mad I was afraid she was going to hit somebody. .

Mom was never really, really happy without the Coors. Her philosophy was that if you got too happy you'd always be let down because the next day or week something bad would happen. She believed that if you stayed only medium happy, the letdown would be less painful.

I'm afraid I grew up with the same philosophy. On those rare moments when I have been ecstatic, I've managed to quickly talk myself down to a smile instead of a laugh. If something good happened I would go through a brief bout of excitement, and then tell myself to cool it. I grew up and older with that trait.

Mom and Dad couldn't have been more different. Where she was prickly and moody, he was always happy. It used to drive her crazy because there was simply no way she could pick a fight with him. Anger wasn't part of my Dad. It was pointless to try. He'd say, "Odease, sweetheart, it'll be ok." He was always a schoolboy in love, and she loved him back even more.

I cannot remember Dad losing his temper with Mom, although there were times she deserved it. He never lost his temper with my sister Jackie, and she probably never deserved it. She was the good girl. I was always in trouble.

Mom met Dad in San Diego during World War II. He was in the navy. She was a waitress. My Dad spent most of his childhood in Oceanside, California. He was the only child in an upper middle class family. Dad played the clarinet and got a music scholarship to the University of Southern California.

His father Charles was a prominent businessman. In pictures his mom was beautiful. They both died when Dad was in his early teens and so he grew up longing for a family. There was never any question that when he found one, he would never let it go.

When I was a year old, we moved to Virgin where Dad bought the only store in town. It burned down a couple of years later and so he built another, bigger one. The store was called the Mohawk and it had a bar, café, grocery store, tiny service station, and four cabins.

We lived in two cabins that were connected like a train. I grew up looking forward to living in a square house.

Mom hated the business and I couldn't blame her. The Mohawk's hamburgers were legendary and everybody seemed to like Mom and Dad, so business was always humming right along, much to the chagrin of Mom. That meant she was in the kitchen cursing to herself and frying hamburgers.

One time, I made her mad during an especially busy time. I saw her pick up a butcher knife and throw it in my direction as I headed for the exit. The knife barely missed me as it clattered against the screen door. Out of the corner of my eye I could see Mom rushing to try to try to catch it before it hit me. I never let her forget it.

Queenie's favorite time was in the evening when Dad would slip away for an hour or so to take her for a ride. There weren't that many roads around Virgin and they traveled them all, my mom with a couple of cans of Coors to boost her spirits. Sometimes Mom would spot a black cat up ahead. Dad knew what to do. Even if it meant a detour of several miles. Mom was a superstitious, headstrong woman. We dreaded lightning storms, not so much because of the danger, but because she would make us get off the phone, away from the window and then under the bed.

A newspaper article about a football game Dad played for USC described him as "dynamite in small packages. He loved all sports and played with the local kids although he wasn't always invited—he was just too damn rough. Most basketball games he played in ended early. The court would be littered with hurting bodies. You'd hear kids twice as big as Dad saying "Geez, Jack!"." Everything he did, he did with all his heart. That included the Virgin dances on Saturday nights. Dad loved to dance but by the end of the evening the dance floor looked a lot like the basketball court: Injured bodies everywhere.

Dad fell in love with Virgin in almost the way a man truly loves a woman. He sucked in the fresh air every morning and pronounced to anyone who would listen that Virgin was the most beautiful place on earth. He was known throughout Southern Utah as a one-man chamber of commerce.

But, Dad could have lived in Virgin one hundred years and he would never have fit in. The locals accepted him—although I'm not sure how much that mattered to him. He didn't know what end of a cow to milk or what end of a gun to shoot. They would kid him and he would laugh, but he knew he was never meant to be a cowboy or a farmer. He was in Virgin because that was where Queenie wanted to be and because he was enthralled with the beauty of the place.

Most people thought Dad was an alcoholic when he first moved to Virgin. He probably was. One night as I was sitting in our store with my mom, we heard a rattling coming down the highway. We walked outside to see Dad driving our poor Nash Rambler with the bumper torn off and clanging against the highway. He got out with the sheepish grin that made it impossible to get mad at him. He was looped and had hit a cow on the way home. Dad said, "Odease, I had a little mishap."

When he sobered up, he felt terrible about the cow and reimbursed the farmer and sincerely apologized. After a few years, Dad all but gave up drinking, except a rare beer and a less rare cigar. He loved his cigars. He gave up booze at the same time he was selling beer at the bar. Never talked about it, just did it.

Dad knew that when he was drunk he wasn't a good mate or a good husband so he decided to sober up. It wasn't for religious reasons or because Mormons disdain alcohol. Throughout the remainder of his life he kept a bar stocked in the house for anyone who did drink. I never, ever heard him cast judgment on anyone for anything.

Dad had one fundamental goal: to live each day a little better than the day before. Each day he would rise about five in the morning to listen to big band music and read an inspirational or self-help book. Then he would give Jackie and me a thought for the day that we were supposed to memorize by that evening. Mostly he gave us thoughts about love.

As I grew older, I realized that he was a remarkable man, in some ways too good for this earth. I worried constantly that he would die young like his dad who passed away when he was forty-one. It was a thought I never got rid of and it haunted me from when I was a young teenager. I loved my Mom. I was closest to Mom. I idolized my Dad.

I never once heard him swear. I never heard him say a lewd or suggestive thing the whole time I was growing up. He would always fade away from a group if one of the men started telling a dirty joke.

Once when Melba, a cute relative through marriage, was tending the bar, a loud-mouth customer became abusive with her. Dad overheard his comments and suggested evenly but firmly that he should discontinue his remarks. Instead, the man—who was much larger than my Dad—started swearing even louder. In the next instant, Dad jumped over the counter, grabbed the man and threw him against a booth 10 feet away. He told the customer to get out and never come back. Then he apologized to everyone, especially Melba, and went back to work.

Dad owned a gun but I never knew why. It was a small .32-caliber pistol located in the bottom drawer of the bedroom chest. One night late when Mom thought she heard someone outside, Dad got his gun out and, according to a witness, was very fortunate not to have found the intruder because he likely would have shot himself. That was the only time he reached for the gun.

Guns were a big part of life in Virgin. Almost every male from twelve on up owned at least one gun. You would see the rifles in the gun racks in the back of their pickups. They were considered a necessary part of life, although not for my parents. Other than the old green pickup my mom and I used to take the trash to the town dump, we had no use for a pickup or a gun.

It was odd that Dad knew so little about guns, because the Mohawk was hunter-central during the yearly deer hunting season. The place was crawling with deer hunters from all over the country. They knew my Dad knew nothing about guns and kidded him endlessly, but each year they would also brag to him about the six-point they had just killed.

One California hunter liked Dad so much he left instructions for his ashes to be buried next to my dad's grave. So now when you go to Virgin you'll see Jack and Odessa Severson, along with Henry Schmidt. What do you say when someone asks to be buried close to your dad in what was supposed to be your place?

Dad carried a tab for all his customers at one time or another. If they told him things were tough, he said they could pay him later. Some did. Many didn't. And when he did say no, Mom would usually override him. But if he caught someone lying, he would never forget—another trait he shared with Mom. That was a cardinal sin. He wouldn't say anything, but he would never trust the person again. He didn't cheat on his income taxes and he didn't overcharge his customers. There were so many times in my life, even when I was much older than he was when he died, that I thought to myself, "What would Dad do?"

My friends from the city always told me how lucky I was to grow up in a small town. But I always felt that there had been a mistake, that I didn't belong there. I didn't have the kind of dreams that I assumed other kids had, like growing up to be a great athlete or politician or world-renowned physicist. I wanted to own a Thunderbird convertible and have a cute girlfriend. I did look up at the sky, at the contrails of the commercial jets flying overhead and wonder where they were heading, but I didn't picture myself in one of them.

I was in trouble most of the time either at school or at home and everyone in town knew about it, and told my mom about it. She knew I was stealing beer out of the backroom and drinking it while I was taking trash to the dump. She knew when I secretly borrowed the family car to visit my girlfriend. She knew when I lied, which seemed necessary most of the time.

She knew when I took the bucket out back to feed the pig that the bucket was empty. I just didn't want to carry smelly, disgusting slop. I could never figure out how that pig grew so huge. Mom knew when I said I had done my homework that I never did. She knew when I skipped school, which was more than I attended, and in a just world I would never have graduated. A couple of teachers actually expressed their indignation that I did graduate. If I learned anything in school it was unintentional.

It seemed that everything Mom knew about my wayward ways, the whole town knew, often before she did. So, I spent the best part of my youth looking over my shoulder. In the big city nobody notices you. It's easy to get lost in the crowd. In Virgin, people cared about everything everybody else did. There wasn't much else to care about. I'm convinced it's why I grew up so self-aware, and with so little confidence. I knew people were watching every move I made.

Why I ever got into anything as public as television will always be a mystery to me. I've never overcome serious stage fright. Unlike most of my colleagues, I never got used to live television. I hated it. I was terrible at it.

As far as I knew—and everyone thought they knew everything about everybody—all the girls in Virgin were virgins. If they weren't, it wasn't my fault. When I left Virgin I was still one, a fact of life that has troubled me ever since. It was only when I left the place that I learned that "Mormons don't drink or smoke but screw like rabbits." That's why the people up in Idaho refer to Utahans as "carrot eaters." My view of Virgin might have been different if I'd screwed like a rabbit.

I think the reason I was so careful about sexual exploration is that I knew if I messed around, the whole damned town would know about it. Mom and Dad never discussed the birds and the bees with my sister or me and I would do anything to avoid the conversation. The closest Mom came to talking about sex was telling me not to come home if I got my girlfriend pregnant.

One reason I didn't like Virgin was because it seemed that most people in town didn't like each other very much, or at least didn't trust one another, especially when it came to water. That was the big divider. Virgin had too little of it, especially for irrigating. I was always surprised that people didn't get killed over water.

In as much as Virgin was my whole world and the only one I knew I had no idea how strange the place must have seemed to tourists passing through. Over the years when I've traveled through small towns all over the country for my work, I always think of Virgin and how the people in the town I am passing through seem very much like the one I grew up in, trapped in a bubble while the world flew by us at fifty miles an hour.

Overshadowing Virgin was a red mesa that jutted a half-mile into the sky. We learned in the late 1950s that it was going to be the site of some very important research. At that time, most jet pilots who bailed out of their plane going past the speed of sound died instantly. It was crucial that the government remedy that situation and Stanley Aviation out of Colorado proposed a series of tests on the Hurricane Mesa.

First they built a two-mile track along the top of the mesa that ended in a pool of water at the mesa's edge. Then they ran a rocket-propelled sled along the track up to 600 miles an hour. The water acted as an instant break, at which point the seat occupied first by a dummy and then a chimpanzee, would eject out over the edge of the mesa and parachute to the ground several hundred feet below. It was quite spectacular and caused a major stir throughout Southern Utah.

It put Virgin on the map, though not always as you would expect. A number of people in Virgin and from surrounding towns thought UFOs were landing on the mesa and conspiring with high-level government officials. Some people in Virgin still think that way. That was the level of paranoia and distrust toward anything that smacked of the federal government.

If the locals had known what was going on behind the scenes, they would have really been upset. I got a summer construction job on the mesa and was shocked when I encountered the CEO along with some of his employees and visiting government dignitaries running around naked. Every afternoon at the end of the workday he would take his entourage down the treacherous windy road to the Virgin River where they would frolic in the muddy water in the nude.

28

I attended elementary school in Virgin's two-room schoolhouse. I couldn't imagine schools with hundreds of students. I think we had fewer than twenty. The attitude I got from my teacher was similar to what I encountered from my high school teachers—that I was lazy and didn't give a hoot about learning. Some attitudes are deserved.

High school was in a town called Hurricane, a much larger community of about 2,000, ten miles away. Getting there and back each day by school bus involved negotiating switchbacks on a narrow highway that hugged the edge of the mountain. If the brakes gave out, we went over the cliff. It didn't seem treacherous at the time. It does now.

I graduated from Hurricane High School in 1962. Most of my friends and their parents would have been more convinced that there is justice in the world if I had been held back. I deserved to flunk. I think I was graduated because my teachers all realized that there would nothing gained by holding me back. Nobody skipped school more than me. Nobody had more creative excuses. I wasn't obnoxious, I wasn't loud, and I wasn't a troublemaker. I wasn't much of anything. I was a good bullshitter, but the teachers caught on to that.

The girls liked me almost as much as I liked them. I was apparently kind of cute. For a while I was so popular I was elected school cheerleader. I hasten to say I never ran for the position. I never tried out. I was soooooooo embarrassed. I stood before the student body and sternly announced that I was not going to be a cheerleader, period, and walked off. I still get a sick feeling when I think about it. I'm surprised when I look back to see that I was president of my sophomore class.

Public high school in Utah, then as now, included seminary: elective classes about the Mormon gospel that every kid elected to attend. Even in seminary I wasn't much of a student. I got in trouble at my senior year-end seminary party when I spiked the punch with Everclear, a potent alcohol that will knock you on your rear end. It didn't take long for the seminary teacher to track me down.

The premonition that haunted me as a kid that my Dad would die young came true when he died at age forty-four. I'm looking at a picture of him as I write this and it seems as though he can see right through me. At the time he died I still hadn't amounted to much. I was married to a sweet girl named Sandy of whom he was very fond. I still hadn't gone to a real college, but I had a job at a solid Mormon company called U and I Sugar, working in accounts receivable. I felt at the time that in Dad's mind the sugar company was about as good as I was going to get.

Dad had a heart attack on New Year's Eve in 1967. It was a shocker even though we knew he had a bad heart, probably from the rheumatic fever he had as a kid. His doctor, one of his closest friends, allowed my father to continue to lift weights even as he waited for open heart surgery scheduled for April 16, 1968. I remember visiting him and watching him work out. He didn't look good. He was pale and sweated way too much. Dad never did anything half-hearted. He was lifting heavy weights.

On April 10, Dad called me in Salt Lake and we talked for about five minutes. It was in the evening. I remember him telling me he loved me, which was something he said fairly frequently. After he hung up, he called my sister Jackie, and a second or two after he told her that he loved her he handed the phone to Mom and keeled over.

My sister was listening as Mom screamed and then hung up the phone so she could call the fire department. And my sister was on the phone when the doctor pronounced him dead. At times like this, you always ascribe more to it than really existed, but we all believe that Dad knew he was about to die. Death for the survivors is always a dreadful experience, but when I hear of someone who's loved one died at age eighty, I can't help but think that they lived almost 40 years longer than dad.

The funeral service was held in Hurricane where there was a larger chapel. By then, Dad had become a Mormon. I always had the feeling that it was because he wanted to belong to some church when he died. It wasn't that he didn't take it seriously, but I always thought it was an odd fit.

We buried him in the Virgin cemetery. I was angry that the world didn't stop to pay tribute. I swore at the time that I would remember every single person who didn't take the time to attend the funeral. For a week after we buried Dad, I was too sick to get out of bed. I had a broken heart. I knew that no one could ever replace him. I knew also that I had let him down.

Mom wanted to stay in Virgin, to run the Mohawk café she hated so much. A few years before Dad died, they built a cute little home right next to the store. It was only a couple hundred yards from the cemetery so Mom wanted to stay there. We invested the money Dad left in mutual funds certain that Mom would be ok financially. Within two years, the money was gone. She didn't spend a penny of it. The market went to hell.

It turned out Mom was six years older than Dad. I'm not sure he ever knew that. She was an exceptionally attractive woman and even though she was only fifty when Dad died, there was never any question that she would marry again. My sister and I encouraged it but she could love only Dad.

Mom and I were extremely close but fought constantly. Then I would take her for a ride and buy her a couple of beers, and we would make up. She had amazing compassion. I remember several occasions when I would leave her in the car while I went in the market, and while I was inside, she would spot a homeless person and dispatch me to give that person money.

In 1990, Mom got gallbladder cancer. The doctors said she could do chemotherapy but it probably would only prolong her life a little while. She said no. Mom stayed at my sister's house and wouldn't let friends visit her while she was sick, because she didn't want them to be sad. Mom went pretty quick, within six months.

I was living in Washington, D.C. Just a few days before she passed away, I went out to spend some time with her. She was in great pain and was barely conscious. That Sunday I went home, and during the night she died. I've always felt guilty that I wasn't there for her in the end. She deserved more.

We buried Queenie next to Dad at the Virgin cemetery. It was an amazing service on a gorgeous day. Orville and all of Mom's special people were there. There was no pomp or circumstance at the Virgin cemetery that day. People cried and told 'Odessa stories,' everybody but me. I loaded up on Valium. It is one of my regrets. I never cried. In the years since, I have been back to the cemetery many times, but I still can't cry.

QUEENIE & DAD

The Mohawk Café has seen better times It was once a thriving place

My wife Karyn and me atop Mom and Dad's grave. The can of Coors was in honor of mom

I WAS BORN LUCKY

It wasn't until I moved away from my hometown that I fully realized what an unusual name my parents gave me. It wasn't unusual to me; I'd grown up with it. It wasn't unusual to my friends who had grown up with it. But then when I went away to college I started noticing folks chuckling when I was asked to stand and introduce myself, and especially when I said I was "Lucky from Virgin."

I have always felt that most people think I wear that name because I won a quarter or a dollar playing poker. Truth is, I was never a very good gambler. My Dad, on the other hand, was as good as anyone I ever saw. He was a pro. I watched him in Vegas and I watched him in small poker games, and I never saw him lose.

I'm almost positive it was my Dad, not my Mom, who gave me my name. I say that, in part, because when I called my mom to tell her we were going to name our oldest daughter Brandi, she said, "Why don't you just call her gin or vodka." I'm sure she was just humoring Dad when she agreed to name me Lucky.

Dad died so young, and I didn't become really curious about the origins of my name until he was gone. My mom was always sketchy, even evasive, whenever I would ask her. That may have been because she didn't want my friends to know. We lived in a very tiny town where everyone knew everything about you, and Mom, who was only marginally a Mormon, didn't want the whole town to know I was named because of my dad the gambler. It wasn't until many years after my childhood, and after Dad died, that I started to ask questions.

I heard of two scenarios. One was that Dad won $17,000 or $27,000 the night I was born. I've not been able to verify that but shortly after my birth he had enough cash to pay for a small café on the main road through Virgin.

The second scenario is that I was named after Lucky Luciano, the mobster. At the time of my birth Luciano had not yet been deported to Sicily. It was near the end of the war and Luciano's racketeering sentence to Sing Sing was on hold because he and the mob helped authorities catch enemy spies along the New York waterfront. So for a while, Luciano was considered a good guy. That is the only reason I can imagine that my dad would name me after a gangster.

It seems odd that the career of someone named Lucky would begin in a conservative place like Utah. Maybe the first news director who hired me figured I wouldn't be around long enough for anyone to notice my name. There's no doubt in my mind that the name ended up helping my career. How can you forget a reporter named Lucky?

By the time I left Salt Lake City ten years on, I was pretty well known—a big fish in a small pond. I'm sure there were many households where my name was taken in vain because I was not very reverent about things held sacred in Utah, and almost everything in Utah is sacred.

When I got the call from NBC News that they were interested in hiring me, I almost immediately started having second thoughts because it dawned on me I would either have to give up my beard or my name. I don't think there were any bearded correspondents for any network at the time and I'm damn sure there were none named Lucky.

When the senior vice president Tom Pettit offered me the job, he told me my new name was going to be John. I said "Why John?

Why not Jack?" which was the name of my Dad and the name of my son. Tom said, "No, it's John."

John is not a bad name. In another life I wouldn't complain if my name were John. But if you've grown up as Lucky, John is not who you are. I didn't feel like me at all. I felt like I was in the wrong skin. I felt bland, and I thought it reflected in my work. From that experience I've come to feel quite strongly that people often become what their name implies, especially if the name is unusual or quirky. I once had a producer whose name was Twinkle, and she did.

NBC News staffers were always asking me about my name. Was it true that it really was Lucky? Why did I agree to change it? At the time, none of the networks had correspondents with unusual names, not because they weren't born with those names but because the network would simply change them to something more acceptable. John seemed to be NBC's favorite name for this purpose. Bud Dancy, for instance. NBC didn't like "Bud" so they named him John. There were others. Today anything goes. Today I could sport a beard and call myself Lucky and nobody would think twice. But, if I added that I grew up in Virgin that might cause them to pause.

One time I was working for an NBC magazine show hosted by Roger Mudd and Connie Chung. I had always been a fan of Roger's work. He was one of the Old Breed. I knew no one who embraced the traditions and mission of journalism more than Roger. One day he came up to me at the water cooler (yes, the water cooler) and said, "I heard you let them take away your name." He said it in a way that I knew he thought less of me. Later I learned the story behind his name.

When Roger went to work for the CBS affiliate in Washington, DC, the station manager wanted him to change his name. He just didn't like the sound of Mudd, as in "Your name is mud." Roger, a southern gentleman to the extreme, indignantly refused.

The station manager didn't realize that it was Roger's ancestor Dr. Samuel Mudd who fixed John Wilkes Booth's leg after he shot President Lincoln, ending up on a prison island off Key West, Florida. President Andrew Johnson eventually pardoned Mudd but his conviction was never overturned.

Roger apparently complained to the NBC brass about taking away my name. Others complained as well. I had some supervisors who wanted my name changed back to Lucky because it was much easier to promote while I was working on a magazine show.

After it was finally changed back to Lucky, I saw research that showed my name recognition shot way up, above correspondents who had been in the public eye for years. Tim Russert told me on several occasions that he was the reason NBC finally decided to change my name. I think there was some truth to it because Tim had NBC News president's ear. Tim had everyone's ear.

At any rate I was notified two years after going to work for NBC that my name would henceforth be Lucky. I felt free at last but not for long. Within a day or two, a memo came down from the news vice president. It said, "What if Lucky is doing a standup at the White House and President Reagan's dog 'Lucky' goes running between his legs?"

Suddenly, I was no longer Lucky. I was John again. But then the NBC News bosses agreed to compromise and let me call myself Jack. That actually felt pretty good. Jack is more informal than John. Two months later, I was allowed to become permanently Lucky. That's why some of my friends call me J.J.L. for John, Jack, Lucky.

Throughout my life, I've met dogs, parrots, and horses named Lucky. I've met a few humans with the nickname Lucky but only one little boy whose real name was Lucky, in Okemah, Oklahoma. Even more strange is that his mom actually named him after me. But even before, my sister named her middle son Patrick Lucky Hadley. And then Patrick, who has a PhD deep in the Greek classics from Toronto University, named his first son Raylan 'Lucky' Hadley. He has brilliant red hair. And my daughter Miss named the oldest of her three sons Maxwell 'Lucky' Bradshaw. Pretty cool.

I know my Dad would have been immensely proud to have three grandkids and ten great-grandkids. Without a doubt, he would have thought that giving up gambling to raise a family was the best bet of his life. I've done my best to see that my kids and grandkids, and anyone who will listen, look at Dad as their ideal.

MY MISSION

After I moved out of Utah I tried to avoid doing stories about Mormons because I had done so many when I was living and working in Salt Lake City. One story I went back to report was about a new Hare Krishna temple in Utah County, the epicenter of Mormondom. The temple was highly visible from the freeway, definitely a head-turner, only ten miles south of BYU and the Provo Mormon temple. This part of the state has far more Mormon influence and members than Salt Lake County. And there it was, quite a lovely example of a Hindu temple, the first of its kind built from scratch in the US of A.

But what made it a story was that the Mormon Church had donated $25,000 to the construction of the temple and its members had invested most of the sweat and labor on their days off, Sundays excluded of course. It was a rare story of harmony among churches. And these two religions made it particularly interesting.

It started when the Church asked its local leader, a stake president, which is a position above bishop, to drop by and check out rumors of a new temple that clearly wasn't of Mormon origin. Locals had heard about the plans for a Hindu temple, and they were concerned. They'd even signed a petition against it, although they never gathered that many signatures.

Construction began and seemed to be going in bits and spurts and then it stalled altogether. So the Church was very curious about when it was going to be completed, if ever. It would have been embarrassing for the community and the Church to have a foreign temple so prominently displayed but standing there unfinished. Stake presidents are often successful businessmen, and Dr. Stan

Green, a radiologist, was no exception. At first blush Dr. Green seemed friendly, even sweet, with a meekness that belied his accomplishments, which were impressive—including thirteen children, five of them adopted.

It turned out that Dr. Green and Caru Das, the president of the Hare Krishna temple, developed a close friendship and Dr. Green became a strong voice in favor of completing the temple, especially because it wasn't Mormon. Now it has become a source of pride not only for the Hare Krishna's, but even more so for the Mormons who can point to the onion-topped temple as an example of how open their culture is. In fact, I'm aware of many times the Church has contributed money and church manpower to other religions in Utah and other states.

While we were riding through the countryside with Dr. Green, we spotted two Mormon missionaries. These had to be two of the most unlucky missionaries in the world, getting sent on a mission to convert new members in an area that must be at least 99.9 % Mormon. It might take their whole two-year mission just to find someone who was not a member. One missionary was from Tahiti, the other from Switzerland.

Whenever I see missionaries, it always brings back strong and mixed emotions. I have rarely told anyone, even friends that I was once a Mormon missionary. Although I would have if someone asked. I had knocked on doors looking for converts. I had ridden on bikes in a suit and tie. I had people yell at me and ridicule me. I got up every morning and prayed and prayed before I went to bed and prayed in between. I was not only a missionary, I was a pretty good one.

I escaped Virgin when I was eighteen to find myself and make my fortune. Mostly I wanted to have fun, and I did. Learning wasn't something that motivated me, as my experience at the business school in Salt Lake aptly proved. At that point, I was serious only about having fun and my cup runneth over.

I remember with surprising clarity the night I headed south out of Salt Lake City to join some friends at a party on Utah Lake. I pulled into one of those quick stop convenience stores and then backed out across a four-lane highway in front of a Utah highway patrolman.

I thought he was a very nice guy even when he asked me to touch my nose as I tried to walk a straight line. That must have been quite a sight. I couldn't even find my nose, let alone touch the end of it. But I wasn't worried. The cop asked me what was in the cooler in the back seat of my grey rear-engine Monza two-door sedan. I told him with some pride that it was filled with all kinds of beer as well as the rest of the bottle of sloe gin that I had been drinking.

I had always heard that sloe gin has a way of sneaking up on you and I can now vouch for that. Anyway, the officer turned out not to be my friend after all. He took me to the police station where I was given a breathalyzer test, one of those gadgets where you blow into a straw and the liquid inside gets darker the drunker you are. Mine went black.

It wasn't until the officer was taking me to a cell that I realized he wasn't my buddy, and that's when I swung at him. He didn't seem too concerned, though. I don't think he even ducked. I must've missed him by a mile. I didn't realize I had swung at him until I talked to him the next morning when I was sober.

That was one of the longer nights of my life. I was throwing up and when I wasn't, I was sure that my life was over because the only person on earth who could or would bail me out was my Aunt

Adeila, my Mom's sister in law. My Mom and my aunt hadn't spoken for years because of a misunderstanding I never understood.

Aunt Adeila was the one person on earth my mom most of all didn't want knowing our family secrets. I cannot stress that enough, But there was no one else unless my parents drove 300 miles to bail me out. It turned out Aunt Adeila was wonderful. She got me out, gave me no lecture, and sent me home to face Mom and Dad.

They weren't happy but they weren't shocked either. I'd spent most of my high school days preparing for a night in the drunk tank. Dad didn't say much at all but I could tell he was, once again, disappointed in me. My mom was also uncharacteristically quiet. I seemed to be the only one with a level head. I told them I wanted to go on a Mormon mission, but only if I could go outside the country because I was undoubtedly going to lose my driver's license. That surprised them both, but they weren't opposed to it. I would be out of their hair for two years.

The bishop in Virgin was Uncle Bill. He was a good guy. I'm quite sure his younger years were not spent in church. I later learned he might have been inebriated when the elders came to ask him to be bishop. Uncle Bill didn't even preach when I told him why I had to go. I'm sure he, too, was relieved to be getting rid of me. He told me to start going to church, paying my tithing, etc. and he would put through the papers for a mission. I requested an English-speaking country as far away as possible.

After I got my mission call to New Zealand, I knew there was a God. English is the national language of New Zealand and I would have no trouble getting a driver's license. I was as pleased as could be under the circumstances.

At the same time, when I got "the call" it was as if the devil himself had decided to devote his devious charm to stop me from going on a mission, to disqualify me. Suddenly, I had more girlfriends than I knew what to do with. They were coming out of the woodwork, but I knew with a certainty that if I had sex before I went on my mission I would go to hell for sure.

It may have been more superstition than religion but the temptation and the punishment was right there in front of me. And that's what my uncle told me would happen. "The devil will tempt you," he told me.

There was one girl I had a crush on for two years. She was so cute and suddenly really liked me. I still can't believe that I actually sneaked out of her house when it seemed certain I was going to get 'lucky' (This is the first time I've ever used my name in this context.) I confess I'm not sure I would run away again. But it was only a few days before I was supposed to report for my mission.

In those years, all missionaries, no matter where they were going, first had to check themselves into the mission home in Salt Lake City for one week of intensive orientation. That was also the first time we were eligible to go through the temple. I was never very comfortable with the temple experience. It was too full of ritual and secret signs for my liking.

Back then, there were actors in the temple who re-enacted ancient rites. Some of these actors were so ancient themselves it wasn't clear they could survive the re-enactment. Today, ' live' actors have been replaced with a highly produced film. In essence, the enactment is about moving from this life to the next. It's a very fundamental part of Mormon doctrine.

The temple is also where members are baptized for the dead. Young men who hold the lowest level of the priesthood are baptized for those who have passed on. Their baptism by another church doesn't count. According to Mormon belief, only those sanctioned by the Church and its prophet are recognized by God and so millions if not billions of people need to be baptized vicariously if they're going to get into the highest degree of heaven.

One of the things that really put me off during my first temple visit was that there were hardly any pictures of Christ and many, many pictures of Joseph Smith and Brigham Young and other Mormon prophets. I went to the temple in New Zealand two or three times. There were no amateur living history actors in New Zealand because it was a more modern temple with an instructive film.

The night I drove to the mission home for orientation I was drunk, but they allowed me in anyway. The week was intense with all kinds of instructions and lectures. It was also the week when we elders were first introduced to garments. Non-Mormons and some Mormons call them "angel chaps," among other things. Garments are underwear: white, covering most of the torso down to the knees.

Mormons believe these garments will help keep you safe and pure and discourage temptation. Both men and women wear them. You get into a garment that way you would a jumpsuit. The only opening is in the rear so using the bathroom requires practice. They aren't very manly or sexy and it's not difficult to understand how they could discourage temptation.

I was not taking the mission home experience as seriously as I probably should have. Less than a block from the mission home there was a novelty store, which sold sneezing and itching powder. I bought both. After we were introduced to garments I sprayed itching powder on the toilet seats. It was like a pandemic of itching. Elders throughout the building were walking along scratching their rear ends. Somebody told on me. I was called in and chastised, but it wasn't a capital offense.

The last evening, we had a very important speaker: the president of the Council of Twelve Apostles who later became the prophet, Joseph Fielding Smith. About fifteen minutes into his speech, the sneezing powder was everywhere and so everyone was sneezing. It worked its way from the back of the audience all the way up to the podium. They could never prove it was me, but there was a strong suspicion and I think it influenced the decision about what kind of missionary companion I should have to begin my mission.

I was met at the airport in New Zealand by the mission president, Elder Reed Kohler, who was a Utah farmer, and his wife Elda. President Kohler was known to be pretty strict. He had heard of my misbehavior in the mission home and so he assigned me to a district leader who was the son of five generations of Mormon farmers from Cache County, Utah.

Cache County is very Mormon and people there take the religion very seriously but no one more seriously than the first 'companion' I was stuck with. He smiled, but it was only a half-smile. I never heard him laugh. When he shook my hand, I thought he was going to squeeze so hard he'd break my fingers. I think it was from milking cows. He looked me hard in the eye, helped me load my bags in his car, and off we went to my new life. Most missionaries in New Zealand got around on bikes but since Elder Rich was a district leader, he also had a car.

It was apparent my companion had been assigned to straighten me out even if that meant misleading me. The first time was when he told me that I had one week to learn six thirty-minute lessons missionaries recite when they are invited to people's homes. One lesson each visit and then, hopefully, after six lessons, a baptism.

I memorized the six lessons in one week without too much trouble. I always had a very good short-term memory. Then I learned that missionaries were actually given six weeks, not six days, to learn the six lessons. When I memorized them in a week, I became something of a celebrity.

I should have been grateful to him for getting me off to such a great start, but I was more of the mind that I should kill him for causing so much stress. I can remember riding back to our apartment in Auckland one beautiful Sunday afternoon under the soft glow of sunset, when I couldn't hold my anger any longer. I leaped from my bike onto him and his bike and started pounding him as we both fell to the ground in the middle of an intersection. The melee didn't last long but it tore both of our suits and damaged my bike.

In another world in different circumstances I would have respected him. In fact, I started to like him more after I jumped him. I always thought he would make a perfect assistant to the mission president; much better than me.

Because of my quick memory, and the attention it drew, I seemed to advance up the mission hierarchy quite quickly. By the time I had been in New Zealand eighteen months, I had advanced to become the top missionary, with the title of second counselor to the president. That's as far up as a missionary can go. I wrote weekly newsletters and would visit a different set of missionaries almost every morning to share prayers and inspiration.

I was a good missionary. I knocked on a lot of doors, which took a little getting used to. I remember that some of the first greetings threw me completely off guard when the woman of the house answered in her robe and all I could see were her very hairy legs.

I think American missionaries were a novelty—objects of curiosity. Occasionally, I would see a Catholic priest walk down the opposite side of the street sprinkling the same front porches where we were standing, with water. I assumed it was holy water to ward off whatever evil spirits my partner and myself may have left behind.

There was no question that we were treated much better than the Catholic and Church Of England missionaries who first proselytized New Zealand in the 1800s. Back then Maoris were cannibals and fiercely proud of their own religion. They see God's spirit in almost everything animate and inanimate, much the same as Native Americans. I think one of the things that ultimately appealed to Maoris about Mormonism and other Western religions were the doctrines promising rewards in the hereafter for good behavior in this life.

New Zealanders were generally friendly and receptive. They spoke the Queen's English and favored the UK culture. Sadly, though, the food was also very English. Breakfast was bangers and stewed tomatoes. Lunch and dinner and most every other meal were lamb, and more lamb. And they favored these Gawd-awful spaghetti squished between white bread sandwiches. When I think of New Zealand, I don't think of good food, although I understand it's become much more international and edible.

I don't know whether it's because I was a good BS-er or that I genuinely like people, but I didn't get many doors slammed in my face. I was quite successful convincing people to talk to me and eventually joining the Church. I believe I set the New Zealand baptism record, and I don't think it's ever been broken.

I found it to be more complicated and difficult trying to convert Maori who have their own culture and traditions. For instance, I might be meeting with a family with six kids only to discover the parents had never married. It wasn't a big deal in their culture. So then they would marry and within months get a divorce. They wouldn't split up, but they couldn't live with the thought of being married. My job was to convince the local bishop to waive the rule requiring that couples with kids must be married.

For two years I became a different person, totally absorbed in my mission. I can't quite explain what happened to me. I think maybe it's because I had never been in a Church leadership position before. I know I didn't want to fail. I read the bible and all the other church books, like the Book of Mormon.

I didn't cut corners. I prayed. I did about everything I was instructed to do. I confess there were moments I sinned, at least in my heart, like the time I saw a beautiful redhead on a city bus. It was unusual, but at the time I was traveling alone. Anyway, I stayed on that bus an extra hour past my stop just so I could look at her.

Every few weeks we would have a zone meeting where the mission president would have a private session with each missionary and in every meeting he would grab the young man's hand and while he was shaking it and looking into his eyes, he would say: "Elder, have you been masturbating lately?" I was never quite sure why he asked that question. Did he want us to, so we wouldn't have more dangerous urges? Or was he asking us to do the impossible? I never dared ask.

There weren't many female missionaries when I was in New Zealand. Back then it was not very common for young women to serve on a mission. Where there was often pressure on young eighteen-year-old men to serve on a mission, at that time there was little or none on young women. As the assistant to the mission president, I got to know them all. I think it was harder being a woman missionary in the macho culture of New Zealand.

The Church underscores the importance of the priesthood and women are not eligible. They couldn't baptize new converts. Only the men could. Today it is much more common for young women to go on a mission. The Church encourages it. There are now several thousand in the mission field, although their missions last only eighteen months instead of the twenty-four required of male missionaries.

Each missionary is paired with a companion (of the same sex) for two or three months at a time and then dispatched to another companion. I ended up with more companions because I was apparently pretty easy to get along with and because I was supposed to be a role model. I also had my share of gay companions. Being gay was not only taboo, it was a taboo subject. You just didn't talk about it. The mission president would do his best to pair a gay missionary with one who was decidedly not gay, so I guess I'm decidedly not gay.

Who knows if serving on a mission nurtures gayness or makes the young man feel even more like a sinner? The Church still considers it a grievous sin. It wasn't until I returned home that I realized what a huge problem the Church has with gays. I think I was naive growing up in Virgin where we never spoke or even knew of such things.

Salt Lake City hosts the second largest gay pride parade after San Francisco. The current mayor is a lesbian. Gayness is the elephant in the room. Some church officials still believe that being gay is an acquired life style, and just as it can be acquired, it can be overcome.

That ridiculous and ignorant theory drives me round the bend. "Go straight" programs are now illegal in several states.

Before I left for my mission, my Dad, who was not Mormon, told me he was fine with my going and would support me, but he didn't want me to come home intolerant and narrow minded. I'm sure he had some questions about my open-mindedness the first few weeks I was back home because I was still in the proselytizing mode, still "filled with the spirit."

Because I had a successful mission, I was in demand to talk in church groups throughout Southern Utah. The pivotal speech was when I spoke to a high priest quorum. High priests are usually quite ancient and rigid. If you tabulated the total age of the audience it must have been over ten thousand. I should have known better, but I spoke on my pet subject.

There's a traditional ritual in Mormon churches where the first Sunday each month, members of the congregation are encouraged to stand and give a short, extemporaneous, inspirational speech that usually ends with the individual "bearing" his or her testimony. They would say something like: "I know Joseph Smith was a true prophet, I know the gospel is true with all my heart. I say these things in the name of Jesus Christ, amen."

Most everyone would say something similar, including kids in their teens and preteens. So in my speech to the high priests I said, "I think it's wrong to tell your kids to say they 'know' these things are true because they don't." I knew that I didn't know and I was one of His missionaries. I didn't think the elders in the room knew either.

I said, "When you tell your kids to say they 'know for sure,' then in their minds they have no reason to find out." I suggested that instead they should teach the kids to say they believe the gospel is true and they hope they'll become worthy enough to know for sure one day. At the end of my speech I was met with stony silence. No one came up to me to tell me what a great job I had done, not one person. A fundamental precept of the Mormon Church is to "know the truth and the truth shall make you free." Turns out it did make me free although not in the way intended.

I will always have mixed feelings about whether the mission experience was good for me or a waste of time. I certainly gained self-confidence, knocking on doors of folks who didn't want to be bothered. I greatly exceeded my expectations and many others' when I advanced to be the top missionary.

I'll always wonder about the people I helped convert and then baptize. I wonder if their life is better than it would have been. What if I converted them to something that's not true? Will they go to hell because of me? Will I go to hell because of me? The more I've thought about it, the more I've decided that the Mormon Church is as good as any, and probably better than most, so I'm not racked with guilt.

MY JOURNEY INTO JOURNALISM

By the time I had been married to my first wife for three years, I had gone through three jobs and a tanker full of booze. My ulcer was bleeding and I felt like a loser. I kept thinking that this was not the way it was supposed to go. Actually I had no idea how it should go. Growing up I had very small dreams. You get married and bam! you get kids and a job and live happily ever after. The only thing I knew was that I wasn't happy. I hadn't liked any of my jobs, and I still didn't know what I wanted to do when I grew up.

My first job was with U and I Sugar, at the time a major national sugar company owned by the Mormon Church. The headquarters where I worked was located directly across the street from the Salt Lake City Mormon Temple. The senior VP Reed Smoot was a Mormon official. No one could accuse me of pursuing a company or a job just because it looked fun. There wasn't much fun around U and I Sugar, especially in the accounts receivable department.

I don't think I ever realized that time could move so slowly. Every afternoon by two-thirty, I would fall asleep going over the numbers. My job consisted of adding and subtracting. We had a foosball table near the lunchroom and that is where I really excelled. There wasn't a soul I knew at work who didn't live the Word of Wisdom—no drinking or smoking—except for me. I worked right next to a woman, who was a few years older than me. She had the nicest set of breasts I'd ever seen and they may have been the reason I stayed in accounts receivable as long as I did, which was all of about nine months.

I heard there was an opening in the traffic department, and since I would still be able to ogle Jean on my way to the men's room and when we played foosball, I applied for the job, and to my surprise, I got it.

I'm still not quite sure what my job entailed, but at least one part of it required that I keep track of the hundreds of rail cars filled with U and I sugar that were dispersed around the country. Inasmuch as I had not exactly shined over at accounts receivable, I was determined to excel in the traffic department.

Even I could tell right away that we needed a new system to track our train cars. As it was, we simply had a rotating card system that would show approximately where each car was located. For instance: car number 116, destined for the Hunt's condiment company, was somewhere near Baton Rouge. We could never be more precise than that, and to be honest, rarely did it matter.

My plan was to build a tracking board that would hang on the wall directly behind my desk. It was a big and colorful board, and I built it entirely by myself. There were those who complained that the project seemed to take forever and kept me out of the building for days at a time. That was part of the plan. When it was all done, even my critics were impressed. It was a multi-colored board with movable blocks that represented one or a series of cars, and the blocks were brilliantly colored as well, so my board looked more like a moving work of art than a practical tracking system.

I was proud indeed. But as soon as the project was over, I hated my job. Any idiot could keep track of railcars. That's what I told myself.

Then one day, I couldn't find a train. I'm not speaking of a train with a couple of our cars. I'm talking about the whole damn train. Every car in it belonged to U and I Sugar, and I couldn't find it. There was a disconnect in my system. When something that big disappears eventually someone finds out about it. And to my deep embarrassment, everyone at Headquarters found out. For about a week, I was unable to sleep. I was so preoccupied I didn't even notice Jean's assets. Then one day, we got a call, "Were you missing a train?" I was so relieved I took the rest of the day off.

The next week I made a rather poorly calculated decision—to go into the vice president's office and ask for a raise. If ever a single individual personified a Mormon official, it was Reed Smoot. He came from a long line of prominent Mormons who valued a hard day's work above almost everything but God. Mr. Smoot was also a very smart man. He actually got to be where he was not because he went to church every Sunday, which he did, but because he was darned good at what he did.

Unfortunately for me, he was a good judge of character, and when I walked in and asked for a raise, his face grew quite red. He stood up and circled his desk as he asked how in the "Hell" I could ask for a raise when I nearly lost a whole train full of sugar. I didn't have a good answer. I can't remember whether he fired me or demanded that I start looking for another job.

By the time I got my third job, selling H.J. Heinz Ketchup, I was drinking about a half a gallon of wine a night. But at least being a regional representative for Heinz got me out of the office and out of the house. I didn't tell many friends what it was I was doing, because when I did, they wanted to know if I knew the secret to getting the ketchup out of the bottle. Needless to say, they were not impressed with my career track.

I sold only to institutional warehouses and not to restaurants. The truth is, there wasn't much sales involved. The company either wanted the ketchup or it didn't. It was kind of a rough and tumble business though, and I didn't really fit in. I had no idea of what job would fit, but I knew it wasn't a ketchup salesman.

The last three months with Heinz, I rarely left the house. I drank cheap wine and nurtured an ulcer. To say that I was unhappy would not be saying enough. The only spark I remember during that period was the night Armstrong walked on the moon. I got up and opened another bottle, but I think that momentous event had an impact on me. I was proud to be an American, proud of Neil Armstrong. Somehow I felt a glimmer of hope, not that I could walk on the moon, but that I could do something beyond my limited dreams. I felt a stirring.

Finally. Even I couldn't hide it anymore, and though I was still too depressed to look for another job, I called my boss in Denver to say I was quitting. He said, "You can't quit, I want to fire you." His name was Mike and Mike was a very big, gruff sonofabitch. We were never close, but we didn't have to be. Mike told me he was getting on a plane and I was to meet him that night at the bar at the Ramada in Salt Lake where he would be staying. I did, and he told me I was the worst hire he'd ever made. He was really disappointed that I had quit before he fired me. Then he bought me another drink and we got drunk.

The most important job I had in those three years was the middle one with an employment agency that specialized in hiring reps for national sales companies. Actually that's how I got the job with Heinz. It was one of those firms that charged the company and not the potential employee for making a placement.

Even in the haze of my life at the time, I discerned that most of the men who were looking for a different job had spent their entire career unhappy. Many were in their forties and desperate to find another line of work but they were trapped. They were supporting kids in college and couldn't afford to take a pay cut or move to another part of the country. The experience had a strong impact on me.

I didn't want to spend my career, whatever it was, unhappy. I didn't want to get trapped. I didn't want to be bored. I wanted to have fun. More than anything I wanted the freedom to say "Go to hell." Even though I was discovering a little more about who I was and what I didn't want, I still needed a job. We had just purchased a little Tudor home for $13,700.

After Heinz, I stayed around the house another three months. I was deeply depressed. I was doing a lot of drinking and when I wasn't too drunk, thinking. What did I really want to do? I had always been interested in what was going on in the world. Even in Virgin, I read the *Salt Lake Tribune* every day. Maybe that was what I should grow up to be—a newsman, a television newsman.

I was far from graduating from college but I had nothing to lose, so I started knocking on doors at TV stations. In fact, Salt Lake City was an unusually good television news market, primarily because the Mormon Church owned one station and pumped a lot of money into it. Another station was owned by a man who became my hero. He was probably the richest Democrat in the state and he was determined to compete with the Mormon Church.

But when I knocked on those doors, I was told to leave my resume and someone would get in touch with me. They never did. I can't say I blamed them because my resume did not contain one single thing that would qualify me to be a TV newsman. I had no experience. I had no degree. I had a funny name. It was like looking for a job completely naked. The only thing about me that could possibly have been impressive was that I must've had balls to even be knocking on doors.

The third station I went to had the least resources and the least commitment to news. It was number three, even though the news director there was one of the most respected newsmen in Salt Lake. His name was Roy Gibson and he was also a journalism professor at the University of Utah. In fact Roy had more qualifications than the other two news directors combined, but eventually he agreed to talk to me.

Roy was very blunt. He asked me why I thought anyone in television news would hire me. I said I just had a feeling that I would be good at it. In the end he agreed to let me hang around the newsroom and help out if needed so long as I didn't get in anyone's way. I think he expected me to stay around a few days and then disappear.

I hung out at KCPX for 30 days, usually tagging along with the city/county reporter. He was very good at what he did and generous in his advice to me. I'll always be grateful to him, although I'm not sure he remembers me fondly. One day he got a call that his mother in Dallas was very ill so he asked for time off to be with her. Roy told me he'd let me try the beat for a week. Two weeks later he hired me as the city/county reporter.

At the same time I went back to school at the University of Utah to get a degree in journalism. Roy taught a course in writing and was easily more instrumental in my style of writing than any other individual. Roy was an excellent writer, unusual at the time, because he wrote in active voice whereas most TV journalists were still writing in passive voice, the style of most print journalists at the time.

Roy's bible was *Sports Illustrated*, because the writing was all active voice. My first assignment was to read *Sports Illustrated*. When I would turn in scripts either at school or at work, they would usually come back with so many comments in red ink you could not read my original script. He beat the hell out of me. I even started thinking in active voice.

I took to television like a moth to heat. I wasn't bad on camera. I have always had a very good short-term memory so I could memorize my on-camera "standups" in no time. My stories were a little different, a little more wry and cynical and I was more inclined to empathize with the little guy. It was who I was; I can only imagine it came from my mom. It was not the things she said to friends, but I came to realize it was that she harbored a healthy distrust of sacred cows, and so did I. Within a few months, I was one of the best-known reporters in town—partly because of my name I'm sure.

For some reason, maybe because of my experience growing up in Virgin, I've never felt the need to fit in. With few exceptions, I never hung out with other newsmen, not even later in my career. Maybe it's because they were real newshounds and I'm not. I'm less interested in headlines or short stories. I want to know why they're important.

I'm not knocking "crash and burn" reporters. I admire their skills, but I don't have them and I don't care. It's not for me. I want to tell a story people will remember. I like to let it unravel from the beginning to the middle to the end, and hopefully the end will have much more meaning than it would have without all the unraveling that came before. I need to emphasize that I consider myself a journalist first, a story-teller second.

Although I was off to a good start, my new career was not without some serious bumps along the way. One I won't forget occurred when news broke late in the day that a popular lake in the middle of Salt Lake County was totally polluted. My cameraman and I rushed out to the scene, which was only a few miles into the suburbs, but we couldn't find a good vantage point. So I knocked on the door of a nearby farmhouse and asked if we could shoot from the loft in their barn above the corral. They agreed. We ran to the barn, shot my on-camera appearance and drove like madmen back to the station, which was downtown.

We were working with film in those days, so the first thing we had to do was get it developed. By then, we were barely minutes away from the 6 p.m. newscast and my story was the lead.

Roy asked me to come in his office to watch the story, which I was happy to do because I knew we had beat the hell out of the competition. The anchor led to my story. I popped up at the top and begin to lay out the story. As I talked, the cameraman did a 360-degree pan of the polluted lake area. For the first 10 seconds everything seemed to be going ok, until I screwed up my lines and said "Goddamn Son of a Bitch start over."

Normally that would have been cut out but we were so late the editor missed my screw up. So I started over. The cameraman started his circular shot again and I screwed up again with expletives not deleted. Remember, this is going out over the air in the heart of Mormondom.

Even when I got it right, you could barely hear what I was saying because of the cows mooing down below in the corral. By the time Jon was through with his 360-degree pan, the viewer was too dizzy to understand what was going on anyhow. It grew very quiet and very tense in Roy's office that evening. His face was redder than I had ever seen it and it could get red. He looked at me and said, "Well that was embarrassing." I made it a policy to never swear when a camera was around even if I knew we could edit it out—a policy I have been known to break.

I have always been amazed that I chose television for a career because I'm a very shy person. Doing a standup on film or tape, where you can screw up and do it again then edit out the screw-ups, that's one thing I can do better than most. Doing something in the studio 'live' was quite another matter, and is to this day.

The weatherman was always one of the most important figures in local news and when Weatherman Morgan decided to move from Salt Lake back to Albuquerque, the station manager asked me if I would give it a try one weekend. He knew that I was also producing the weekend newscasts (while I went back to school) but told me I could prepare the weather before I started working on the newscast. Well, Weatherman Morgan was something of an artist and he would draw wonderful cumulous clouds and green mountains. It was colorful stuff and one reason Morgan was so popular. So he was my model.

Before the show I drew the clouds and the mountains and the rain and so forth on the board in the studio, then I put together the newscast. I was so nervous I sneaked in a bottle of wine and consumed most of it in the control room before it was time for me to walk into the studio and do the weather.

When the floor director cued me to start the weather I did just fine until I got to my artwork. And then I couldn't figure out what were the mountains and what were the clouds, and I forgot to give the forecast. It was the only time the station manager asked me to fill in. I'm convinced my stage fright is a result of growing up in Virgin where I knew the whole town was watching me screw up.

I worked at KCPX for seven years, until an executive producer for KUTV, the liberal station at the time, offered me a job. I'll never forget when I told my news director (by then Roy Gibson had left) that I was leaving. He asked me how much the new station was going to pay. When I told him it was double what I had been getting he said, "Hell, I would have paid you that." There's a lesson there somewhere and I keep learning it.

My new job was one of the best I ever had. I started out a director of documentaries and was given a free hand once a topic had been agreed on. For the most part, in the beginning I did documentaries about the environment at a time when people were just starting to pay attention.

The owners of KUTV, an NBC affiliate, were serious environmentalists and they wanted me to do subjects like zoning, pollution, you name it. There was only one taboo. I couldn't do anything on any of Utah's five national parks. The station's owners, the Hatches, didn't want the rest of the world to discover the unmatched beauty of these parks. They wanted them left unspoiled.

The best part of my new job was that I got to know Trent Harris. He's one of the best producers I know and became one of my closest friends even though I told him he was fired when we first met. I didn't like his project. He replied, "You can't fire me, because I won't leave." And he didn't.

Trent graduated from the American Film Institute, the best film school in the country. He's made several movies, cult movies, that enjoy a devoted following, worldwide. I loved writing with him because he was the only one who could keep me from wandering off the map. Trent is his own man, a crazy sonofabitch, but I know of no one with more integrity. We hooked up again about twenty-five years after KUTV and traveled the world doing some really good work and drinking beer.

What I did probably more than I should have was tweak the nose of the prevailing religion, which was still nominally my religion. I did an hour about the Church's doctrine denying African Americans the priesthood. It was called the "curse of Cain" and it held that blacks couldn't hold the priesthood because they were descendants of Cain, who murdered his brother Abel. For years I thought I shouldn't have done that documentary because, if it was church doctrine and it didn't hurt anyone, why was it anyone's business? Then I realized that what the members learn inside church influences their attitudes and actions on the outside. So now I wish I had done more stories on the subject. The same rule applies to the Church's position regarding women.

The Mormon Church will righteously defend its policy regarding women, saying they are held on a pedestal. Those who obey are. Those who don't are called before the elders and told they'll lose their eternal blessings if they don't get in line. Elders hold the priesthood, which is everything in the Church.

I witnessed it in the marriage and divorce of my oldest daughter. During the divorce, which was bitter and resulted in several visits by the local constabulary, church elders almost always sided with the husband because he held the priesthood. Mormon women are second class citizens. The Church will deny it. It's subtle but I've seen it up close.

I think I may have been the first television reporter in Utah to do a story about the Mountain Meadows Massacre, a horrible bloody mass killing perpetrated by Southern Utah Mormon settlers against an Arkansas wagon train in 1857. This was during a time of very tense relations between Brigham Young's Utah and the United States Government.

The settlers schemed with local Paiute Indians to get members of the wagon train to throw down their arms. When they did they were systematically murdered. Seventeen of their younger children were kept by Mormon families and reluctantly returned when they were older.

I also did the first stories about how Utah school textbooks airbrushed the truth of the massacre. I wasn't trying to be the first to do these stories—I couldn't understand why they hadn't been done before. Then I realized that I didn't know about the massacre until I moved out of Virgin.

People knew about it, they just didn't talk about it, even with each other. I grew up about fifty miles from where the massacre took place and I never heard it mentioned. I never knew that the man accused of orchestrating the massacre hid from authorities in the hills overlooking Virgin.

I produced and hosted an hour special called *Polygamy, Prospering In Exile*. It was always a wonder that that one didn't get me excommunicated. When it aired, my bishop told me I ought to keep a low profile for a while. By that time I wasn't attending church but the bishop was a friend.

In the beginning I thought the story was a good idea because polygamy was so awful. In some communities today I think it still is. But not the community of about 400 polygamists I visited in the Bitterroot National Forest south of Missoula, Montana. The sect's leader Dr. Rulon Allred was a handsome older man and the two wives I met with him in the suburbs of Salt Lake were both over fifty, well-spoken, erudite, and attractive.

We hooked up with Dr. Allred and another wife, Mildred, in Missoula and drove to Pinesdale about sixty miles south. Pinesdale had its own church, schools, construction companies, and some extra-large homes. It was a lovely, neat little community nestled in the pine trees. After a few days I became convinced that these polygamists ought to be left alone, that the only thing harmful about the lifestyle was the way its adherents were treated by outsiders as shameful sinners.

Within a year of my time with him, Dr. Allred was shot to death in his Salt Lake office by a polygamist from another fundamentalist group who said he had been told by God to kill Allred. He also killed other polygamists before he ended up in the Utah State Prison.

After a few years producing, writing, and hosting documentaries, I became convinced that documentaries were not an effective way to get an audience. They take weeks and months to produce, then pop up for one showing and disappear. Other stations had reached the same conclusion and were experimenting with a magazine format.

These were weekly shows under the same title with the same reporters and the same approach. The theory was that gradually these programs would build a loyal audience. A weekly show is also much easier to promote than a one-shot special. Every week, same time same channel, same reporters.

Finally after considerable pleading, I convinced the station owner and manager to allow me to start a magazine show. I chose the name *Extra*. The station let me hire four producers and a couple of cameramen, then we went to air. It was one of the best times of my career. The people on the show, with the exception of the two I fired, were some of the best people I ever worked with. It was so much fun, I couldn't believe I was getting paid to do it.

Some thought I had too much fun. There was a story going around that some days I would sneak out of the window of my office and spend the afternoon shooting pool. Those stories were greatly exaggerated though occasionally I did find inspiration in a bloody beer. And I wasn't a bad pool player.

One of the best parts of working in a city like Salt Lake is that almost everything is sacred. I don't think we missed anything. When Harvey Milk, the gay San Francisco supervisor, was assassinated we devoted the whole show to him. Remember we were in Utah. We did stories about the Equal Rights Amendment, gay rights, and abortion.

We did stories all over the globe. I remember one day George Hatch the station owner called me into his office and said in his very high pitched voice, "Luckeeee, I want you to go to El Salvador, there's a big story about to happen down there." I said, "George, our viewers don't give a damn about El Salvador." He said, "Well you better get on down there." So we went. Not long after, El Salvador was in the midst of a civil war and I was there covering it for NBC News.

One day a friend of mine, the son of the governor of Utah for whom my wife Karyn worked, told me about a program for journalists at the Yale Law School. He was about to be a senior and was on the *Yale Law Journal*. He encouraged me to apply for the program. I kept putting it off because there was no way in hell Yale would accept someone like me with a name like Lucky.

At my wife's insistence, I finally did apply several days after the deadline and was stunned silly when I was notified that I was one of five journalists from around the country who had been accepted. KUTV agreed not only to let me take a year's leave but also to pay my salary, and I could keep my company car, which was a BMW. Not many reporters had company BMWs. I was aware that I would never have a better deal than I had at KUTV.

Yale was the most difficult year of my life. What scared me the most were not the professors who were so much better than any I had ever experienced before (except for Roy Gibson). What scared me were the students who had been programmed since they were two or three years old to attend a top school like Yale. They had been tutored and prepped and they took their assignments so very, very seriously.

I will relate only one story from Yale that explained the fear I lived with that year. It was the first day of Contracts, which was the school's most popular class because it featured the most popular professor, Arthur Leff. He wrote the textbook and was absolutely the most brilliant professor I ever experienced. On the very first day, Leff looks down at his list of one-hundred-plus students and calls out my name. I knew he wanted to see what kind of person Yale would admit with a name like Lucky.

The case Professor Leff wanted me to brief was called Hawkins v. McGee, "the Case of the Hairy Hand." It was about a man who scarred his hand from contact with an electrical wire. Dr. McGee told Mr. Hawkins he could make his hand "one hundred percent good" by performing a skin graft from Hawkins' chest area. Sadly Hawkins' hand sprouted thick black hair and he sued. He won, by the way.

Fortunately I had read the case, although I did a miserable job briefing it. After a while we moved on, but a few minutes later I noticed that I had broken into a cold sweat. I was drenched. As it turned out, the Hairy Hand case was the most popular of the semester and student after student brought it up almost every day. Every time I broke into a cold sweat.

Professor Leff had a terrible tic, almost violent. He wore glasses and whenever he took them off, he invariably poked himself in his eye

69

when his head jerked as he tried to put them back on. Turned out he had a brain tumor and died shortly after I was at Yale. He, more than any professor, taught me how a good teacher can inspire even a bad student like me.

Going home from Yale was a miserable experience, partly because Karyn was so upset. She kept asking me to promise that we were not going back to Salt Lake City to die. By that point, I wasn't up for that either. So when I returned and heard that KUTV was going to open a bureau in Washington, I applied and got the job.

Ronald Reagan had just been elected and Utah's two Republican senators were going to have a lot of clout in the new congress. Several western television stations sent reporters to Washington for the first time that year.

For three years, I sent home a story almost every day about what Washington was doing and how it affected Utah. It was a fun time and we did some good reporting. About that time John Hinckley shot Ronald Reagan and since Hinckley's family was from Colorado, the NBC station in Denver worked out a deal where I would also report for KCCO. It started out as Hinckley-only stories but before long I was doing the same kind of reporting for Denver as for Salt Lake.

Although every local reporter dreams of working for The Network, I probably dreamed less. I had it good—a clothing allowance, a company BMW, even a travel allowance of $6,000, which at the time was a lot of money.

When NBC called to offer me a job, I wasn't quite sure I wanted to go. In fact it took six months to decide and the only reason I accepted was that I was thirty-nine and thought if I was going to do anything I better do it before I died. It was always in the back of my mind that my dad died when he was forty-four.

Because as I was leaving an NBC affiliate to go to work for NBC News, the two worked out a deal. For the first three months I would work for NBC News out of their Washington bureau by day. At night I would drive across town to the KUTV Washington bureau and co-anchor the "local" news at midnight my time (10 p.m. in SLC). It was one of the most miserable periods of my career.

The NBC Washington bureau was never meant for fun. It was a serious place—at least the people who worked there thought it was pretty serious. During those first three months, I was assigned an office that belonged to Bernard Kalb of the Kalb brothers. Marvin was already heading to the JFK School of Government at Harvard. Bernie was the State Department correspondent and he spent his days at State, which, in my view, was pretty close to hell. Bernie was the fun one, a very cosmopolitan dresser who loved to talk about his worldly experiences. I liked Bernie.

I did not like the State Department. When I was asked to fill in at State I could never figure out what they were talking about. It was a language I couldn't comprehend. When they said yes they meant no. But it was better than being stuck in that office with no windows, looking at a map of the Middle East that I could not have cared less about. I won't forget the endless afternoons waiting to anchor KUTV's late news, wondering why in the hell I hadn't stayed where I was.

I knew immediately that the bureau was not a place for me. Sitting around and shooting the breeze with secretaries and producers is something I'm not very good at. Shooting the breeze with anyone longer than a few minutes is painful for me. There were a number of correspondents in what I called the "Hall of Horrors" whose work I had known and admired for years, but there was always a tension amongst correspondents—we talked but rarely became close friends. I think it had more to do with ego than anything. Correspondents were the "cocks on the walk," especially then. We rode in Town Cars and private jet airplanes.

NBC had two White House correspondents on the A team. For *Nightly News* it was Chris Wallace, son of Mike Wallace. Chris is one of those driven people, driven to become like his father, and driven to carry the coveted title "White House Correspondent." I like Chris. I think he's one of the best interviewers in the business. The White House correspondent for the *Today* show was Andrea Mitchell, and Andrea was a presence to be dealt with. She was always nice to me but I was sure I would never be on the "A" list of her party invites. I always admired Andrea because of her drive, and I do mean drive. Women in our business had to work twice as hard men, usually made half as much, and did a better job.

One of my favorite stories that really describes Andrea's ambition was when I was filling in for Chris at the White House, stuck in the same small glassed-in cage as Andrea. First thing that morning I couldn't help but listen in as Andrea pitched a story she had been working on for *Nightly News*. It became pretty clear that *Nightly* wasn't interested. Then she pitched the same story to *Today*. Again no interest. She was becoming desperate. She called the executive producer of *Sunrise*, a show that came on earlier than the *Today* show. *Sunrise* never turned anyone down but there was no interest in Andrea's story.

Finally she called a show that was on the air during the wee hours of the night, called *Overnight*. She actually shed tears during that pitch. Lo and behold *Overnight* bought the story. When she hung up she looked at me and said "Damn, today's my birthday and I'm supposed to be at a surprise birthday party tonight. What am I going to do?" That is how much Andrea needed to be on air.

Getting my face on camera was never a priority for me. I've seen it. One time I was filling in as anchor and while I was reading, I looked up and saw myself on the monitor and lost my place. My producers were constantly upset with me because I didn't rush to see our story on the air. They would be even more upset if they knew how many times I never saw the story at all. The fun for me was reporting and writing the story, end of story.

NBC News assigned me to the campaign of Jesse Jackson and then George Bush senior in 1984. The traveling press called Jessie's campaign the "cycle of pain." We rarely knew where we were going to spend the night. We constantly worried about the plane breaking apart. We were so worried that the three networks and the *Post* and *Times* went in together and rented a plane of our own. It was a BAC 1-11, a little smaller than a 737 but much cooler. Our main cabin looked like someone's living room with lamps and couches. When Jesse came aboard, he asked if he could ride with us instead of on his own plane.

Jesse was tireless. He always had something to say and the talent to make it rhyme. I didn't dislike Jesse, but I always wondered how sincere he was. I did agree with his political positions. I definitely felt I was at a disadvantage being one of the few white reporters on the back of the plane. I think we experienced a little bit of what black reporters have long experienced on campaigns with white politicians.

After Jesse, I was assigned to Vice President Bush. The press plane was an old 727 with a Pan Am crew. The Pan Am crew were the best. They looked out for us. Every evening after a long day of several stops, when we got off the plane the crew would hand us either a bottle of wine or a bottle of liquor. We knew we would always be spending the night in a nice hotel, usually a Westin.

The Secret Service were always there to meet us when we landed (several times a day). They were there when we departed and agents were also often on board the press plane.

Over the course of the campaign you get to know these agents and without thinking, you become their eyes and ears. You become paranoid, always on the lookout for someone who shouldn't be there. Some of these agents became my friends but my overall impression of the Secret Service was not positive.

They were very serious about their work but when they weren't working they acted like a bunch of frat guys. The last night of the campaign after Reagan and Bush won, the party ended up in my room and it was totally trashed by the Secret Service. The hotel wanted to charge me for it.

On a flight from San Francisco to DC, the lead secret service agent came to me and asked if I could vacate my seat next to a female correspondent whose birthday it was. The agents wanted to wish her "Happy Birthday." She was very popular, very fun. Anyway, I vacated my seat and the agents surprised her and wished her happy birthday. When I went back up front I expected to find her happy with the special tribute. Instead she was crying. They had touched her in places they shouldn't have.

After the campaign I was stationed in Chicago as a general assignment reporter in what was known as a "fireman bureau." When something would break out they would send us. One of my first stories had appeared that morning in the *New York Times*. We were always chasing stories after they were in the *Times*. This one was a feature, not a hard news story. Didn't matter, I found myself on my first Lear jet flying through the skies to report a story that could run almost anytime. Those were the days.

It didn't take me long to realize that I should not be doing hard news, in part because the stories were so short, usually about a minute and a half. I've always hated to give any part of my story to the anchor. I want to tell the beginning, the middle, and the end. It seemed like I always had to give the best part of the story to the anchor in the studio and I would just add the details. It was not very satisfying. Anybody could do it. Probably anybody could do it better than me.

I remember a story about a fireworks factory explosion north of Pittsburgh. We boarded a small jet and flew as close to the location as we could. Then we borrowed a car to take us to the site where nine people had been killed. We got our footage, returned the car to the airport and took a helicopter to our affiliate in Pittsburgh. It was so late we were forced to bulk-feed our raw footage to NBC New York for it to be edited there. I added the narration from the station.

Then the producer and I jumped in a Town Car destined for the Pittsburgh airport, where our private jet awaited us. I'll never forget getting on the plane, fixing a drink from the bar, lighting up a cigar, leaning back in my plush seat and thinking, "Wow, this is the life." But the only thing I did was meet the deadline, get the story done in time to make *Nightly News*. It was a "manly" experience but not very satisfying. The most fun was when we could convince the pilot to take off like a rocket, but it really used up the gas.

After a couple of years I was assigned to do documentaries, or specials, which was the best job in the news business. I did some hour-long programs with Tom Brokaw and other reporters and some just by myself. My favorite was a special I did with Tom called *Home Street Home.*

The best part, by far, working out of the Washington bureau was getting to know my favorite producer in the business and one of my closest friends. The way to explain Ray Farkas better than anything, is the way he dressed. He wore tennis shorts year round. In fact he was an excellent player, but he wore the shorts to make a statement. Remember this is Washington where the dress rules call for drab grey and boring. Ray wore shorts to say he was his own man. I remember a Christmas party where suits and ties were expected. Ray wore black tennis shorts.

The first time I worked with him was on a long piece about a dying town in North Dakota. Ray shot four standups with me and used them all, but you never saw me once without looking real hard. Once I was so far away I could only speak with him via a walkie-talkie. You might catch a glimpse of me through the rearview mirror or see my shadow. I think he was worried that my correspondent's obsession with "facetime" might get in the way of the story.

He was the ultimate stylist and he knew how to use natural light and sound better than anyone in the business, although I had friends who did not appreciate his work. They hated it. Sometimes he made the viewers search for the headline. You had to pay attention. Maybe it wasn't for everyone, but it worked for me.

Ray taught me how to have a conversation on camera rather than the typical TV interview where the interviewee is pasted against the wall. Ray lectured in film schools around the country. I could always tell when I worked with a photographer who had taken one of his classes. They were a cut above. Photographers were always showing up at the office we shared, and Ray would always have time to review their work and give them advice.

He used sound better than anyone. He loved to put a wireless mike on a subject and leave it there so long the subject would forget it was hanging around his neck. I remember a documentary he did about abortion. Vice President Dan Quayle was speaking at an anti-abortion rally on the mall. The vice president forget about the wireless.

The crowd wasn't nearly as big as projected. You could hear Quayle in the huddles saying, "What are we going to say?" The huddles continued with the VP getting more and more desperate. I think he settled on 500,000, which was about twice as large as the crowd actually was.

Ray did not exaggerate or distort the truth. He amplified it. He did not like cheap gimmicks. I listened to him on one occasion when I'm sure the producer in New York, one of NBC's finest, was ready to jump off the balcony at 30 Rock, after Ray critiqued his primetime special that had just aired. Ray thought it used gimmicks just for the sake of using them. He figured that if your film didn't further the art it was a waste of time and money.

Ray's parting shot was a six-camera shoot of an operation to install electronic plugs into the brain to see if it would stop the shakes from Parkinson's disease. The story was titled *It Ain't Television…It's Brain Surgery*. Ray was the subject. When the implants were plugged in and turned on, Ray's shakes stopped. What a moment.

When he died of colon cancer, a couple hundred of his fans from around the country showed up for a memorial service. There were no tears. Just story after story of what a remarkable man and artist we had the pleasure of knowing.

After working on several documentaries, I was assigned to the *Today* and *Weekend Today* programs. I would usually have one story a week. It was a great gig. During the winter I looked for stories south of the Mason-Dixon line. During the summer I looked north. Sometimes, if a story turned up in an area I hadn't visited yet or wanted to visit again, I'd forget the weather.

While I was working for *Today* and *Weekend Today*, I got an offer from a well-regarded producer, Chris Koch, asking me to host a new program he was producing for the Discovery Channel called *Invention*. Chris had been the executive producer of NPR's *All Things Considered*, as well as many documentaries for almost every media outlet out there. The president of NBC News, to my surprise, said he would allow it. *Invention* became one of Discovery's most popular programs and was on the air five years. I think one of the reasons it worked so well was that if I could understand the subject matter, anybody could.

I did very little field reporting for *Invention*, most of it was studio work—not my favorite, but we had one helluva studio. The Smithsonian gave us permission to record the show's studio segment inside the National Museum of American History. The crew wouldn't start setting up until after the museum closed for the day. Then we would spend most of the night recording my on-camera intros. There was always a lot of downtime for me, and so I was able to wander the place at will. There were several guards on duty but they were always downstairs drinking coffee.

By the early 1990s I knew my time at NBC News was running short. NBC had a new owner in General Electric, which was about the exact opposite of RCA. When RCA was the owner, NBC was referred to as the "family network." It was a good place to work.

When General Electric took over we learned why GE CEO Jack Welch was called Neutron Jack. His strategy was to blow up the people and keep the buildings. I saw firsthand what happens to a company when the bottom line is more important than anything else. It wasn't pretty. I saw the dark side of human nature: colleagues who were very good at their jobs suddenly cared less about journalism and their colleagues and more about pleasing their boss and getting a paycheck.

We got a new NBC News president. Michael Gartner came from a small paper in Ames, Iowa, where he was the editor and publisher. We were optimistic: a small town editor had to be good and solid. We were wrong. Gartner had disdain for what it is we do. His mission, which he seemed to relish, was to turn NBC News into a bottom line enterprise. Employees who were loyal team members were promoted. Those who weren't, were let go. My last meeting with Gartner's vice president went like this: "We need to know if you're a team member. Are you?" I said I would try, but neither one of us thought it would work out.

Days before I was to split sheets with NBC, I got a call from Cheryl Gould and Bill Wheatley, both news vice presidents, telling me that Gartner was out and the brand new news president Andy Lack wanted a correspondent in Japan right away. Would I be interested? I was, but not excited. My wife was even less excited. I had been in Japan a couple of times and I thought it was a very foreign place. When I got there I realized just how foreign it was.

I was told that I could report stories the way I like to report them, which is usually not very conventional. I like a little humor, a little wry (and a little rye). I like stories told through people.

Most all the reporting I had seen from Japan was about imports and exports and trade deficits. I wanted to learn about the Japanese people themselves. I have always been fascinated with their stoicism, as we saw after the Fukushima Earthquake. How come they could compete in the world marketplace without taking over companies and firing employees as we did in the US?

If I had been a little smarter I would not have accepted the job without first meeting the new *NBC Nightly News* executive producer, who's really the most important person in the news hierarchy

After I had accepted the Tokyo job I dropped by to visit him and it did not go well. It became immediately apparent that this guy thought I had been hired over his head, without his approval. I would have been pissed too. I assumed he had approved the decision. If I'd have been smart, I would have walked away right then.

He told me the kind of stories he wanted me to report and how to report them, which was not the job I thought I had accepted. Anybody could have done reporting the way he wanted and probably better than me.

That first meeting, as bad as it was, was much better than all our subsequent encounters, which usually took place over the phone since I was in Asia. He didn't like me or my style. I didn't think he had any. He liked to load up stories with facts and figures he would pull from the New York Times, and God knows where else. I like facts and figures but not when they become a crutch for good reporting.

When I first went to Japan, NBC's satellite bill some days was over $25,000. That was the tab for stories for *Nightly News*, *Today*, *Sunrise*, and whatever other requests there might be. I hasten to point out that *Nightly News* was on at six-thirty in the evening in New York, which was (except for Daylight Saving Time) seven-thirty in the morning in Tokyo. When the *Today* show came on at seven in the morning in New York, it was eight in the evening in Tokyo. By the time I left Asia, we rarely had a satellite bill because we were Fed-Exing our stories.

When there was news, the days were long, accommodating the bosses who left 30 Rock in New York for the night before 8 a.m. Tokyo time and didn't return to their offices until at least 10 p.m. our time. For the first several months there was lots of news.

I learned how sleep deprivation can affect your outlook and attitude. I learned that I should not talk to New York after not sleeping for twenty-four hours. I knew before I agreed to move to Japan that it was almost always a dead end for correspondents. It was a career ender. One problem is the time difference. It's very difficult to maintain any kind of connection with the people who matter under these circumstances.

While I was in Asia, NBC, like the other news networks, had hired very much the same consultants who made local news "happy news." These consultants convinced management that Americans were much more interested in the fire down the street than what was going on in other countries, like Japan for instance.

The four lowest selling *Time* magazine covers one year during that period featured foreign leaders, including Yitzhak Rabin after he had been assassinated. Had Rabin lived, we might have peace in the Mideast, but viewers were more interested in the fire down the street. It was true. I remember when my dad got a ticket chasing a fire engine. It's also true that too many folks today only know what's happening in their neighborhood.

I went to Asia with a business card that read "Chief Asian Correspondent" until I pointed out that I am not Asian. By the time I got there, General Electric had learned how to use the bottom line to determine how important a story was to them. The whole four years I was in Japan I never once went on a feature story outside Japan except once when I paid my own way to Hong Kong.

The New York desk only moved us when at least two shows wanted the story enough to agree to share the costs. They would want it only if it was so big it couldn't be ignored. We made lots of trips to Korea, usually over threats from North Korea. We'd arrive in Seoul about 10 p.m., and would be expected to have a story ready by six the next morning.

The only place we could go in the middle of the night where there were people and enough light to shoot was the red-light district and nobody there ever gave a damn. We kept going to South Korea because the *New York Times* and other publications said South Koreans were really on edge. We never found an edge even when we were shooting in broad daylight, and definitely not in the red light district.

There's also a problem with the language. Japanese is very circular, very indirect, which is why when you watch the movies the generals are always yelling and gesticulating, because there aren't words that adequately express their anger. There's another reason: It's described in Japanese as "honne-tatemae," which means: "The public face does not reveal the inner heart."

So when you interview someone who has just lost their family in an earthquake and they say, "This has been the worst day in my life," and you put that in the script, the producers in New York say "Sounds good, go ahead and edit the piece." Then when they see it they hate it because the person has a big grin on their face while they're talking about their horrible day. "The public face does not reveal the inner heart."

Another problem is that many Japanese don't like to appear on camera as much as they like to take pictures of everything that moves. They simply don't like to stand out. You'd think they would come running when you request an interview but they're running the other way.

Most Japanese spend eight years learning English, but they learn it by rote and forget it. Even in Tokyo understandable English is hard to find unless you're at a hotel or using public transportation. Outside of Tokyo it's almost impossible. In China, even in the most rural parts, people seemed to speak and understand limited English and instead of running away, they surrounded us, begging to be interviewed.

Near the end of my tenure in Tokyo I did a story that nearly gave the executive producer a heart attack and probably hastened my exit. I don't even remember what the story was about but as usual we didn't get script approval until about four-thirty in the morning. I rarely did a standup that wasn't in the middle of the night.

On this night, it was raining hard and very dark so we did what we usually did in the middle of the night—we went to the red-light district where there were a few red lights here and there. We did my on-camera in about 10 minutes and beat it back to the bureau to edit it into our story and satellite it to New York.

I always listened to the footsteps of my bureau chief as she walked into my office with the feedback. I could usually tell by her walk how much the executive producer liked or hated the story. This time she was running, pitter-patter pitter-patter. She said, "He says you look like Goddamn Mary Poppins." I said "What?" She repeated herself. It turned out that when I got out of the van to do the standup, Yashi the cameraman handed me an umbrella from the back seat. I

83

grabbed it. Problem was the handle was white and the umbrella was transparent. I did look like "Goddamn Mary Poppins."

By the time I got back to the US the writing was on the wall. My days at NBC News were numbered. My contract was up. My agent was no longer optimistic. I was waiting for the phone call.

It didn't help when the story broke that I had been arrested at the Salt Lake airport for carrying a small amount of marijuana in my backpack, far less than an ounce. That was in the late 1990s when marijuana was considered evil, no matter the amount. I had some friends in Salt Lake who usually had a little extra "smoke" and gave me some. I left it in my son's home and went off to our cabin in Idaho.

Then I was back in Salt Lake on my way to a story in Pasadena and when I stopped by the house, the door was locked. By the time I got the door open I was running so late I tossed the baggie of less than a third of an ounce in my backpack and the security lady spotted it instantly. The airport police arrested me but, because the amount I possessed was so small, didn't think it was necessary to book me. So off I flew, badly shaken, to Pasadena. I kept my fingers crossed that just maybe the word wouldn't get out. The airport police seemed sympathetic.

About a week later, Salt Lake's *Deseret News* ran the story of my arrest. Before long it was picked up by papers around the country. NBC News never fired me. I never heard a word but I noticed the next morning that I was no longer listed as an employee. And there were no more paychecks.

My kids seemed okay with their dad's arrest. My wife was definitely not. She hadn't been a practicing Mormon for years but many of her relatives on her mom's side were good LDS and I had embarrassed them and her mom and dad, especially her dad who was not even a Mormon. I don't think my wife has ever forgiven me, and I feel bad about it. But I never felt guilty.

The laws prohibiting marijuana were completely unjustified in my view. To begin with, marijuana is not a gateway drug that leads to other more dangerous drugs. No matter what the DEA tells you there's never been a definitive study that proves a connection. Mostly I thought the laws were hypocritical.

I remember one night when my wife and I, my producer and his wife, and our two-man crew were at a social hour at George H.W. Bush's summer home in Kennebunkport, Maine. My wife was on the porch drinking beer with the future president George W. (that was before he quit drinking) and I was inside where we were drinking the hard stuff. I listened in on a righteous conversation where the wobbly participants condemned the scourge of marijuana. I was thinking to myself that the man should not be driving home.

If there was an upside to my arrest it was that I learned a lot about my friends. Some I had thought were good friends suddenly disappeared. To this day I have not heard from them. I remember my first bureau chief in Chicago who had become the weekend show producer. After he read the newspaper accounts he sent me a note saying, "Say it ain't so." I said, "I'm afraid it is." I never heard from him again. Others I had worked with but did not consider close friends stood by me and we have become very good friends. I will always be there if they need me.

Within a couple months of my public marijuana arrest I was working for a program on PBS called *Religion and Ethics Newsweekly*. I couldn't have imagined it. If they googled my name, one of the first things to pop up was my arrest, still is.

R & E was hosted by Bob Abernethy, a colleague of mine at NBC News. Bob was in Russia while I was in Asia. I didn't know Bob well but I liked what I knew then. Now I'm a huge fan.

Bob had a master's degree from the Woodrow Wilson School of Public Affairs at Princeton and had studied divinity at Yale. After he left NBC News he persuaded the pharmaceutical company Eli Lilly to sponsor a weekly national news program about religion. There wasn't anything on the air like it at the time.

The first story I did for the show was on polygamy, at topic I was quite familiar with. I thought it would be my first and last story. I couldn't imagine someone from a program called *Religion & Ethics Newsweekly* would want to hire someone like me, and I was quite sure I didn't want to work for a program called *Religion & Ethics Newsweekly*. Turns out I was wrong on both counts.

Over a period of twenty years I did many, many stories from all over the globe. When I left NBC I thought my career was over. Truth is, I enjoyed my work far more at *R & E*. The stories were longer and I'm long-winded. They had meat to them and relevance. Relevance is always important, especially if there is a lesson involved.

The executive producer of *R & E* Arnie Labaton is a Jewish scholar and an atheist. Going through a script with Arnie could be an ordeal. I had to justify every statement. Was the sky actually blue? How did I know that he or she actually felt a certain way. We always had a discussion over qualifiers like 'many' or 'most.' But when our session was over, I knew I was on safe ground.

I also became more understanding of other people's beliefs. Bob did not like stories that were downers. It was okay to criticize as long as there was light at the end of the tunnel. If there was no lesson or moral to the story, what was the point? On top of that I was able to do longer stories with excellent producers and good crews. It doesn't get better than that. As I have been heard to say many times, God bless Eli Lilly.

I was sorry when Lilly pulled its sponsorship, but it was understandable. The program was not promoted. It may have seemed other-worldly, out of another era, but when you got beyond the surface there was some very good reporting on subjects that were not covered anywhere else.

The staff of Extra, a magazine show where nothing was sacred, in Salt Lake City where everything was sacred

With KUTV at the 1980 Democratic convention in NYC

Interviewing Vice President George H.W. Bush. The more time
goes by the more I appreciate the integrity of this man.

PLACES

Place plays a key role in stories and our perspectives. I traveled all over the world, always comparing other people's places to my hometown, wondering if theirs had hope and opportunity, and if the people knew there was another world in another place.

TROUBLE IN PARADISE

When I first read about Everglades City I was instantly hooked. Here was a tiny town, surrounded by a national park, whose people hated the federal government and weren't terribly fond of each other. Seemed an awful lot like my hometown. My producer, Michele Dumont, had a more romantic view of it. She thought it was Florida before it was tamed, with not a retirement village in sight. I guess I'm not much of a romantic. I couldn't imagine anything but the dead fish I could smell even before we got there.

There were a couple of cafés in town where you can get seafood, but only hardcore fish eaters could wade through the smell to eat it. Everglades City was a fishing village almost in the middle of Everglades National Park. It wasn't quaint. It wasn't charming.

There was something unique about the place, something else in the air, and it wasn't friendliness. The first thing I sensed when I stepped out of the car was suspicion. People looked at you then looked away. For a town of only 500, where everybody knew everybody, nobody seemed to know anybody. The only thing lacking in Everglades City was the theme music, something like "The Good, the Bad and the Ugly."

I've always been fascinated by what it is that causes seemingly ordinary, law-abiding citizens to cross over the line and commit crime. Everglades City was that in spades. The crime spree there began with only one individual and then spread through the whole town.

As in Virgin, the people of Everglades City relied on tourism to make a living but the better paying jobs were disappearing under suffocating federal rules and regulations. The better paying jobs were all related to the fishing industry.

When you think about it, what happened was easy enough to explain. The local economy, like the national economy, went to hell, and it was pretty clear that it was only going to get worse. As the national park surrounding the town grew more and more popular and besieged by tourists from all over the globe, the park service was forced to impose tighter and tighter regulations on just about everything, including fishing. It got to be so restrictive, fishermen could no longer make a living no matter how many hours they worked, couldn't even sell their boats and get the hell out.

For Totch Brown it was a sad end of life as he knew it. Not only was his livelihood disappearing several years before he was ready to retire, but his favorite pastime was also in jeopardy because of encroaching park rules and regulators. Totch was one of the best alligator poachers in the Everglades.

When he took us for a boat ride it was clear he knew where they were and how to lure them to the surface in the dark of the night so he could shoot them and sell their hides. Unfortunately for Totch, park rangers were aware of his nocturnal activities so not only was his fishing career in jeopardy, his cash-generating hobby was not generating cash.

It wasn't just bad for Totch. The whole town was struggling and like most everyone, he blamed the park service and the nosy rangers. It's the same most everywhere. Find a national park and you'll find it surrounded by locals who hate the National Park Service almost as much as the bootleggers hated the feds. Some of the animosity, of course, is warranted. Park service officials can be arrogant and arbitrary.

Locals don't see the beauty around them, or the clean tourist dollars that support the local economy. They see blind bureaucracy and they see red. They bitch and complain from sunup until the bar closes, but they don't normally go out and deliberately break the law.

Remember, Totch was an alligator poacher so the notion of breaking the law was not an aberration to his outlook on life. I could have sat and listened for hours to his stories about leaving the law in his wake. He was a world class storyteller. But Totch went a step further, actually several hundred miles further south in his fishing boat to Cartagena, Colombia.

He did it knowing what he would find when he got there— something far more valuable that a catch of fish, something called 'Square Grouper.' Of course a boatload of prized 'Ganja' (marijuana) could land him in prison for a long time. But Totch was desperate and if he didn't get caught, he'd be rich.

Hardly anyone knew the bays and coves and inland waterways better than Totch and so even though drug enforcement agents operated boats, planes and surveillance balloons all along the Florida coast, Totch had no trouble evading detection, traveling in and out of Everglades' Ten Thousand Islands. He would travel close to shore at night and park his boat in the thick brush along the coast by day.

Once when I was traveling on Air Force Two with Vice President George Bush into Miami for a conference on drug trafficking, we flew by two of the surveillance balloons tethered near Marathon Key. While we were watching, one of the balloons accidentally came untethered and simply drifted into the heavens. It was a sight to see. I heard Vice President Bush say, "There goes 180 million dollars into thin air." Apparently there was no way to re-harness it.

Back to Totch. Before he headed south to Colombia, he had made some contacts with strangers who hung around local hotels and who he suspected were middlemen for the drug cartel. So when Totch snaked his way back to home territory, a journey that took a couple weeks, he already had a buyer, a very happy buyer. Not very often did such a large amount of dope slip through the most watched drug corridor in the US unmolested.

Totch started making regular trips to Colombia, sometimes harrowing cat-and-mouse adventures with DEA agents tracking him until he got inside the maze that is the Everglades.

He was prospering beyond his wildest dreams, so much so he needed help manning and unloading the boat. So he started hiring some of the local fishermen, who of course were no longer fishing, and before many months it seemed that Totch employed much of the town. There was work for everyone.

The change in Everglades City was not subtle. The town and its fishermen no longer stank of fish. Some started sporting gold chains around their necks. Some started driving Mercedes Benz automobiles instead of old rickety pickups. Others built add-ons to their house that dwarfed the existing structure. Some purchased brand new boats that were designed for speed, not fishing.

There were stories of $100 tips for a cup of coffee, bedrooms with sunken bathtubs, chandeliers hanging over worktables and swimming pools. Some folks made as much as $50,000 in one night carrying bales of marijuana off the boat. At first it was only Totch's boat. Before long there were others.

If Totch had employed the whole town, maybe no one would have tattled about the city's booming underground economy. But envy and jealousy, human nature being what it is, eventually overcame those who were left out of the gold rush and slowly the word got out that something was amiss in Everglades City.

One early morning just after dawn, dozens of DEA and FBI agents and local constables invaded the city and arrested fourteen adult males. Another eighteen were arrested from nearby communities. I couldn't verify if any women were arrested. Totch was the big catch but he got off with only a year and a half in prison and a fine of two million dollars for evading taxes. Inexplicably, authorities could never come up with enough evidence to convict Totch of actually ferrying tons of drugs on his fishing boat.

What happened to his associates is a good example of really stupid justice. For those who would give information implicating their neighbors, their sentences were relatively light, two to four years with time off for good behavior. Those who refused to squeal on their neighbor got a much harsher sentence even though they were charged with the same crime. Some were sentenced to as long as forty years.

So for a few years the town was populated mainly with women. There were households where the convicted head of the house had served his reduced time and was comfortably at home living next door to a house belonging to the neighbor he ratted out who was still in prison.

As you might suspect, there was a good deal of tension in Everglades City. Imagine what it would be like looking across the fence at the neighbor happily enjoying his family, knowing your dad was still behind bars for the same crime. Imagine the loathing.

There were situations like this in almost every block of town. Neighbors getting in fistfights was not uncommon. And it was not unusual to see boats moored at the dock riddled with bullet holes.

Along the inland waterway you could see the burned out hulls of boats that belonged to those who sold out their neighbors. This might explain the lack of friendliness in the air around Everglades City.

Where I grew up, there were no bullet holes or boats, nothing that violent. There was no gold, but water was almost as important and there was never enough of it. The town was divided over water. People fought over it but the weapon was usually a shovel, not a gun.

The good thing is that Everglades City no longer stinks so much of fish. Now, people go there to look for hidden treasures. There are rumors and stories of strong boxes filled with drug cash hidden deep in the surrounding marsh. Every city and town is looking for a way to stand out on the map. Everglades found one, not to mention being surrounded by the greatest road free wilderness in the U.S. of A.

Everglades now offers eco and nature tours, and hiking and kayaking and a pretty good museum. The old timers will still complain about encroaching government regulations. But like my home town, it's probably much better than it would have been without these regulations.

Unlike some of the folks who worked for him, Totch went on to live comfortably in Everglades City. He wrote a memoir called *Totch, A Life in the Everglades* and started a touring company called Totch's Tours. Not long before he died of a heart attack, Totch was honored as the grand marshal of Everglade City's Seafood Festival. For an old alligator hunter and a convicted criminal, life turned out pretty good. I don't remember him expressing any regrets, except that he got caught.

CHINA

Through my eyes the rush of China from a third world country into full bore capitalism has been nothing short of miraculous, but it's capitalism with an edge. You can still get in trouble without breaking the law. China remains a communist country, determined to stay that way, although history has shown it can change on a dime.

The changes I saw there over a decade were mind-boggling. During my first visit in the 1980s, private cars were scarce. There were new highways and freeways, but hardly any cars. Many Chinese wore nothing but blue and green Mao suits. The average person on the streets of Beijing seemed course and crude.

Restaurants were scarce and when you found one it was almost impossible to get service without tackling a waiter, and then when you did, they were rude. Maybe they didn't like being tackled. I had heard that waiters spit on the floor. It was true. The food was usually good, maybe because by the time it arrived, you were famished.

A few years later, I was traveling to Beijing once a month after Deng Xiaoping became the paramount leader and embraced capitalism with a passion. Then, I was physically accosted by street peddlers who wouldn't let me pass without looking at their wares. I remember walking down a steep hill from one of the entrances to the Great Wall when a vendor would not let me pass until I bought something.

Each time I would visit, there would be new monumental changes. One morning I was standing at one of the city's busiest intersections with thousands of people coming at me from every direction and I knew something was very different. Eventually it dawned on me.

Since my last visit, Chinese women had discovered lipstick. I suddenly realized I was surrounded by what seemed like zillions of ruby red lips.

The highways that were so sparsely populated during my first visits were clogged with carbon monoxide-spewing, Chinese-made automobiles. I went to Mexico City once to do a story on one of the world's most polluted cities. It was during the dreaded inversions of the winter months. The pollution was terrible but nothing compared to the skies over Beijing.

There were many days when I couldn't tell whether the sun was shining or not. Some days I couldn't see across the street. The air was tangible and suffocating. It wasn't just automobile pollution. Most residences and apartments were heated with coal. Add to that the dust blowing in from the Gobi Desert and it was difficult to breathe. It became a ritual: every time I flew out of China, the very first thing I would do was go into the lavatory and wash the dirt out of my eyes.

During my stays there I kept my eyes open for some of the cool products I purchased in the US that carried a Made-in-China label. I never found one. Everything in China was a knock-off, including some cars. The Jeep Cherokee, for instance. You could buy the real thing in Beijing, but you could also purchase a knock-off manufactured by the government.

We went with camera to one of the government stores and listened to a sales pitch for the jeep. It came loaded with air conditioning and electric windows for only $8,500, about half the price of a real one. It looked exactly like the real one, but when I took it for a test drive I couldn't get it out of first gear. I never even got out of the car lot. Two-hundred yards away, there was a real Jeep dealer who tried to sell me one of his products but didn't dare criticize the phony government jeep down the street. I asked, "Doesn't it hurt your business?" He responded as if I was an idiot. "It's not my business!" he screamed. "It's the government's business!"

Then I went to the Chinese equivalent of the Better Business Bureau, the Bureau of Consumer Complaints. It consisted of one room with two men, two phones, but only one line. They took turns answering. When I explained my problem they told me if I purchased a fake jeep, I should simply go back and demand a real jeep. They, too, acted as if I was some kind of idiot and then they shooed me away.

China is two worlds: one in the city, the other in the countryside. The current population of 1.4 billion is about equally divided, although that's changing as more people move o he cities for jobs. As in most countries, progress reaches the rural areas much more slowly, which is why China's leaders are always looking over their shoulder to make sure there's not an uprising brewing.

One day, my editor Richard Kipniss and I were invited to dinner with a family in the countryside. It was a Sunday and, as always on weekends, the main attraction in the village was an old cement pool table in the town square.

Since Richard and I had both spent too much time in pool halls we were a little better than average. It turned out to be a very physical experience. As the crowd gathered around, both men and women, elders and children would offer suggestions as to how to shoot the next shot. They pushed and shoved and pinched. If you lost, they treated you like a loser. They ignored you. Losing was no fun.

Outside the house where we were having dinner there was a brick wall. Almost every home in rural China has one. Behind it is the toilet—a hole in the ground and a ditch. The stench was nauseating.

I can't imagine getting used to it. The house had only one big room, a combination kitchen, living room, and bedroom. Although it was bitterly cold outside, inside was toasty. It took a while to realize that the heat was coming from the parents' cement bed, which also acted as a coal-fired stove. I imagine the bed must have gotten pretty warm.

The room had one lightbulb and one water faucet. The wood stove was outside. I expected to get food poisoning, but the food was tasty and apparently quite safe. The family was unusual in that there were two daughters.

This was during China's "one child policy" and normally if there was only one child, it was a boy. At the end of the meal, the mother chided the youngest daughter for not finishing all the food on her plate. The mom said, "Think about all the starving children in America." She wasn't being cute. I heard other parents say the same thing.

I spent most of one year in China going back and forth from my home in Tokyo, waiting for Deng Xiaoping to die. It was a deathwatch, and I wasn't the only network correspondent doing it. Back then it would have been embarrassing not to have a correspondent in-country when the leader died. That is no longer true. When Deng did die in 1997, it was the last story I reported for NBC News out of China.

After all that waiting we almost missed the story. About two in the morning I received a call from the New York desk telling me that wire stories were reporting Deng had died. I started bouncing off the walls because we had less than four hours to write a story, get it approved, do a standup, cut a narration, edit it, and then rush to CCTV (Chinese government TV) and satellite it to NBC in New York.

The only serious problem was I couldn't find my editor or cameraman. Apparently they had been out getting thoroughly soused and when they got back to their rooms they had fallen into a deep, inebriated sleep.

I finally roused them by banging on the door so loud the hotel security guards came running and were demanding to know, in Mandarin, just what in the hell was going on. If Kyle Epler, the cameraman, hadn't come to the door, they were going to take me away. That was the good news; the bad news was when I looked in Kyle's eyes, they were not in focus. He had no idea where he was or who I was. He was my cameraman.

Finally, my editor opened his door dazed and bleary-eyed. The pressure was on him more than any of us and he was not always great under pressure. We had talked about it several times. He was a very good editor, but facing a difficult deadline he occasionally descended into denial. I would say, "We've only got five minutes," and he would say, "Hey don't worry about it." It was a helpless, terrifying feeling. The more I got after him, the more he would slow down.

We did miss a deadline once and there is hardly anything that reflected more negatively on a correspondent and the crew than missing a deadline, which then forces the executive producer to restructure his newscast. They don't like that and they don't forget it.

Because we had so many false alarms (there were no death rumors that day), we had shot very little same-day footage. At three in the morning it's difficult to find any footage. It's especially difficult to find an interview, and nobody was dumb enough to do a pre-interview about the Chinese leader dying. We shot my standup as we always seemed to do in Asia, in the dark. Considering his hangover and the dire circumstances, the editor did a masterful job, but we were running perilously late.

I will always remember the drive to CCTV, thirty minutes of terror. My first thoughts were that we were going to die. Our driver, who was normally very cautious so as not to dent his pride and joy—an old, battered Toyota—drove like a madman. We actually ran a roadblock and I was certain that our car would be riddled with bullets as we raced away. I think we rushed through the roadblock so fast and the Beijing police were so sleepy, they didn't come after us. Amazingly we made the deadline, and the story was not bad.

New York wanted live shots for the new MSNBC channel and the only place we could do those was atop the CCTV building. To get to the top of the building, we had to climb three flights of stairs and then a ladder attached to the side of the building, up two more flights to the roof. (I don't like heights. When I was a kid I climbed a tiny apple tree and Mom had to call for help to get me down.) I ended up spending most of the day on the roof, waiting for the next live shot rather than climb back down and up again.

I spent a lot of time in China running from or dodging the Public Security Bureau police. The PSB are the federal police, a quasi-military unit with very large troopers. They always glared at me as if I was a suspect.

When we were on a story we had to move like bandits, in and out quickly, usually with the police one stop behind us. When they told you to move, you moved, or they moved you physically. There was no negotiating. As they became wiser to our ways and technology, the cops would simply confiscate our shot tape. Again, there was no negotiating.

I remember doing a story in the countryside about how parents were paying their life savings to get a sonogram for the pregnant mom. Sonograms had just become available in China. If the parents found out the baby was going to be a girl they usually aborted it, because of the one-child policy. For they weren't much use on the farm; boys were much more valuable. It was a good story and we had some excellent interviews to back it up, but what we needed were pictures.

We drove from one clinic to another and the folks from the Public Security Bureau were always only minutes behind us. We could look back and see them. It was a hairy, scary day. I don't know how many pedestrians we nearly ran over. That's another lasting impression of China, no matter where you go, there is no end to people. They're everywhere.

Because of the one-child policy and the deadly prejudice against females, China is now facing a crisis. In 2016, there were almost a staggering 50 million more men than women. The Chinese believe as do most Asians that males need sex often or they become bored and violent. One of the only ways to control them is to send them to war. The government has abandoned the one-child policy and is now offering tax incentives to parents of baby females. Chinese males can be found in Thailand, Vietnam, and Korea, hunting for wives.

NORTHERN ADVENTURES

I've stood on the shifting ice at the North Pole. I've been kissed and bear-hugged by an amorous Eskimo woman in Nome, Alaska. I've balanced on an ice floe as my hosts slaughtered a walrus. If someone asked me which of these episodes I would like to forget the most, it would be staring into the eyes of the dying walrus.

North Pole

I went to the North Pole for the *Today* show. This is how I began my first story.

Good morning. You can find this place on your world map at ninety degrees north latitude. It is more commonly known as the North Pole. From where I'm standing there's no east, no west, no north. It's all downhill from here. The closest land is two miles south of me on the ocean floor. The North Pole is one gigantic ice floe.

We were only allowed to stand on the pole a little less than an hour. It was a short ending to a long, tedious ride in a noisy Twin Otter airplane, the workhorse of the arctic region. We—my crew and myself—were without my producer, Ned Judge, because there wasn't enough room in the plane for Ned. He's a big guy and the plane was already full of paying customers who paid through the nose for the experience and the bragging rights that very few humans could claim.

There were five paying passengers. One was a lawyer, another a hotel executive. There was a doctor from Southern California and then a couple who saved for years to make the trip. Bill Robens was

107

a machinist who had lost part of his leg in an accident. This was his first airplane ride. I had the impression he would crawl to the pole if it was the only way. His wife Phyllis was a junior high school teacher. Our tour guide Susan Voorhees was the first woman to stand on the pole.

We made several stops along the way. The first was one of my favorite cities, Montreal. From there we were aboard the Twin Otter on our way to Resolute Bay where it was a balmy twenty five below zero. There aren't many creature comforts at that temperature. One of them is food. It keeps you warm and it keeps you going. Parties crossing the ice on sleds often consume 6,000 calories a day and still lose weight.

It took the early explorers months to make the journey and many never completed it. It took us only three days, but after hours of droning engines, a dogsled didn't sound bad. As we worked our way north, our next stop was King Christian Island. We knew we were headed north even though our compass wasn't sure. The closer we got to the magnetic north pole, the more it confused our compass. We appeared to be going in circles. Fortunately the Twin Otter was equipped with an inertial navigation system which ignored the magnetic pull of the pole and flew us in the right direction, north.

Our last night was at the Eureka Weather Station. It's the last human settlement before an endless horizon of pack ice. Very early in the morning the pilots were pre-heating the turbo-prop for the 3,000 mile round-trip to the pole. We would be making stops along the way but one engine would always be kept running. If they both stopped and would not start in the thirty- and forty-below temps we would be screwed, and then we would die. That was very much on my mind.

When Admiral Robert Peary said he was the first to arrive at the pole in 1909, his expedition traveled with 246 dogs and a host of Eskimo crewmembers. His claim was later disputed by explorers who said it was impossible to cover the last five miles in such a short time.

From the beginning, the National Geographic Society stood by Peary, and when I questioned the magazine's senior editor, he continued his support with the lame explanation that Peary "knew where north was." Even after commissioning an investigation that did not support Peary's claim, *Nat Geo* still stood by him. I cannot understand why.

Instead, the first person to set foot on the geographic North Pole was an insurance agent from Minnesota named Ralph Plaisted in 1968. It took him forty-three days aboard a snowmobile. In between Peary and Plaisted there were many pole attempts, some ending in tragedy. In 1847 Explorer Sir John Franklin's entire expedition of 129 men froze to death on remote islands hundreds of miles south of the pole. Explorers have tried walking to it, flying over it in a hot-air balloon, and one tried it on a motorcycle. In 1958 the submarine Nautilus cruised under the pole but didn't surface.

The North and South Poles are similar in a number of ways. Both are extremely cold, windy, and icy, and basically uninhabitable. But there is one big difference. I would have been happier landing on the South Pole because the ice sits on land, not just ice and ocean.

We departed the Eureka Weather Station with fifty-gallon barrels of gas in the middle of the passenger compartment. The tanks on the Twin Otter couldn't carry enough to get us up and back so we made one last stop at a refueling station known simply as 86 North. There we were greeted by two very alone men who lived there in a tent during the summer months.

They refueled our plane for the last push and we traded our gas for theirs. I tried to talk to these gentlemen. One was a Russian, the other an Inuit Eskimo. Neither was very talkative. They said they listened to the BBC and Russian radio and ate tons of food to stay warm. That was about all they said. I did my best not to show that I thought they were both nuts. No amount of money could convince me spend several weeks of my life staring at nothing but ice. No mountains. The only animal I saw was a snow bunny.

When we finally arrived over the pole it did not look inviting. We saw a white landscape broken up by huge fissures and ice floes that could swallow our plane in an instant. This had been the time of year when the ice was quite thin and appeared to be alive and angry. If this was only a practice approach it wouldn't have been nearly as scary as the realization that our pilots intended to land us on top of shifting ice.

In fact a plane did sink in 1925 on an expedition led by Norwegian explorer Roald Amundsen. It turned out the plane was actually 150 miles short of the pole.

Our pilots attempted four touch-and-go landings before they decided it was safe. On the fifth attempt, the Twin Otter and its very nervous passengers touched down. It was the shortest landing I can recall, including landing on an aircraft carrier. We were told by our pilots that we had a maximum of one hour, no more. I've always thought pilots were a little crazy. This confirmed it.

These are the things the paying passengers did for one hour at the North Pole: The hotel executive planted the Hawaiian flag. The California doctor just kept running around the Twin Otter so he could say he had quite literally run around the world many times. The Robens stood staring at the endless ice. I tried to think deep but was distracted by how much time the passengers spent watching my crew at work. I resolved then that one day I would start a company that would charge people a few hundred dollars a day to carry our tripod and sound gear.

I was wearing one of the most expensive cold weather parkas available at the time, supposedly good for temperatures down to forty below zero. It was very disappointing to discover that the temperature at the pole was almost thirty above zero, almost balmy. We had brought along a bottle of brandy to celebrate our place in history. We would have brought champagne but we thought it would freeze. It turned out we would have been drunk before it froze.

I was moved by what I saw. It was endless and seamless in every direction, the white ice against the bleached, white sky, as if we were at the center of infinity. We could have been on another planet. I have never felt more insignificant or, even though I was surrounded by several humans, more alone. I would have thought that it would be possible to hear a whisper in a place so isolated, but the sound of cracking ice made it difficult even to hear each other speak. That, and the noise of the plane's engines reminding us that we needed to get the hell out of there.

Savoonga

I had misgivings, but who can say no to a story on an island in the Bering Straits of Alaska. I'd been to Alaska before, and it was always a spiritual experience. The landscape overwhelmed me. The chance of seeing animals in the wild excited me—sighting a wild animal always makes my day. And then there are the glaciers. For me, there's nothing more alive than a calving glacier, cracking and spraying for hundreds of yards.

I was going to a small village called Savoonga on St. Lawrence Island in the Bering Sea about 160 miles south of Nome. It was an Eskimo village and the reason we were going there was to document a walrus hunt. The local economy consists largely of subsistence hunting for walrus and bowhead whales, although they kill just about everything else that lives in or on the water. Seals are another favorite but not nearly as prized as walruses and whales.

Hunting these mammals is of course very controversial. It drives animal rights activists crazy. The Yup'ik Eskimos say the hunt is essential to their survival. They say they use virtually every part of the animal for food, clothing or hunting paraphernalia. Killing these mammals was not just a sport.

My own misgivings were twofold. I didn't want to see anything get killed and certainly not a walrus that looks like a couple of my uncles. It didn't really seem fair to me. How is a walrus supposed to defend itself? I have no trouble with people who use rifles for sport or for sustenance. At least that's what I say. I'm not sure how sincerely I believe it. Killing something always makes me feel terrible, but then I've never been that hungry.

Savoonga is not a charming place. You'd think as an island village it would hold some allure, but charm would get lost in this place. It was one of the uglier villages I've ever had the misfortune to visit. It sits on permafrost so the trails are made of wood and where there is no wood, mud. The houses are ramshackle.

Next to the houses were scaffolds bearing the carcasses of dead animals. I saw a polar bear being skinned. Because of the freezing temperatures the carcasses did not stink but they certainly added to the ugliness of the place, along with the trash strewn everywhere. It seemed that almost every one of the 600 or so residents had their own pollution spewing ATV or four-wheeler. We had our own to carry our camera gear.

My crew, producer, and myself were staying in what we called the Savoonga Hilton. It was our attempt at gallows humor. The Savoonga Hilton would make a Motel 6 look like a Four Seasons resort. The rooms were tiny and disgusting. Refinements such as running water, hot water, or any water did not exist. Same could be said of toilets. It was the first time I had the displeasure of using a "honey pot." For those who don't know, it's a bucket. We were stuck in this hole for three days before our hosts spotted a walrus.

Our deal with the tribe was that we would pay $1,400 per day each for three fourteen-foot dinghies, whether we used them or not. We were paying $4,200 a day, walrus or no walrus. We were stuck there in the Savoonga Hilton, essentially prisoners, and the natives weren't friendly. They never invited us into any of their homes, which didn't make us unhappy. There was no TV. There was no radio. There was no toilet.

Finally, a walrus sighting. We jumped in our fourteen-foot dinghy. Our hosts jumped in the two other fourteen-footers we were paying for. There were a couple of other boats joining us. The Bering Sea that day was churning with icebergs, some bigger than a house. We saw plenty of seals riding the ice but that day they were of no interest to the hunters. Our prey was walrus. We only saw one.

Most of our hosts were using lever-action Winchester 30-30s, a rifle I was familiar with. I was immediately uncomfortable when it appeared that some of these hunters were teenagers. That worry was amplified after the hunters, old and young, spotted the walrus and then circled it, firing as they closed in from all angles. In other words, they were firing at each other with the poor walrus in the middle. You could see bullets splashing into the water.

Eventually, somebody hit the walrus and we moved in for the kill. I swear I could see the fear in the walrus's eyes. We later learned it was a male. It was shot several times before it was dragged on top of an ice floe, bleeding. We all got out of our tiny boats and stood there in the bloody water. There's no place I'd have rather not been.

The hunters quickly gutted the walrus and when they cut open the stomach, one of them grabbed a handful of clams and offered them to me as a prize. I was thinking, "Surely they don't expect me to eat these." But surely they did. I smiled my best smile and said no, that I had a very weak stomach from the bobbing boat ride. They laughed but it meant more clams (a delicacy) for them.

We had our story, with great pictures, though I would have never shown them at mealtime. We had interviews explaining how this was a tradition that went back eons and was crucial to the survival of the village. I'm thinking, who wants this village to survive anyway? I did not have a warm feeling for these people and I'm sure the feelings were mutual. It was an unfriendly cold, sterile place.

I can't remember anyone saying "hello" or "welcome." We were like aliens. I remember thinking that they could kill us, and no one would ever know. Remember the wood chipper in the movie *Fargo*? I'm sure the grizzly killing of the walrus didn't help my outlook.

We had chartered a flight to Savoonga and the charter was scheduled to pick us up the next morning. Just one more night at the Hilton. My producer visited the village chief to pay for the boats. It was over $30,000. He came back. We drank a brandy and prepared to depart.

Then one of the villagers dropped by to say the chief was not happy, that my producer had short-changed him. I knew that was not true.

My producer was a stickler about expenses. His denial did not quell the chief's complaint, which gradually grew into anger throughout the village. Before long we grew concerned about the safety of the producer.

Finally, cameraman Jim Watt called a friend of his who was a higher-up with the Alaska Highway Patrol. He agreed to call the chief and calm him down. A highway patrol plane would be available to get us out of there if necessary. It turned out not to be. We spent an uneasy night and then the next morning drove our four-wheelers up the windy road to the plateau where the landing strip was located. I'll never forget looking back and seeing several ATVs from the village following us about a half-mile back.

Happily our charter sat there revved up waiting for us. I don't think we've ever loaded gear so fast. We zoomed away just as the entourage from the village arrived. They weren't waving goodbye.

Nome

At the end of this book, I've included a script I wrote for an NBC News magazine story I did on Nome, Alaska. It was one of my first trips to Alaska, and my first to Nome. A couple of things stand out that weren't in the script.

I had broken my toe the day before my son Jak and I departed for Nome. When we got in the air on the Northwest flight, the pain became so bad I was on the verge of asking the pilot to make an emergency stop. I realize now how silly that sounds—making an emergency landing for a painful toe. I'm sure it would have been a first. I could tell my son was sincerely hoping I wouldn't make such a request. I didn't but I was in extreme pain, probably because of the air pressure in the cabin.

When we arrived in Anchorage my producer Ned Judge was there ahead of us. He was waiting at the curb in a stretch limo. On one hand, I was happy because I knew how much it would impress Jak. On the other hand, I've always hated limos. They're pretentious and they take up too many parking spaces. Ned had the driver take us on a tour of Anchorage while we looked at tapes that had been shot by other crews, and we gulped cold beer. Life was as it should be. The next day we flew on to Nome.

The absence of darkness really got to me. It's a mood changer. The sky would dim a bit but only in the wee hours. It really messes up your body clock. I was depressed most of the time. I guess that's one of the reasons Alaska has such a high suicide rate.

What I remember most vividly about Nome never made it in the script. I had just finished an interview with a park ranger. It was about midnight but it looked more like noon. The ranger had sunglasses on. I walked across the street and into the Board of Trade Saloon where it was coal-bin dark.

I could barely see the bartender when I ordered a cold beer. Cold is no problem in Nome. My eyes had still not adjusted when I heard a very husky voice from the stool next to me. It said, "Ya wanna kiss?" I said, "What?" It said, "Ya wanna kiss?" She reached over to hug me and I mumbled something like "I was just leaving." She kissed me on the neck as I got the hell out of there.

That's not the only reason why there's no place like Nome.

On our way to Resolute Bay with producer Ned Judge in the foreground. After we loaded the fuselage with 50 gallon barrels of gasoline, there was no room for Ned to make the final leg to the pole

The Twin Otter is the workhorse of the Northern Territories. The pilots kept The engines running for fear that they would freeze up

This man paid thousands of dollars for the privilege of planting flags at the top of the world

Dodging ice floes in the Bering Sea off Saint Laurence Island

Looking for walrus with teenage hunters in the Bering Sea

Pulling in the wounded walrus where the hunters then cut open the stomach and offered me a handful of half-digested clams

Palm Beach, Donald, and Me

I visited Palm Beach not long after the future president purchased the Mar-a-Lago mansion from the estate of Marjorie Merriweather Post, heir to the Post Cereal fortune. He got a good deal. Marjorie paid about $8 million when she had the mansion built in 1924. The president bought it for $7 million and that was after it was designated a National Historic Landmark. He did it by playing hardball.

Originally, he offered the Post family $25 million, which was rejected because there were other higher bids. So Trump announced he was purchasing the land between Mar-a-Lago and the ocean and he was going to build a four-story home that would block the Mar-a-Lago beach view. The threat brought an end to competitive bids. The estate had no choice but to sell to Trump. That story alone would have been enough to get Trump elected.

The Mar-a-Lago mansion is huge and sits on seventeen acres of valuable Palm Beach real estate. The building now has 126 rooms (Trump added a few) that include a private club, guest rooms, and a spa. The family lives in quarters closed off from the rest of the house. Trump added a 20,000-square-foot ballroom. The club has five clay tennis courts and a waterfront pool. The place also has three bomb shelters.

Palm Beach is unique. Every community is a little unique for one reason or another, but Palm Beach stands alone. Actually it's an island connected to the mainland by a bridge—a drawbridge. Crime is not allowed in Palm Beach. If the wrong sort began to move onto the island, lifting the bridge is always an option. I'm not the one who said that. I heard it from the police chief himself. He may have been kidding, but it is possible to raise that drawbridge.

The streets of Palm Beach are lined with Rolls Royce's, Bentleys and Mercedes. The main drag, Worth Avenue, is appropriately named. It's known as the Rodeo Drive of Palm Beach and it's a fun drive just looking at the fancy cars and stretch limos. The shops along Worth Avenue have been called the "rabbit hole of high-end shopping." Others have called it "ridiculous." I like Worth Avenue but I wouldn't buy a suit there. I couldn't buy a suit there.

Hollywood is for movie stars, Washington for politicians, New York for financiers. Palm Beach is for the rich. Before Trump (henceforth to be known as BT) that meant old rich, blue-blood rich, Mary Lou Whitney rich. She was the wife of Cornelius Vanderbilt Whitney, the mining magnate and philanthropist.

When I sat in the living room of her home, one of seven she owned around the world, Mary Lou explained that "You can't live in Palm Beach unless you have a great deal of money." She went on to say, "It's not a place to come if you are really on a very strict budget." Over the years I've had the experience of interviewing the truly rich who were born rich and never were average. I used to think they were having me on, that they were making fun of themselves. Then I came to realize they are so shielded from reality they have no idea that people are living in a completely different world just a few miles down the road. They're not bad people, they just have different worries.

While we were in Palm Beach, we attended a charity ball raising money for a big-band hall of fame. I love big bands, but where else would you find a charity to support them. Mary Lou was dancing. So was Colonel Spencer, the cousin to Princess Di. Prince Charles played polo at Palm Beach.

Billionaire financier Henry Kravis played there. The Kennedys had a home there. Brian Mulroney, the former Canadian prime minister, lived in Palm Beach. Michael Jackson lived there briefly and returned for his honeymoon. The Duke and Duchess of Windsor frequently holidayed in Palm Beach. It's an impressive list.

Mary Lou described Palm Beach as a sort of Camelot, "A place little girls and big girls can dream about." She said, "It's sort of a fairy world. It's like something you might dream about as a child when you look at those beautiful pictures in the book and Prince Charming and the queen and all the ladies of court. It certainly is lovely and you forget there's all the wickedness in the world for the short time that you're here. It's a lovely feeling."

One thing that leaped out at me at the ball was that so many of the women were elderly, even ancient in appearance, and they were dancing with very young, virile men. One woman, one of the "grand dames," reportedly well over 90, was dancing with a handsome South American male who was twice as tall. She was literally hugging his hip.

My contact and guide was herself a Palm Beach socialite named Helen Bernstein. Helen had a column in the *Palm Beach Post* called "Potholes in Paradise." She was a philanthropist particularly for the arts, on several boards, including the New York Library, the Vatican Museum, and the Palm Beach Symphony, for which she chaired the annual dinner dance. Helen had a very dry, biting wit. We became good friends.

She explained why there were so many old dames and so many young gigolos: "Because the men that have made a lot of money and have come to Palm Beach don't live very long. They've already worked very hard and they're not... They're older and they die soon. There's a group that, you know, take these women here and there and they're all very nice men."

I think the word got out because there were quite a few of the "very nice men" at the dance. It's the elderly ladies who imported the young studs. Helen pointed out a couple that must've had a seventy-year age difference. She said the woman hired the young man as her driver when she was on a shopping spree in New York. When they got back to LaGuardia Airport to return to Palm Beach, the woman persuaded the driver to leave the car and come to Shangri-La with her.

Helen's husband was an investment banker who took us out for a couple of hugely expensive crab dinners. He was Helen's age. We became friends too. Once when I visited Helen he wasn't around. I asked her where he was. She explained that her former husband had run away with their Brazilian maid. Turns out being rich has its drawbacks.

Helen knew Donald Trump personally and explained why he was having such a hard time getting accepted by Palm Beach society. She said she didn't think that coming into Palm Beach and making a big splash was such a good idea. She said it didn't sit well the way he swished into Palm Beach bragging that he was buying an estate even the government couldn't afford to keep up.

Marjorie Post had willed her mansion to the government but the government didn't want to spend a million dollars a year to maintain it. So the government gave it back. Helen told me, "You can't try to overwhelm the people with your money and your power." And that's what The Donald did, before things went sour.

Here's what happened. First, Donald was told he couldn't land his helicopter at Mar-a-Lago because it wasn't zoned for that. It was a setback but he figured he could maneuver around it. Then he discovered that the water around Mar-a-Lago wasn't deep enough to moor the Trump yacht. Not much he could do about that. Much worse, Mar-a-Lago sits almost directly under the flight path of the Palm Beach Airport. That was huge. Flight paths are usually located over the poorer parts of town where resident protests can't be heard. I was there when jet airplanes took off and landed and it was loud.

Finally—and this was the lowest blow of all—The Donald was not welcome at the Palm Beach Bath and Tennis Club, one of the oldest and most exclusive private clubs in the country. It was a slap in the face that someone so rich and famous wasn't allowed to join.

About a month after I reported the story about Palm Beach and its unwelcome new resident for the *Today* show I was in Atlanta visiting my kids on a weekend. I didn't think even the NBC New York desk knew where to contact me.

I was surprised when the phone in my room rang. I answered. It was Donald Trump. He said, "I just wanted you to know that I could have belonged to the Palm Beach Bath and Tennis Club, I just didn't want to." He was very pleasant. I didn't know what to say. I know what I was thinking. I was thinking, yeah sure. Now I'm not so sure. Maybe he didn't want to join because Jews and blacks and other "undesirables" were not welcome. As I write this I'm just now experiencing my first positive thought about Donald Trump. I expect it will be the only one.

A few years after he purchased Mar-a-Lago, Trump fell on hard times. In negotiating with his bankers, he agreed to divide Mar-a-Lago into smaller properties. That very much alarmed Palm Beach residents. The city council rejected the idea. So Trump decided instead to turn the estate into a private club that, unlike other Palm

Beach resorts, accepts Jews, blacks and even people who like to call attention to themselves.

So Mar-a-Lago is now the "Winter White House" or the "Southern White House." Nixon never wanted to live there. Jimmy Carter was offered and refused. That's why the government gave the estate back to the Merriweather Post Estate. Trump seems to like it. I know a couple reasons why. The fee to join the club doubled from $100,000 to $200,000 after his election as president. The club has 500 paying members. Overnight guests pay up to $2,000 a night.

Over the years, Trump has filed numerous lawsuits against Palm Beach County to try to get the airport to divert the flight path from over his estate. The last one in 2015 asked $100 million in damages because of the unreasonable amount of noise, emissions, and pollutants at Mar-a-Lago. He claimed that city officials actually pressured the FAA to direct air traffic over Mar-a-Lago in a "deliberate and malicious" act.

Here's the kicker. Now that Donald Trump is president, the Secret Service imposed a no-fly zone over the estate so there's no more airplanes zooming overhead, and Palm Beach exempted the president from the ban on helicopters on residential properties, at least while he's president. The president conquered Palm Beach.

PEOPLE

People can surprise me and sometimes people can change me. Sometimes it's our perception of them that changes. You never know for sure until you get there.

SERGEANTS 3

In between my junior and senior high school years, I landed a job working on the production of a movie called *Sergeants 3*. Actually it was two jobs. By day I watched the lunch line to make sure the extras didn't take too much food. By night I worked at a mansion rented by the "Rat Pack". This was one of only two movies starring the entire Rat Pack. The second, *Ocean's 11*, is much better known.

At the time, the Rat Pack was probably the most famous clan of Hollywood's bad boys. They were led by the crooner himself, Frank Sinatra, followed by Dean Martin, Sammy Davis Jr., Peter Lawford, Joey Bishop, and other lesser known luminaries like the Crosby brothers. In case you're interested, the term "rat pack" actually came from Lauren Bacall. When her husband Humphrey Bogart and Frank Sinatra came home hungover and dragging, she said they "looked like a pack of rats." The term stuck although Sinatra never liked it.

My buddy Kenny Leach from Kanab, Utah, got me the job. He was a few years older and had done some work on other movie shoots in southeastern Utah. It was a time when Hollywood was all about Westerns and so many of them were made around Kanab, it was known as Hollywood East. Dean Martin had taken a liking to Kenny, so he got a job and then got me one.

Sergeants 3 was a comedy directed by the great John Sturgess. The plot was not complicated. Sinatra, Martin, and Lawford, the Sergeants 3, were up against some really bad Indians (now known as Native Americans). The sergeants had some help from a black jazz trumpet player and former slave who wanted to join the cavalry— who else but Sammy Davis Jr. Ultimately Davis saves the day when

129

he warns the cavalry about an ambush and he is rewarded with a commission in the cavalry.

At the time, I had no clue about the plot. All I knew was that there were dozens of extras riding horses, or at least trying to. For some of them, it must've been their first attempt. I remember ambulances moving in and out all day transporting injured extras that had fallen off their horses.

Some were hit and knocked off their horse by rubber-tipped arrows. One scene I watched unfold had the soldiers riding through a canyon when they were ambushed by Indians shooting from the other side of the hill. Arrows flying out of the sky; Cavalrymen falling off their horses. It was a disaster. They didn't have enough ambulances. As a bystander it was exciting to watch, probably more exciting than the actual movie.

Although most of the filming took place in northern Arizona, the stars stayed at Parry Lodge in Kanab. It was a cool place featuring a great restaurant with hundreds of pictures of Hollywood stars on the walls. In the middle of the property was a beautiful pool where I got to go swimming one night with Ruta Lee, one of the stars. The Rat Pack stayed in rustic, motel-style rooms connected to each other.

The rooms were spacious and comfortable. I mention them because from time to time the maids allowed me inside. I saw stacks of pink silk shirts Sinatra wore, and pairs of his velvet shoes. Dean Martin wore more manly attire with checkered shirts and leather jackets. Peter Lawford's room had pictures of his brother-in-law President John F. Kennedy.

Sammy Davis Jr. was married to the Swedish actress May Britt, although she never visited him. He had a full-length picture of Britt on the back of his bathroom door. She was considerably taller than

Davis but there was more talent packed in his five-foot-five frame than any man I've ever known. They were a very unusual couple and apparently received a lot of hate mail. At the time, thirty-three states considered interracial marriage a crime.

There were cops on hand whenever the Rat Pack was out in public. I couldn't figure out why. Locals would simply stand and stare. Truth is, they were more in need of protection than the stars. On more than one occasion, folks living in white homes would wake in the middle of the night to find the Rat Pack showing a movie on the side of their house. I thought the stars were actually very gracious to the Kanabites. Sinatra donated several thousand dollars to the local high school.

Every few days a DC-3 would arrive from Las Vegas, a couple hundred miles away. The plane would be stocked with booze (as there was not a good selection available in Mormon country), caviar, and other delicacies and whores.

We didn't know for sure they were whores but they didn't have a role in the movie, and they were really sexy. One afternoon Kenny and myself took two of these young ladies out to show them the so-called bottomless lake outside of Kanab. They seemed to be only interested in how deep the lake was.

The filming took place in several locations in the red mountains surrounding Kanab. The production company had a helicopter to ferry the actors from one set to another. There was also a doctor, in case one of the actors got sick, or was too hungover to act. I was told there was a special injection. From what I could tell, Dean Martin was the only actor who never needed sobering up. His inebriated persona was apparently mostly an act, at least during that period of his life.

By day, I stood around and, as instructed, watched the lunch line to make sure the Indian extras didn't steal too much food. I don't know why the production company thought the cavalry extras wouldn't steal food.

The demeaning view of "Indians" hadn't changed much in the previous hundred years, and still hasn't. Brooklyn-born, Italian-Puerto Rican descendent Henry Silva played Indian Chief Mountain Hawk in the movie. Apparently the director didn't think Indians could play Indians.

By night, I worked in a beautiful mansion about five miles out of town. Some nights I would work in the kitchen, other nights I would serve drinks. I liked those nights best. More than once, Sinatra came up behind me and slipped a fifty dollar bill in my back pocket. He'd say, "Go get laid, kid." I saw him walk up behind waitresses, kiss them on the neck, and tuck a one hundred dollar bill in their belts.

Each night Sinatra and his co-stars would take a look at the day's rushes, the scenes they had shot that day. This was my favorite part of the evening. More often than not, Sinatra would not be happy. He could swear like he could sing. No one was better. It was like listening to an opera filled with profanity. He used words I had never heard before, really crude expletives so articulately spoken— if not opera, it was literature.

One day while I was loitering on location, I watched Sammy Davis Jr. grab a shovel and knock invading Indians off their horses. The metal end of the shovel was actually made of rubber. There was a lot going on in front of me. A couple of workers were throwing sand into huge fans. An NFL quarterback was throwing pretend dynamite through a window, and Davis was knocking Indians off their horses.

Something wasn't working right because they kept doing the scene over and over. On the last take, Davis mistakenly grabbed one of the workers' real shovels and knocked a poor extra off his horse. The Indian extra went away in an ambulance. Davis had a sprained wrist.

Most nights, Sinatra and company would stand around a grand piano and sing while Sammy accompanied them on the piano. That night, with his sprained wrist, Davis could not play. My buddy Kenny said his friend could play. That was me. With more than a decade of piano lessons, I was good at reading sheet music but I had small hands that could barely reach more than an octave.

Fortunately there was a book of sheet music on the piano and so I played a few songs. I was so scared, excited and lost in the moment, I couldn't remember what I played until I spoke about it with Kenny years later. He remembered "Luck Be a Lady" and the "Lady is a Tramp." I'm sure I played terribly, like I was in a trance. Maybe that's why I couldn't remember what I played. I never practiced after that. Anyway I had climbed the mountain. How many people get to accompany Frank Sinatra, Dean Martin, and Sammy Davis Jr.? Peter Lawford and Joey Bishop couldn't sing any better than I could play.

At the end of the shoot, Dean Martin shouted Kenny and me to the Sands Hotel to attend the Red Skelton show. The head production chef agreed to lend us his red Cadillac convertible. Someone must have twisted his arm. Las Vegas was a couple hundred miles away and it meant a drive through the long tunnel and down the switchbacks of Zion National Park. When we got to the exit, there was a ranger standing in the road signaling us to stop. Apparently Kenny's driving scared the hell out of other drivers. The ranger didn't give him a ticket but said he should be in jail.

We had a ringside table at the Red Skelton show. It was by far the crudest Las Vegas show I've ever watched, but Marilyn Monroe was seated only a table from us. We got to meet her and the actor Yul Brynner. Pretty heady stuff for a 17-year-old.

EVEL KNIEVEL

The evening I walked into the bar in Butte, Montana, it was dusk and I had a new leather bag my wife had bought for me in Mexico. I loved bags and it was a beauty. It didn't look like a purse, at least not to me. It was dark inside the bar, with maybe five or six cowboys sipping beer. As I was about to sit down, I heard one say to the others, "Isn't that a pretty purse. It's kind of girlie isn't it?" I pretended not to hear, sat down, ordered a beer.

A few minutes later I got up, went out to the car, and did not return with the bag. I had to go back inside because I was supposed to meet Evel Knievel, the world's most famous daredevil, later that night.

Evel was at the peak of his career. He had completed seventy-five motorcycle jumps from ramp to ramp, setting world records including jumping over fifty stacked cars. He had many crashes and broken ribs, crushed his pelvis, suffered concussions, and had just crashed trying to fly over the waterfall at Caesar's Palace in Las Vegas.

Before that, his jet-powered motorcycle, known as Skycycle X-2, failed to fly over the Snake River Canyon in southern Idaho. His parachute opened prematurely and the drag pulled him down on his side of the river. It was fortunate he didn't land in the river or he probably would have drowned. The television audience for that jump must have been huge. All the networks were there. Even though he failed, he was more famous than ever.

His toy motorcycles were selling like hot cakes. He was earning big money endorsing real motorcycles. The Hollywood and sports promoter Shelly Saltman had just written a book about him that was not flattering but it only made Evel more famous.

I was there to do a profile of Evel for a magazine show I hosted in Salt Lake City. He finally showed up about an hour late and he wasn't friendly. It was pretty clear that either this guy had an instant dislike of me or figured I was a hayseed who should be honored to be in his presence. It didn't matter really because what I brought with me was free publicity and he'd do anything for more publicity. My first and last impression of Evel was that he was a blowhard. I'm sure he must have been a bully when he was growing up.

Evel was drinking Lucky Lager chased with 110-proof Wild Turkey. I was drinking the same. I always liked that combination myself. It was a great way to kick off the evening if you were in a hurry to get it over with. Evel downed several shots and didn't appear to be getting drunk. As long as we were talking about him, the conversation went well. He wasn't interested in anything else.

What was most shocking to me was the way women reacted to Evel. I've been around movie stars, including an evening drinking with Robert Redford, and none of them attracted women the way Evel did. We were sitting at the corner of the bar and women, some with their husbands or boyfriends in tow, would walk up and proposition him—with their "other" standing right there, holding their hand. Some of these women were quite attractive. Evel would flirt with them but he was more interested in getting drunk and talking about himself.

At some point in the evening, early in the morning, Knievel challenged me to light my beard on fire. He said if I'd do that he would light his chest hairs on fire. It seemed like a fair deal to me so I said I would if he would. About that time another woman showed up asking if he needed company. He turned her down and fortunately we forgot all about our bet and continued to get drunk.

About five in the morning, just before sunup Evel Knievel decided we were hungry so we walked to his estate—that's what he called it. His estate was a nice ranch house with a shed and stables and six horses. I assumed riding was his hobby but he said he'd hardly ever ridden a horse in his life. I got the impression he had stables and horses because that's what you were supposed to have when you were famous and rich.

His wife Linda was lovely and sweet. He woke her up and told her we were hungry and she should fix us a big breakfast. Even in my sorry state I was embarrassed by the way he talked to her. He was a bully. I had the impression she was used to Evel barging in in the middle of the night. I couldn't understand how such a cool, classy woman would stay connected to such a jerk. He treated her like kitchen help. Breakfast kind of sobered us up and tired us out so I went back to my hotel room with a plan that we would meet later in the morning and go golfing. My cameraman O.C. Budge would be with me. After golfing we'd do the interview. It was all set.

So we met at the Butte Country Club. If Evel wasn't friendly the night before, he was hostile that morning. He's a good golfer though. I am not, but I don't think that was the reason he suddenly turned on me. He started cursing me, said I had come to make him look bad and there was no way he was going to do a goddamn interview with me. I asked him why he had changed his mind. He said none of my damn business and then he wouldn't talk to me. We got on a plane and went home without a story.

On my flight home, I sat next to a man who looked like he'd been set on fire. His face was seriously disfigured from some sort of burn. As we talked I mentioned my night with Evel Knievel and how he wanted me to set my beard on fire. Turns out that is exactly what this fellow had done and would pay the price the rest of his life.

A few weeks later, Knievel and a friend caught Shelly Saltman in an alley in Los Angeles and beat him senseless. Saltman had written a very damning book about Evel, accusing him of beating his wife and of being seriously hooked on drugs. Apparently Evel took offense. His friend grabbed Saltman from behind, holding his arms behind his back while Evel beat him senseless with an aluminum baseball bat. Saltman's arm was broken in several places. He had a concussion and required several operations.

Evel found himself in the Los Angeles jail behind bars. He was sentenced to three years' probation and six months in the county jail. You'd think that someone who just beat up a defenseless person would be too embarrassed to talk about it on TV but when we called the jail he agreed to do an interview. So I sent down a reporter and cameraman to get the interview I didn't get in Butte. It was quite satisfying.

Years later I did a story with Knievel's son Robbie, who took off after his father. Robbie started jumping his bicycle when he was four, then performed with his father in places like Madison Square Garden. Robbie wanted to become a world famous daredevil like his father but Evel was against it so the two split.

Altogether Robbie made 350 jumps, including over the waterfalls at Caesar's Palace, the jump his father crashed landed. He cleared sixteen buses, jumped over a moving locomotives and over five military jets aboard the aircraft carrier *Intrepid*. I met Robbie at the Snake River Canyon where he planned to do what his father could not do—ride a rocket across the canyon. Apparently he thought better of it and never attempted it. His last jump was 2011, at the age of fifty.

I liked Robbie. He wanted to beat his father's record but did not want to be his father.

TED BUNDY AND ME

I did one of only two television interviews done with the serial killer Ted Bundy. The other was his confession the day before he was executed. Bundy was the most pleasant killer I ever interviewed.

I was a reporter for KUTV in Salt Lake City. By then Bundy was suspected of kidnapping, raping, and then murdering at least two young women from the Salt Lake City area and was the prime suspect of the so-called Green River murders of at least eight young women in Washington State.

People were fascinated with Bundy. He wasn't a typical murder suspect. He was educated, handsome, and articulate. I'm sure if a jury had to choose who was guilty, Ted Bundy or me, they would've convicted me.

I tracked Bundy down inside the local jail in Glenwood Springs, Colorado, where he was being held on one murder charge. Glenwood is right next door to Aspen. First I called the sheriff, who apparently did not have much experience working with news media. He allowed me to speak with Bundy on the phone.

I told Bundy I wanted to come to the jail and interview him to give him a chance to explain his side of the story. Bundy was reluctant but finally agreed I could come the following week.

When I showed up with a cameraman and another reporter who was going to do a shorter story for the nightly news (I was shooting for a documentary), Bundy said he had changed his mind and didn't want to do the interview. I told him we had come all that way at considerable expense for a small TV station. He seemed genuinely concerned that I would be embarrassed if I went home empty handed. Finally he relented. We did the interview in his cell.

He had the demeanor of someone thoughtful and calm. His hair was long, almost to his shoulders, and he had a beard. The women who survived his attacks spoke of how handsome he was and charismatic. It's one reason he was able to get close to them in the first place.

We later learned that he would usually approach his victims—young women and teenage girls—in a public place claiming he was an undercover cop or some kind of authority. Police also found a pair of crutches in his apartment that he used to fake an injury or a disability. He would then coax them to a more private place and overpower them. Of course at the time I didn't know the way he operated and I wasn't a hundred percent convinced he was guilty. He was so damn polite. I cut right to the chase with a question I now find a little embarrassing, but I had to have him answer it.

"You are not guilty?"

"No," he laughed, "I am not guilty. Does that include the time I stole the comic book when I was five years old? No man is truly innocent. I mean, we all have transgressed in some way in our life and, as I say, I have been impolite, and there are some things I regret. But nothing like the things I think you're referring to."

The day before he was executed he admitted to thirty murders in seven states between 1974 and 1978. Police suspect there were more. In his confession he said at first he killed women so they couldn't identify him to the police. But then he said killing became part of the adventure. He said in the beginning he was only an amateur, "impulsive." Then he became a world-class predator.

140

Bundy can be found on most every list of "World's Worst Serial Killers" I have been able to find. The lists include Donald Henry Gaskins, who was accused of killing by torture eighty to ninety people, many of them hitchhikers. He holds the distinction of being the first person to kill an inmate while he was on death row.

Also on the list is *Jack the Ripper*, who was accused in the 1880s of surgically removing his victim's organs. Luis Garavito, also known as *The Beast*, is one of the world's worst serial killers. He confessed to the torture, rape, and murder of 147 young boys, but the number is believed to exceed 300. In Japan, Tsutomu Miyazaki, also known as the *Human Dracula*, abducted and murdered little girls, then indulged in sexual activities and drank their blood.

Bundy was also a necrophile. He told investigators that he would revisit the crime scene and spend hours with the corpses, grooming them and performing sex acts until the corpses had decomposed to where even he couldn't approach them. He kept some of the heads in his apartment as mementos or trophies. In the end, Bundy called himself *"the most cold-hearted son of a bitch you'll ever meet."*

Even while I was impressed with Bundy's pleasant demeanor and good looks, I couldn't get over his cold black eyes. They had a piercing intensity when they weren't darting around. As I recall, he didn't blink and I wasn't up to staring him down. I had dreams about those eyes for weeks. I can see them as I write this. He said he wasn't worried about being executed for crimes he didn't commit.

"I think I stand about as much chance of dying in front of a firing squad or in a gas chamber as you do being killed in a plane on the way home. Let's hope you don't." He laughed. I asked, "But you don't lay awake at night thinking about it?" "Not a moment, honest to God, not a moment."

I think one part of him thought he was telling the truth. He didn't think he'd ever be caught. He had slipped through dragnets several times before and would again. It was like he was disembodied. I was interviewing Ted Bundy the innocent victim, while the guilty Ted Bundy stood by watching. He was so smooth, it was only after I looked at the interview a few times that his dispassionate answers began to reveal a man disconnected from other people's pain. This is what the man who decapitated twelve of his victims had to say about the suffering of their parents:

"I've been told that the parents of these girls are fairly decent people. I don't know. I really feel for them because apparently they suffered some incredible tragedy in their lives. The life of a loved one is probably the most extreme kind of loss you can suffer in this life and I feel as much for them as anybody can."

Bundy was born in a home for unwed mothers and was told that his mother was actually his sister although he eventually learned the truth. His grandfather was described as a bully and a bigot but Bundy spoke affectionately of him. The identity of his actual father has never been determined with any certainty. His mom Louise Cowell said she had been seduced by a sailor.

Louise met the man who raised her son, Johnny Culpepper Bundy, at a singles club. He was a hospital cook and apparently tried to be a good father to Bundy. He formally adopted him and even though he and Louise had four children of their own, they tried to include him in the family. Bundy never accepted his stepfather and reportedly thought he was not very smart.

When I interviewed Bundy, I had no idea he was such a demented, evil sonofabitch. Except for the cold, dark darting eyes, he seemed so calm. The only time he showed real emotion was when he talked about the outrageous allegations and rumors in the media that he was a serial killer. That's when he got righteously indignant. I asked him if he was angry.

"Sure, I get angry and indignant. I don't like being locked up for something I didn't do. I don't like my liberty taken away and I don't like being treated like an animal and I don't like people walking around ogling me like I'm some sort of weirdo, because I'm not."

Bundy was a sociopath and apparently they don't always act weird in public. Bundy didn't until you got to know him better. His girlfriend in Washington State, who stayed with him off and on even after he was under suspicion, finally called the Salt Lake County Sheriff's office to say she suspected he might be the serial killer.

She told investigators she had discovered some odd things in his apartment, such as a meat cleaver, surgical gloves, some crutches, and a sack full of women's clothing. She said she would sometimes awaken in the middle of the night and find Bundy under the covers with a flashlight examining her body.

Bundy rarely had a job before or after he became notorious. He got by borrowing from friends and shoplifting. He told investigators that he had shoplifted practically everything he owned that was worthwhile and that the thing that thrilled him was possessing it. That included the bodies of his victims. He said the ultimate possession was in taking a life and then possessing the physical remains.

At the time I did the interview it would have been unthinkable to imagine so much evil in one individual. I might have asked for a guard to be present during the interview, but of course I wasn't asking very provocative questions.

"You think about getting out of here?" "Well, legally, sure."

Bundy got out but it wasn't legal. A couple of weeks after our interview he was moved to the county courthouse in Aspen for a preliminary hearing. Because he had elected to act as his own attorney, the judge ordered that his shackles be removed and allowed him to visit the courthouse law library to research his case.

From there he jumped out of a second story window and hobbled away to freedom after spraining his ankle in the jump. Bundy managed to stay free by breaking into unoccupied cabins for six days until cops found him in a stolen car and escorted him back to the Glenwood Springs jail.

He escaped again by using a hacksaw blade to saw a small hole in the corner of his cell's ceiling. Bundy deliberately lost a lot of weight to make it through the hole and then made several practice runs before he finally escaped. That night he piled books under a blanket to make it look like he was asleep and escaped through the chief jailer's apartment when the jailer and his wife were out for dinner. He then borrowed some of the jailer's clothes and stole away. It was almost twenty-four hours before guards noticed he was missing.

From Colorado, Bundy traveled through Chicago and ended up in Tallahassee, Florida, where he sneaked into the Chi Omega sorority house and attacked three women, killing one, and then broke into an apartment and bludgeoned a fourth student.

His signature calling card was a nylon stocking and in one case a pantyhose mask. From Tallahassee he drove to Lake City and killed twelve-year-old Kimberly Leach. Her remains were found weeks later in a pig shed.

He said in his interview the day before his execution, after he had admitted to "many" murders, that porn, especially with sexual violence, contributed to his behavior—it fueled it, crystallized it, and then alcohol reduced his inhibitions.

He kept going back to sexually violent porn as the primary motivation for his monstrous behavior. And then he said America needs to wake up about the effects of porn. "There are other monsters out there," he said, "and we are your sons and we are your husbands."

Bundy said after his first murder he got sick at the horrible thing that he had done. He said that each time he killed someone he suffered an enormous amount of guilt but then the impulse would come back stronger.

When asked if he felt pain over what he had done, he said that "through God's help" he was able to come to the point where he feels the pain. He referred to God three times in the interview with radio evangelist James Dobson. When he was asked about killing 12-year-old Kimberly Leach after kidnapping her from a playground, he said he couldn't talk about it.

I ran into Bundy again a few years after the Colorado interview. I was at the Florida State Prison on another story and was stunned to see him in a holding cell as I walked by. I reminded him of our interview years before and he said he remembered me and wished me well. One of the nicest guys you'll ever meet. I reported a lengthy story for NBC News right after his execution. My theory is that Bundy was two people. One was a very polite young man. The other was a cold-blooded killer.

During his trial for the Leach murder, Bundy took advantage of a state law that said a marriage declaration in court is valid, and asked his longtime girlfriend from Washington State, Carole Ann Boone, to marry him. Bundy then declared to the court that they were legally married. And they were. Two years later she gave birth to a daughter and said Bundy was the father.

THE TREE BISHOP

I grew up in one of the most beautiful places on earth although I didn't fully appreciate it at the time. Virgin was sixteen miles from the entrance to Zion National Park and close to Bryce, Grand Canyon, Capitol Reef National Parks and Cedar Breaks National Monument. I was surrounded by so many parks, I rarely noticed them.

We were ensconced in beauty that was regulated in one way or the other by the federal government. We hated the intrusion on our rights. We particularly despised a new movement then called "environmentalism." It seemed the whole world was conspiring against us. Energy companies weren't allowed to dig or drill inside or close to these national parks.

There was always a battle going on between the natural beauty and development. Usually development won. Sometimes it didn't. I remember power plants proposed for Southern Utah that would have been smack in the middle of this natural beauty. They were shot down by "those damn environmentalists" and that was before environmentalism became a swear word.

Then I moved away.

When I returned a few years later I did notice the beauty. It was like my eyes suddenly saw the glory. I also noticed the skies were not as clear as they were when I was growing up, the horizons were more hazy. Then I realized I had become one of them - a damn environmentalist.

Now when I hear politicians worrying about leaving their offspring with huge budget deficits, I think they've got their priorities upside down. I'm much more concerned about not leaving my descendants an environment they can live in. There's no question that my kids and their kids are not going to have the same quality of living I enjoyed.

I have no patience with climate change doubters. Ninety to ninety-five percent of research says man is causing climate change. The other five percent of scientists more often than not are on the payroll of energy companies. Google "climate change" and the most prominent websites will lead you to believe it's a cyclical phenomenon. Check out who sponsors these sites. Almost always it's the energy developers. Even if the ninety-five percent are wrong, why should we pollute our environment? I'd like to take the doubters to Mount Kilimanjaro in Tanzania and throw them to the natives. It wouldn't be pretty.

I've been to the base of Kilimanjaro a few times. It's the highest mountain in Africa at about 19,340 feet, and it's the highest freestanding mountain in the world. Kilimanjaro is actually a stratovolcano composed of three separate volcanoes

The name in Swahili apparently means "Great Mountain." No surprise there. Some locals call it "white mountain" because of the glaciers near the top. Sailors could see the mountain from a hundred miles away in the Indian Ocean. Kilimanjaro is one of the most popular tourist destinations in Africa. Climbers first attempted to scale it in 1861 but it wasn't until 1912 that anyone made it. Kilimanjaro is of huge importance to the Tanzania economy.

For the people who live within a couple hundred miles, it is sacred and crucial to their lives. Without the water from the mountain's glaciers, these people would be forced to move elsewhere. Therein lies the problem.

In the last one hundred years, ninety-two percent of the glaciers atop Mount Kilimanjaro have disappeared. Some scientists estimate there will be no glaciers at all, zero, zilch, by the year 2020. Without the ice and snow, the rivers that flow down the mountain that nourish millions of Tanzanians will simply dry up. This land of wonders, of animals roaming uncaged, is losing its shining top.

Don't tell the people here that global warming doesn't exist and that man isn't causing it. They blame industrialized nations like the US and China for polluting the air that finds its way to East Africa. They also blame themselves. The forest that surrounds Kilimanjaro is disappearing at an alarming rate, clear-cut by poachers in the dark of the night. Trees are an important part of the ecosystem because they trap the moisture that helps create glaciers.

Without the forest's humidity, the winds blow dry. The timber is valuable for the construction of wood homes throughout Africa and the world. Another problem is that whole forests have been cut down to make room to grow food. And the timber makes good kindling for their stoves.

About a million Tanzanians living in the shadow of the mountain would freeze in the winter without indoor heat; it gets that cold around Kilimanjaro. It is illegal to cut down trees but greed and survival Trump the law.

I heard about a Lutheran Bishop who preaches more about trees than morality, although he connects the two. His name is Frederick Shoo, a bishop with the Evangelical Lutheran Church of Tanzania. We joined him when he was visiting some of the 164 parishes and half a million members in his diocese at the foot of Kilimanjaro.

At our first parish we were greeted by a small but rambunctious crowd that treated Bishop Shoo as if he was the African version of

Johnny Appleseed. Around here he is known as the Tree Bishop. Bishop Shoo was surveying local lay leaders about how many trees their parish had planted. The number at this particular parish was 46,083. Think about that, 46,083 new trees. When the bishop congratulated the members, they beamed with pride as if they had just baptized 46,083 souls.

Bishop Shoo is a tall, handsome man who speaks very good English. He says when he first started preaching about the environment and disappearing trees, his fellow pastors thought he had lost his way. He told me "They were saying, instead of preaching spiritual things, now he's talking about the environment. What does it mean? I mean, they thought [. . .] maybe I was out of my senses." They actually called on the bishop to repent but he kept on preaching about trees, and climate change, and their connection to God.

"At the beginning of the bible, in the book of Genesis, it is well stated that God created human beings and other creatures but he gave the human being the greatest responsibility to take care of the creation. When we care for creation, I would say that we care for life," the Tree Bishop preached.

Today he has an easier sell. Tanzanians and the Maasai natives may not have seen the NASA pictures showing time-lapse photography of their mountain's dwindling snowcap, but they know it's much hotter than it used to be. In their bones they know something is wrong.

As we drove along the foothills, we crossed puddles that were once streams. We saw creeks and rivers that are dry gullies now. Bishop Shoo mourned over the loss of each one. It was personal for him. He knew the inevitable. "It does not need a PhD to see that already people are experiencing the impact of global warming. A simple farmer in the village now can tell that something is wrong with our climate."

The church now operates a nursery—actually a mega tree garden that nourishes millions of saplings waiting to be planted. There are orange and avocado trees and mangos. The diocese had 152 more nurseries planned at the time of my visit. The prison sends orange clad inmates to load up the saplings and deliver them to local villages. The Mayor of Moshe, Bernadette Kinabo, said the city has set a standard for each resident to plant eighty trees each year. That year Moshe citizens planted one million six hundred eighty thousand trees.

We were there when Bishop Shoo joined local officials at a ceremony planting trees in a clearing in downtown Moshi. They were planting hundreds of trees. The bishop had a big smile on his face. He told me it made him "very, very happy."

In the beginning, parishioners were upset that a religious leader was preaching trees. Now it's a familiar Sunday topic. Now, those who chop trees illegally are considered sinners. There's so much demand, the "sinners" move in during the dark of the night and move out before they're discovered.

Bishop Shoo adopted a plan to plant trees in local cemeteries. He figured no one would dare cut a tree in a holy place and that cemeteries are holy and God clearly loves trees. It turned out to be an inspired idea. No trees have been cut from the cemeteries, but there aren't enough cemeteries.

Pastor Ndosa, speaking from the pulpit, told his congregation that God created trees before he created man. In Bishop Shoo's church, young men cannot be confirmed until they have planted a tree. Pastor Martha Dusiri said some young men even planted trees in their homes. Bishop Shoo wants to change the thinking of a generation, for church members to feel the joy of planting a tree and watching it grow, "the joy of seeing a life."

It will take some time to replace the number of trees that have been cut down, let alone those that are being poached every day. To an outsider it might seem that there is no shortage of timber. There is still a lot of forest, but every year more trees are being removed than are being planted. In Shoo's mind if Kilimanjaro loses its ice caps the whole world will feel the blow. "If there's no snow there," he said, "can you imagine what it will mean."

Bishop Shoo is a man who loves most living things except those critters who chew on trees. He does not like gophers. As we walked by the gopher holes, he would poke his stick in the hole, muttering, "This is terrible, this is terrible."

We attended a wedding for a prominent local Maasai couple. I've not witnessed an event that can match the pageantry of a Maasai wedding, the horn blowers wearing wildebeest headdresses. At this wedding there was an additional ceremony, a tree planting ceremony at the end of the wedding. Bishop Shoo insisted on it. If the bride and groom wanted to be married in the church, they needed to plant a tree. There was no other way he was going to bless a marriage.

I can't imagine his despair when he learned that the United States had pulled out of the Paris climate change agreement.

HONORING A HERO

I won an Emmy for a story I reported about a combat photographer and correspondent. I wrote the twenty-minute segment, which aired on an NBC magazine show, in about four hours. That's a pretty quick write for a piece that long, but it's what happens when you're handed a terrific story with a beginning, middle and payoff at the end, and the pictures to back it up.

As with any award I have received, the people who deserve it are the producer, cameraman, soundman and editor. I'm not playing humble here. It's the truth, but I get the credit. Of course when stories don't work out, I get the blame.

The correspondent and hero of my story, Neil Davis, was an Australian, a big, good looking, manly man, kind of like John Wayne but without the swagger. Davis was also a gentle man. But when it came to covering war, he had a way of placing himself in the middle of the action.

Unlike most western journalists, Davis preferred being imbedded with the South Vietnamese soldiers or the black-suited Viet Cong. By 1970, Davis was a legend. No other cameraman could match the pictures he sent to NBC news. His camera was rolling as many of his friends were killed or wounded. Neil himself was wounded several times.

After the war Neil operated as a freelance cameraman until he became chief of the NBC News bureau in Bangkok. I went to the little bar that became his headquarters, across the street from the famous Cowboy bar in the infamous Patpong sex district. In one corner there were three TV sets showing old NFL football games. In another, three young women were gyrating to the music.

Not paying much attention to the gyrating or the game was a group of war worn freelance journalists standing in the middle of the room telling war stories. They spoke of Neil in rare, reverential terms. Journalists are not usually very reverential. They said they wouldn't have gone where he spent most of his time covering the war, which was ususaly closest to the action. He was the only cameraman to capture the famous pictures of the Viet Cong tank crashing through the gates of the presidential palace during the last days of the fall of Saigon.

Davis usually liked to work alone because he didn't want to endanger his colleagues and because it's easier to get in and out if there's only one of you. But in 1970, he needed a driver and guide. He ended up hiring a Cambodian named An Veng. Over the next few years they became inseparable. Eventually An Veng became Neil's driver, soundman, eyes, and ears.

The dynamics of a camera crew are fascinating to watch. Even domestic crews not covering wars often become closer than man and wife. Almost always the cameraman is the main man. I've worked with some pretty amazing camerawomen but they are still greatly outnumbered by the weaker sex.

The soundman acts as the manservant, carrying equipment, watching the cameraman's rear end and deferring to his or her judgment. Soundmen don't get as much credit as they deserve. They're always in the background. Sometimes I never learned their last name, but my stories were always better when I had a good soundman.

Partly because An Veng and Neil Davis were in so many dangerous situations, their bond grew especially close. One day while they were shooting a firefight between Viet Cong and South Vietnamese soldiers Neil was seriously wounded in the stomach by shrapnel from a grenade. He instructed An Veng to rush the battle film back to the NBC bureau in Saigon. An Veng refused to leave his side; there was no way he would leave his friend.

In 1975 the Khmer Rouge captured the Cambodian capital of Phnom Penh. They were led by a madman named Pol Pot who declared 1975 Year Zero, the beginning of time, the dawn of a new Marxist utopia. He ordered the extermination of all external and internal influences. The "internal" influences were the Cambodian elite, especially those who were educated.

In Phnom Penh there's a high school known as S21, which was used as a prison and torture chamber for the Pol Pot regime. Altogether seven thousand Cambodians were imprisoned in S21. Seven made it out alive.

The torture implements are still hanging on the walls. The memorial to the killing fields is a twenty-foot tall glassed-in box containing hundreds of human skulls. These killing fields were situated throughout Cambodia and were powerfully depicted in the 1984 movie of the same name, about another war journalist and his interpreter and fellow journalist.

The Khmer Rouge murdered or starved to death as many as two million Cambodians, but only a handful of the guilty have ever been brought to justice. In an interview before his death, Pol Pot expressed no remorse whatsoever. All he was concerned about was his failing health.

When I was stationed in Asia, Pol Pot was still alive and in hiding. I tried to get an interview with him and thought about what I would do if I succeeded. Would I report his location to the new Cambodian regime? It would have been a favor to mankind but probably not good for my career. Hitler, Stalin and Mao were the evil of another generation. Pol Pot was one of the most evil of mine.

When Phnom Penh fell, Neil Davis had a helicopter standing by just outside the border gate to transport An Veng, his wife Gia, and their four children to safety. The scene was chaotic. Everyone in the city wanted out. They knew what awaited them if they didn't get out. In the mad crush, An Veng and his family never made it through the gate. The scene was eerily reminiscent of the one where US and South Vietnamese citizens were desperately pushing and shoving to get the hell out of the country before the Viet Cong and North Vietnamese soldiers rolled into Saigon.

Over the next few years, Davis returned to Phnom Penh searching for his friend. He visited old hangouts but never saw An Veng. He left money with mutual friends hoping it would reach An Veng. Then Davis would return to Bangkok.

An Veng knew Davis was looking for him. He actually watched from the shadows. He didn't dare approach Davis, afraid that it would put both men in danger.

During that time An Veng and Gia suffered the worst kind of hell. Three of their children were beaten to death by the Khmer Rouge. They decided that the only way to save the fourth child, Meng, was to get him out of the country. That would be a very dangerous and difficult journey through the killing fields and then across the border into Thailand.

They had no choice if they wanted to save their remaining son. Imagine the pain when An Veng and Gia decided it was best that she stay in Phnom Penh while An Veng took Meng to safety. They traveled by night through extremely dangerous regions.

It took them weeks to negotiate their way to a refugee camp just inside the Thai border. The minute they arrived, An Veng found a phone and called his friend in Bangkok to come get him. Davis was ecstatic. We had pictures shot by an NBC crew of An Veng crying with joy. Davis said he would make the drive to the refugee camp early the next morning.

Davis headed for the camp just after sunrise. Along the way he heard over the radio that there was another coup attempt. They were common during the 1980s, almost comical, but covering them was very dangerous. He had no choice but to turn around and document the fighting near the Thai presidential palace.

His soundman at the time was an Aussie named Bill Latch. As always, Davis got as close to the action as he could, closer than anyone else, across the street from a government tank that was spraying the area with machine gun fire and blasting through the walls with the tank cannon.

The camera was rolling when the tank aimed its gun almost directly at Davis and Latch. Then it fired. In the commotion that followed, Neil's camera fell to the ground but continued to roll. The viewers saw Davis fall in front of it, obviously wounded. Then as the camera rolled, Neil's good friend Gary Burns, another Australian cameraman, dragged him out of the line of fire, leaving a trail of blood. Bill Latch, also wounded, crawled after them.

The camera continued to roll, which was the way Davis would have wanted it. He always lectured other cameramen to keep the camera rolling no matter what. I can imagine him saying, "Even if you're filming your own death."

Next on the film, we saw Gary Burns leaning over Davis and crying, telling bystanders to stand back. His buddy was dead. Soundman

Latch died six hours later. It was just another stupid coup attempt. There were several others in the years to follow.

When An Veng heard that his friend had been killed, he cried like a baby. That's not hearsay. The NBC bureau had sent a camera crew to interview him. First he lost three sons, then his best friend, his only friend. His wife remained trapped in Phnom Penh. Now An Veng, with his son Meng, was stuck in a refugee camp with little hope of ever getting out. There are still such camps in Asia housing refugees from later violent conflicts in Myanmar and Bangladesh. Some Cambodians lived in Thai camps for 20 years.

Normally that would be the end of the story. The knight in shining armor was dead. An Veng was only one of thousands of people displaced by war. Displaced is such an awful bureaucratic term. Displaced and forgotten. But in a turn of events that still amazes me, An Veng was not forgotten. He had friends he had never met, Neil's friends at NBC News.

It was Gordon Manning, the ageless senior vice president of NBC News and the cheerleader for all NBC correspondents, who contacted me about doing the Neil Davis story for a magazine show. He told me that Davis was his hero and that NBC felt obligated to help get his friend's wife, Gia, out of Phnom Penh and then get the family out of the refugee camp. It was an impressive and costly effort, possibly one of the most expensive venture NBC News had ever undertaken without expecting something in return.

NBC hired a young woman who had experience as a volunteer in refugee camps. Chris Jackson's job was daunting to say the least. First she had to find Gia in Phnom Penh, get word to her, and then get her out. It took months. Eventually Chris managed to get Gia transferred from one prison to another and eventually to a prison in

Bangkok. We had a camera crew there to show her behind bars. From there it was easy.

We also had pictures of her finally connecting with An Veng and Meng at the refugee camp. Their reunion was both touching and heartbreaking: they were together, but still stuck in a place they couldn't leave without some very high-level help. They couldn't go back to Cambodia. Thailand didn't want them. The US already had more refugees than it could handle. Most countries simply weren't interested.

Chris managed to locate Neil's friend, cameraman Gary Burns, who had moved back to Australia. Although Australia was not, and is not, known for its enlightened immigration policy, the government finally relented after Burns agreed to sponsor An Veng and his family.

We met An Veng at the camp the day the bus was to take him to the Bangkok airport. He had been told what was happening but still couldn't understand or believe. We flew with him to Sydney. The family huddled together looking out the airplane window, wide-eyed and unbelieving.

Chris Jackson no longer had a job, but she married my cameraman Leigh Wilson. They settled down in Chiang Mai, Thailand, until Chris died quite suddenly from a brain tumor. I really liked and admired her.

After uniformed immigration authorities sprayed the interior of our plane for some sort of disease (I've always thought it was peculiar that the Aussies were so paranoid because Australia is home to just about every insect known to man), my producer Mike Mosher and camera crew and myself were allowed to go through immigration ahead of An Veng. We were there with camera rolling when An

Veng walked through the gate, saw Gary Burns, ran at him and hugged him as if he would never let go. Both men were wet from An Veng's tears. I cried too.

I heard from a reliable source that NBC News spent about a quarter of a million dollars getting An Veng and family to safety. It was a proud moment for the Peacock.

Producer Michael Mosher, cameraman Leigh Wilson, researcher
Chris Jackson and myself working on the Neil Davis story

With An Veng and what was left of his family before departing to
their new Home in Sidney. Australia

PEOPLE & THEIR ISSUES

Sometimes people want their stories told. Sometimes they just want their passion, something larger than themselves, shared. When they care more about the story or their cause than getting fifteen minutes of fame, I care more about them.

WANG DAN

One of the most memorable individuals I met in China was a twenty-seven-year-old man named Wang Dan. He was one of the student organizers of an extraordinary outcry for reform that started in Beijing universities and gained popular support until it was brutally put down at Tiananmen Square in 1989.

The world was transfixed by the pictures of students protesting against one of the most oppressive regimes in modern history. Who will forget the scene of the young man with shopping bags in his hands stopping a convoy of tanks heading straight toward him? He even climbed aboard the lead tank.

He became an unnamed international hero, never to be heard from or seen again. We will never know how many students were actually killed in the Tiananmen Square massacre, some machine-gunned, others crushed by tanks. Most of the student leaders who survived were arrested and sent to prison.

Wang Dan served four years in prison before he was released back to what amounted to house arrest in a large apartment complex in Beijing. He disobeyed orders and refused to stay quiet. Instead, he continued to write for underground newspapers even though he was constantly under surveillance and arrested time and again and taken in for interrogation.

I was asked to prepare a story for the upcoming round of hearings in the US Congress about whether "most favored nation" status should be renewed for China, considering its abysmal human rights record. It was a yearly process. Renewal meant that China would receive trade perks on par with some of America's closest allies. Eventually the status was conferred permanently.

My idea was to interview a dissident, and the man who ran our bureau in Beijing, Eric Baculinao, had some contact with dissidents. Eric, like the other network bureau chiefs, was from the Philippines. Eric and his friends were communist sympathizers and during the Marcos reign had received permission to attend a convention in China. Unfortunately for them, during their stay Marcos declared martial law and they were not allowed to return home. Some, like Eric, were married but never saw their wives or children for years. Eric ended up with a second family in China.

They survived in a country wary of outsiders and became very street smart with exactly the kind of skills required to run a foreign news bureau. Eric said he was in contact with Wang Dan and thought he could arrange an interview, which he did.

We should have realized how irresponsible we were when we showed up at Wang Dan's huge apartment complex with a camera crew and a van full of video equipment. We stood out like what we were, a Western camera crew with a ton of equipment.

We should have known the Bureau would be watching Wang Dan. We should have known we could get him in serious trouble. Wang Dan greeted us in a tiny, spotless apartment and didn't seem at all nervous about our visit. He was very friendly and offered us tea. He had the bearing of someone comfortable in his own skin and I was struck by his quiet dignity.

During the interview I had the feeling that I was in the presence of someone who stood above the rest. Now and then you meet someone like Terry Waite or the Dalai Lama or the Aga Khan. That was the way I felt about Wang Dan. Even though I did the interview through a translator, it was clear that Wang Dan could understand English. He would usually start his answer before the interpreter had translated my question.

When we were through with the interview, the crew took pictures of his apartment, his photos, and of me listening to him and vice versa. Things were going well. We had a story. I would just need to find a university professor and most likely an "expert" from the US.

It was difficult to sell a story to New York that included only an interview done in a foreign language. Some executive producers didn't even like English with a British or Australian accent. It's no wonder so many Americans are uninterested and ignorant of other cultures.

As we were about to wrap up, there was a loud banging on the door. When Wang Dan opened it, six rather large men from the Public Security Bureau barged into the room and confiscated the interview tape before our cameraman, who was very experienced in such instances, could hide it.

One of the men spoke quite good English and told us to come with him. He made it clear with his loud voice and body language that arguing was not an option. So my producer and camera crew and myself were escorted out of the apartment complex. I noticed that none of the bystanders looked at us. It was like we weren't there.

At times like this I was happy to be carrying an American passport. I was more excited about the adventure than worried about my safety. My producer, Kiko Itasaka, was a little less confident. The Chinese have not been fond of Japanese since the Rape of Nanking in the 1930s. My cameraman, Gary Fairman, was an Australian who felt superior to Asians anyway, so he wasn't very worried. Then there was Eric. He could be deported, even jailed.

We were marched through the narrow streets to the local police station, which also served as a jail. We were questioned separately about our intentions with Wang Dan. I learned later that the cameraman had been quite belligerent during his interview and threatened to get his captors in trouble. They were not intimidated.

Because I was the only fully accredited journalist in the group, the task of writing a confession fell to me. I was told that I was breaking the rules by contacting a dissident and that I should confess my sins.

I had gone over the rules before the interview and I knew I wasn't breaking any. I wasn't worried because I was one of a very few bona fide accredited foreign journalists in the country. Actually even that was a fiction. As an accredited journalist I was required to live full-time in China. But I lived in Japan and commuted and the Chinese authorities knew it.

The first confession I wrote, I wrote in a circle. I'd heard about these confessions and I didn't take them too seriously. I admitted to nothing. At the time I had two interrogators and they didn't seem particularly happy with my confession. Then they left. A few minutes later another older man walked in.

If it were possible for me to have a Chinese uncle, I would have chosen him. He had one of those avuncular smiles and he spoke English fluently. Smiling, he told me that my confession was gibberish, and that I should try again. I started to argue that we were innocent of any wrongdoing and that's when I saw the other side of my uncle.

He became quite menacing. He told me I was not taking my situation seriously enough, that I was in real trouble and could end up in prison. I took another stab at a confession. Again, I admitted nothing but this time my attitude changed from flippancy to one of cooperation. After adopting a few of his suggestions, we were all allowed to leave but told we were under hotel arrest until we were notified otherwise.

China is such a big place; with a bureaucracy so vast, it's understandable why the right hand often doesn't know what the left hand is doing. We were convinced that the Foreign Ministry had no idea that the Public Security Bureau had detained us. I met with officials of the Foreign Ministry three or four times after the incident and it was never brought up.

Had the ministry known of the contents of my interview with Wang Dan, I'm sure they would have happily returned the confiscated tape. In the interview Wang Dan told me that for dissidents like himself, life in China was quite miserable, although bearable. But, he said, for millions of ordinary Chinese, if you consider running water, food on the table, and jobs as human rights, life was much better than before. And yes, he said, the US should renew "most favored nation" status because that was the best way for the US to continue to exert pressure on human rights issues.

It was a message Chinese Foreign Ministry would have loved to send to the U.S. Congress if Chinese cops hadn't confiscated the tape.

As we were walking out the door Wang Dan said to me, in English, "I hope you'll be okay." It occurred to me that Wang Dan had far more to lose than we did and yet he was worrying about us. At the time it didn't seem that he was going to be arrested. We learned later that he was also detained for a few days and then released.

After several more arrests, Wang Dan was sent to prison for fourteen years, ostensibly because he had subscribed to a correspondence course from Stanford University. He was finally released early, in 1998, because of deteriorating health—a few days ahead of Chinese President Jiang Zemin's state visit to the US. The last I checked, Wang Dan was living in Boston and aiding the dissident movement any way he could.

As I was walking out the door, he handed me his business card. It is one of my most treasured artifacts. It was light blue, an ordinary-sized name card. On it, was his name, Wang Dan, and at the bottom it read "Free Man." "Wang Dan, Free Man." Still gives me cold chills.

DO-GOODERS I HAVE KNOWN

Some of the most fascinating and generally happy people I have known are crusaders, individuals who devote their lives to a single cause, greater than themselves. For many, their lives took on meaning when they veered off the projected path—investors who decided there was something more valuable than money, people of fame and acclaim who subjugated themselves for a greater cause.

Sometimes a do-gooder is reborn out of tragedy, after the loss of a loved one, or simply a commitment to right a wrong. I call these folks "monomaniacs" because they are so committed to only one cause, nothing else seems to matter. It is an inelegant phrase but descriptive. I often find myself admiring these people the most.

As for me, I probably found the only vocation that would have kept me happy. It's embarrassing how much I've come to require constant stimulation. I'm always curious about anyone who works an 8 to 5 job and does the same task each day over and over. Are they happy? Are they as fulfilled as I am? I know that sounds as though I'm looking down on those people, but I'm not.

I have some very content friends who have 9-to-5 schedules doing the same thing day after day.. A good friend, a telephone lineman from San Francisco, loved his job. I've had several conversations with myself about the degrees between content and happy.

I'm wary of talking about my travels with some people who don't travel. Do these experiences I've had, of meeting fascinating people, witnessing terrible poverty and beautiful spaces—do they mean I should be more fulfilled than someone who has never left their community? The answer of course is no. We can find fulfillment in many ways.

I do think that the experiences and adventures that come with travel ultimately change who you are. Nothing seems quite as black and white as it once did. Rarely is one side all good and the other, all bad. I think it's one reason I've gone from a conservative upbringing to what some people might call a bleeding heart liberal. Although I would disagree with that. I'm sure some friends think of me as a turncoat and a sellout.

I've felt trapped in my career because I like what I do so much. I've not wanted to walk away from journalism because there was nothing else as fun and satisfying to walk away to. I have, however, come to realize that if there is one other thing I'd rather do with my life, it would be to become one of them, one of the people I write about, the monomaniacs who leave the world a little better place. As I have said in this book and to myself." The only thing more fun than writing about them is becoming them.

Scott Neeson

One of the realities I've learned along the way is that rarely does anyone turn out to be as bad or as good as you had thought in the beginning. Often they start out good, with their heart in the right place, but after a little publicity, it goes to their head. Actually it's rare when that doesn't happen. It's always a pleasant surprise when I'm not disappointed by what I find when I get there.

So I was a little more than concerned when I made plans to do a story on a do-gooder I had read about named Scott Neeson, a Scotsman educated in Australia who was living in Cambodia.

It was a bigger gamble than usual because he was half a world away and I only had a couple of short news stories to go on and I had a difficult time getting in touch with him. I suppose it's human nature to become even more interested when the person at the other end isn't clamoring to get back in touch with you. After all, I was offering free publicity.

An hour after we met, we were standing knee-deep in garbage, literally. It was at the city dump outside Phnom Penh, Cambodia. As dumps go, this one was big and ugly, one gigantic mound of trash about a half-mile in diameter. I've never had a very strong stomach, but what I was seeing was so overwhelming I forgot all about my misery.

Scott had given Trent, my cameraman, and myself each a pair of rubber boots to wade through the muck. It turned out that the ones he gave Trent were way too small, but Trent had no other choice so he wore them the whole afternoon. His toes were still black and blue days later.

The dump was an ant's nest of activity. Every few minutes a truck loaded to the brim with garbage would drive up and unload and the mountain would grow a little larger. I've been to town dumps before, although none quite so huge.

The image that always comes to mind is of gulls swirling about the trucks as they unload their garbage. At this dump it was not gulls. It was kids pushing and shoving and fighting to get the most valued junk. More than one child there had been run over in the melee.

There were upwards of one thousand families living in tiny huts surrounding the rubbish, often sharing their shacks and beds with pigs and lice. There was a runoff little stream that meanders through the village. You could see the women wading through the filthy water washing the family clothes. It was especially odd because the place didn't seem depressing.

When we walked around at the end of the day, families would be sitting on their porch in their shanty neighborhood adjacent to the dump, greeting us as if we were in a typical neighborhood anywhere in the world.

What I'll never forget were the sweet smiles as if they had nothing to complain about. It wasn't the first time I realized how fortunate my life and my family have been. I think parents would be wise to take their kids not only to Disneyland, but to neighborhoods where life is very real.

Neeson took us to the dump to show me where he found most of his kids. When he did find one, he tried his best to lure them away. It wasn't easy. Some had families, many did not. Neeson is not a pedophile—although God knows there are pedophiles from all over the world that are drawn to Cambodia by the sweet little lassies and boys whose parents, at least many of them, would sell or loan their child to some pervert just to put food on the table.

Cambodia is still a very, very poor country. Neeson said he had seen pedophiles at the dump. He seemed especially concerned not to be seen as a dirty old man that used his charity to get close to little kids. If ever I harbored that concern, it disappeared before I left Cambodia.

Before he moved to Cambodia, Neeson was a big shot Hollywood executive, President of 20th Century Fox International. And there he was, sloshing through the most disgusting, vomit inducing landscape I have ever seen, looking for kids who spent each and every day at the dump, earning maybe eighty-five cents a day collecting recyclables. Unlike dumps in more modern countries, this one mixed everything together, including dangerous chemicals that collected in little bubbling pools.

I saw several kids who had chemical burns on their bodies, and several who had ugly growths on their faces. Maggots were crawling all over, including on the kids. These were children as young as five and six years old, kids who either had no parents, or parents who forced them to spend their childhood in this squalor.

When Scott first visited Phnom Penh on a backpacking trip, he was taken aback by the number of kids begging in the streets. It's a very uncomfortable feeling saying no to a kid begging for just a few cents to feed himself or his family, especially when you're on your way into the Foreign Correspondents Club to have a beer and a burger that would cost more than it would to feed a Cambodian family for a week. The problem is, if you give money to one, you're physically overwhelmed by dozens of others who expect the same. If you don't get a little calloused, it will break your heart.

Most try to sell something like postcards, for which there is no longer much of a market. Unlike any other country I have been in, newspapers are also a hot item on the streets. You could buy an *International Herald Tribune*, or *Phnom Penh Daily*, or *Cambodia Weekly* for exactly one dollar.

There's only one catch. After you read the newspaper, you have to give it back. That seemed only fair. And then there were the shoe shiners. When you took a seat at a sidewalk café it was not unusual to feel a hand on your ankle as your shoes were eased off for a shine while you ate. The charge again was one dollar.

Scott tried to get to know as many of the kids' parents as possible. At first, he would give the parents money, and buy their kids clothes. He even gave them money to put the kids in school. Then a few days later the parents had spent the money, sold the clothes and pulled the kids out of school so they could either go back to the dump or became a child prostitute.

Those were the options. It seemed as though he took two steps backward for every step forward. It was frustrating but the smiles on the young faces were enough to make Neeson think maybe he had found a new calling, something in his life that had been missing.

At the time, he was in between jobs, moving from 20th Century Fox to Sony Pictures Entertainment. He was, by most any standard, extremely successful. He had a mansion in Brentwood, fancy cars including a Porsche, and of course a big boat. Every Hollywood executive needs a big boat. He traveled first class or in private jets and hobnobbed with the world's elite. He had everything a man could ask for, but he wasn't happy.

Neeson felt conflicted. He wanted to stay in Cambodia but he had just accepted the new job as head of Sony. He decided he would give the new job a year and then see if he still felt the urge to start a new life in Cambodia. During that year Neeson returned to Cambodia a dozen times and started what was essentially an orphanage and school called the *Cambodian Children's Fund*.

The place offered a topnotch education, warm beds, good food, medical care, and during the evening hours, lessons in Cambodia's culture. During the bloody Pol Pot regime, hundreds of thousands of the country's most educated citizens were slaughtered in an attempt to cleanse the country of Western influence. As a result, much of the written history is gone and most young Cambodians have little or no knowledge of their past, their traditions or their culture.

It was on one of his trips to Phnom Penh that Scott received a call that would change his life completely. It was from one of his aides who was on a promotional tour of a new movie with one of the film's stars. They were traveling by private jet. The aides were very distraught because the star was threatening to cancel the tour because he hated the small jet. The aide recounted that the young star had whined that "Life wasn't meant to be this difficult."

There Neeson was with kids who had disease, few had parents, and none had any hope of climbing out of their circumstances. And here was a spoiled American who felt life had treated him unfairly because he was traveling in a private plane that wasn't big enough. That did it for Neeson. He felt a much stronger need to stay in Cambodia than to go back to the good life. He had found the good life in the most unlikely place.

You can get an insight into the Hollywood culture by the immediate reaction from Scott's friends and acquaintances when they heard he was moving to Cambodia to operate an orphanage. The word on the street was that he was doing this just so he could become a darling of Hollywood's liberals. He would go over there for a few months and come back a hero with a wonderful future ahead of him.

Neeson bought a big house in a residential neighborhood in Phnom Penh and turned it into a school and orphanage. It wasn't exactly an orphanage because some of the kids had parents they could visit on the weekends. It was a very cheerful place. The kids were dressed in uniforms, appeared to be well fed, and wearing smiles which were never evident when they were scavenging at the dump.

You could watch the kids soaking in an education they wouldn't have gotten otherwise. Their education was very important to Neeson, because without it he knew they would eventually end up back at the dump where they began. In the evenings the children would learn traditional dances or put on plays they had written themselves about their country. One night we were there, they performed a play about a drunken father who constantly beat his kids. It was all too real.

Now this former Hollywood exec who made his fortune off the movie business no longer believes that Western entertainment is good for families. First, he thinks that if kids at the dump had access to television they would realize how miserable and unfortunate they are.

As it was, families at the dump, however desperate their circumstances, spend every evening not watching television but sitting around talking to each other about what they had done that day, and about their dreams. Even kids in dumps have dreams.

While we were at the dump with Neeson, he came across a young twelve-year-old girl named Tola who had attended his school for two months and had been doing very well and seemed quite happy. Scott even featured her on the front of a brochure he had published about the Cambodian Children's Fund. Then her mother had pulled her out of school because she was losing eighty-five cents a day while Tola was in school. As it turned out, Tola's mother was also at the dump while we were there so Scott went looking for her. When he finally found her, he sat down and started bargaining to get her daughter back.

We were listening in on a wireless mic Scott was wearing. It was pretty clear that Scott felt deeply about getting the little girl back in school and he was overjoyed when the mother finally relented with a little bribe. He loathed offering the mom money and made us promise we wouldn't discuss the amount in our story. He also made the mother agree to sign an unbendable contract that she would not pull Tola out of school for at least six months.

Tola's father brought her to school the following Monday morning and you could see the smile on the little girl's face knowing that she was going to sleep in a clean bed and eat a square meal. You could also see the smile on Scott's face.

Before long, Scott went through most of his own money and so he started a nonprofit foundation to collect funding and build yet another orphanage. Some of Hollywood's most powerful people who were originally skeptical of Scott's commitment have become believers and contributed substantially to the Cambodian Children's Fund.

The last time I checked, Neeson is now providing education for 2,500 students. Two hundred have gone on to university. He operates the only clinic in all of Cambodia offering free treatment to all families whether their children attend his school or not.

He's now building an academy atop the dump, which has since been covered over, where he found so many of his kids. His charity is always listed among the best in the world. Any misgivings I had in the beginning about Scott Neeson's staying power and commitment have disappeared.

I was so impressed with the *CCF* program that for several years my wife and I been supporting one of the students. Her name is Lida and she writes me wonderful emails. I've been to her home, if you can call it that. Even calling it a shack would be too kind. It's a one-room hovel for Lida and her six siblings.

She goes home from the *CCF* school for holidays. I've watched her grow. I knew what she was like when she was nine years old and now she's fourteen. One day Lida wants to be a singer but she says she'll go to college first. I'm not sure about her singing but I aim to make sure she goes to college. It won't be easy. Few of her friends go on to school and she needs to make money to help feed her family.

Scott Neeson looking for kids scrounging at the Pyongyang dump for 80 cents a day

Neeson visiting a family in a village with sewage running through it next to the dump

George Weiss: "Say Yes to Education"

The first time I met George Weiss was at the Apollo Theater in Harlem. It was a surprise event he was hosting for 425 kindergarteners from five Harlem elementary schools. It was a daytime event and the kids must have thought it was just another field trip as they trooped off the yellow school buses.

Neither they nor their teachers had any idea what was in store. Even when the event was over most of the kids didn't understand the significance of what had just been given them, nor did their parents. George Weiss had just guaranteed them free schooling as far as they wanted to go, to law school or medical school or beauty school. He was also offering financial aid for their siblings and continuing education for their parents. It was a gift that just kept giving.

I think one of the reasons I found this story so appealing is that, as a student, I was a poster child for underachievers. I never really got serious about learning until I was at Yale. It's always been one of my biggest regrets. I never realized how much fun learning could be.

My dad went to USC but my mom only made it through the eighth grade. They certainly didn't discourage learning, they just never got through to me how much more I could get out of life if I actually did learn. I've been trying to make up for lost time and my grandkids all think I'm a broken record.

I first read about George Weiss several years earlier and then spotted periodic articles about his "*Say Yes To Education*" program. From the beginning I wondered how long it would last. How long before he went broke? How long before he gave up? When he first announced that he would start a "Say Yes" program in the Belmont Elementary School in West Philadelphia in 1987, there were plenty of naysayers.

One columnist wrote that Weiss was arrogant to think he could swoop down on one of the most troubled neighborhoods in America like a fairy godmother and turn around such miserable lives. And he was criticized for choosing kids at random who had done nothing to earn the privilege of a free lifetime education.

Once they were in the program, he hadn't set standards they would have to meet to stay in the program. It all sounded much too idealistic to work. I remembered how good I was at getting out of learning.

When you look at the statistics of that first sixth grade class of 112, it seems the critics were right. More ended up in jail than in college, three for murder. Twenty graduated from college and twenty-four received two-year or trade school degrees.

The good news was that the dropout rate was much better than most all the other West Philly high schools, and the statistics would have been better if the original class had not included forty-four special education students with learning disabilities. Some could barely recite the alphabet. They told him he could reject the special education students but he said to exclude them would be to admit that there is no hope. In George's view there is always hope.

George Weiss is the son of a research chemist who had been smuggled out of Austria to the US during World War II. The younger Weiss bused tables in high school. That's what he was doing when a business professor from Boston University, who was a customer at the restaurant, suggested he go to the Wharton School of Business at the University of Pennsylvania. That was after Weiss told him he wanted to be an entrepreneur. Weiss's friends say he is the ultimate optimist and was scheming to give away his money even before he had any.

To hear him tell it, the event that changed the course of his life was when Weiss was a sophomore at Penn and his fraternity sponsored a Christmas party for twelve inner city kids. They were known as the twelve apostles and they were about seven years younger than George himself. Over the next few years, he got to know the twelve apostles quite well playing basketball and pool with them. Weiss kept in touch with the kids, even after he graduated from Penn.

On one visit, he discovered that all twelve had graduated from high school, which was quite remarkable for the neighborhood. When he asked them how all twelve managed to graduate, one of them told him it was because of him and all his preaching about the importance of schooling. "We wouldn't have been able to look you in the eye," one of them said. Weiss says at that moment he made a pact with God that he if ever had the financial resources he would make a difference in inner city neighborhoods.

George Weiss is a good-looking guy with salt and pepper hair and expensive suits. When I first met him, he was loaded. He had given $40 million to his alma mater the University of Pennsylvania, a Quaker school. His money market company, George Weiss and Associates, has offices in New York City and Hartford, Connecticut.

He rides in limousines and hobnobs with leaders of the corporate world and academics from America's top universities. Over the years, he has given over $34 million of his own money to Say Yes and pledged $20 million more. But it takes many millions to finance the expanding program, so Weiss is always hitting up friends and business associates for more money. As one donor told me, "How can you say no."

He also started *Say Yes* programs in Cambridge, Massachusetts, in Hartford, New York, and a second program back in Philadelphia, totaling almost 800 kids. He never offers a program without the close cooperation of a topnotch local university, like Harvard or Penn or Columbia. George Weiss provides the money, the university provides the support and expertise.

Weiss has learned lessons along the way. In the beginning he started the kids in the sixth grade. Now, as with the Harlem elementary schools, they're enrolled in kindergarten. He has learned what the Catholics have known for centuries—the younger you can get a child, the better the chance of shaping their character.

Weiss has also learned that it does little good if the kids get way ahead of their parents, so he now provides education for the mom and dad. And if the brothers and sisters show an interest, their education will be subsidized.

I visited with Natasha Johnson in West Philly who had only gone as far as the sixth grade. But after her son Romie was enrolled in Say Yes, she went back to school and was taking college classes and helping her fourth grader with his homework. Sometimes he helped her with her homework. Both said they intended to graduate from college.

One of the biggest reason girls drop out of the program is they get pregnant, and when they do, it makes it almost impossible for them to break out of the ghetto. I'll never forget Jolena Fuller, mother of five well-mannered children.

If you ever saw a picture of a dead-end neighborhood, they lived in it. Jolena got pregnant several times and had to drop out of the program. When she first met George, she asked him how much jail time he had done because almost everyone she knew had been in jail. Even though she had dropped out of the program, she preached constantly to her kids about the value of education.

The graduates we spoke with expressed a desire to pass their good fortune on to others, to give back to the community. Kids like Harold Shields who graduated from Penn and was working on a graduate degree in social work. He was sponsoring a $10,000 scholarship for inner-city kids, even though he can't afford it.

Then there was Kimberly Carmichael who told me, "Where I grew up, you would think there were only black people and the only white people that were around were the cops." She was one of the original Belmonters who has since graduated from college and was working on a master's. Her dream is to "do what George Weiss has done and be able to give back."

The kids knew George Weiss personally because he invested more than just money in each one of them. They told of late night phone calls to see how things were going or a drop-by visit to ask why they hadn't been to school. He visited some kids in prison.

There was never any doubt that he cared genuinely for each kid. Kimberly Carmichael said, "They constantly stayed on us, okay. 'You guys have this opportunity, you need to do something with it.' They were always there."

And when the kids got in trouble, Weiss, his staff, and volunteers were the first ones there to try to get them back on track. Like the young mother of two children who earned an associate's degree and was bailed out of jail several times and *Say Yes* was there waiting for her.

Weiss had grown so close to one boy, Walter Brown, that he had invited him to his home in Hartford. Walter was a very unhappy young man, but George Weiss saw something more in him. He described him to me as a philosopher and a very, very wise young man. Weiss even had Walter's picture on his desk. He was like a son and when he was killed in a terrible accident in a car he had stolen, Weiss gave the eulogy and he cried. Walter was one of several *Say Yes* kids who died way too young.

But consider the other statistics. In Hartford, out of seventy-eight Say Yes students, forty-eight were in college at the time of our story. In Cambridge, of the sixty-seven kids in the tenth grade class, there had been no pregnancies.

Students have gone on to become aeronautic engineers, lawyers, and doctors. Weiss was personally involved with many of his kids and proud as a father of their accomplishments. But he was always frustrated that he can't help more.

So he expanded the program to include whole communities in low-income neighborhoods. Say Yes now covers more than 130,000 public school students. When I talked with him, he was searching for other communities. He said, "There are a lot of great kids in the country that are just falling off the cliff." He would sometimes lie awake at night worrying about how he was going to raise enough money beyond his own to keep the program going, and to expand it. He worries more about the kids themselves.

Wayne and Ann Miller

When I told Wayne that I was writing a small chapter about him and his wife Anne and the God's Love shelter, he said "Oh, that's nice," and changed the subject. The last thing he cared about was credit for what he and Anne have done and continue to do. We were at the Wayne Miller Coin shop in Helena, Montana. He explained that there are hardly any serious coin collectors anymore and it's very difficult to make a dime. But Wayne is a smart cookie and he's managed to make many, many dimes over the years and he's given a good share of them to the poor.

I first met Wayne and Ann Miller in 1988 when I was doing a story for NBC News about their charitable endeavors in Helena, Montana. They lived in a very nice home overlooking a pool and Jacuzzi located above a river. I was in the Jacuzzi drinking a glass of Rothschild 34.

That night I joined the family for dinner. I commented about one of the paintings on the wall. Wayne would buy the works of young artists he thought showed promise as a way of encouraging them. A month after I was in Helena, the painting I admired arrived at my doorstep. That's not the reason I'm writing about the Millers.

I had seen a blurb in a Helena paper featuring the Millers and the fact that they were about the only charity in Helena, although hardly anyone in town knew. The Millers preferred to keep their donations anonymous. That's what brought me there. I was doing the story for the *Today* show.

At the time, the Millers funded almost entirely the city's Sub for Santa program. They paid for kids' tuition when parents couldn't, provided clothing and food for those in need. They even imported string quartets to lend the state capital some finer culture. But you would never hear them talk about it.

Then they started the city's only homeless shelter called "*God's Love,*" which is right downtown. The city was worried that the shelter would cause "undesirables" to populate the downtown park so Wayne bought the property next door and built a park just for the shelter.

It's not an eyesore. It's become an icon, a homeless shelter like no other. It's more like a home and you can feel God's love in it. Whenever I visit homeless shelters around the country, I always recommend a trip to *God's Love* to learn how to do it right.

Wayne and Ann met while they were getting their master's degrees at Catholic University in Washington, DC. After graduating, Wayne opened a little coin shop in downtown Bozeman and is apparently very good at spotting rare coins and investing in gold and silver.

Those who meet him might guess that he's a few steps away from being homeless himself but when they speak with him they find a very bright, intense man with a wry sense of humor. He has a very dry, self-deprecating wit. Drama is not part of Wayne's personality.

Both he and Ann are deeply religious but not preachy or self-righteous. They had five children of their own and adopted four more. Six went on to get college degrees. They both appreciate "the good life" but it isn't the most important thing.

Since its opening, the shelter has grown to add a second floor that houses nine families. Downstairs there are thirty-seven beds. Most people who come through have a job but don't make enough to live off the street, or can't get a job. The Millers' son Dave, an evangelical pastor, runs the place. There are no limits on how long someone can stay there as long as they're actively looking for a job.

Wayne's fortunes ebb and flow with the economy. Sometimes he's rich enough to afford the fine wines he loves. Sometimes things are tight, and then he'll forego the wine to spend what he has on the needy. When the price of gold goes up, Wayne will give five or six thousand a week to help people who drop by the shelter simply looking for help. The last time I checked, there are three charities in Helena—The Salvation Army, the Good Samaritan clothing store, and Wayne and Ann Miller.

If you go to Helena, visit God's Love. You'll remember it. Better yet, leave a donation. And if you're a hobo and want to catch a freight, Helena is a great place to do that.

MAASAI

I was in a remote part of Tanzania near the foothills of Ol Doinyo Lengai, known to the Maasai people as the Mountain of God and the center of their universe. When it spews lava, the Maasai think God is angry. The last angry eruption was in 2007. Legend has it that centuries ago, God dropped cows from the sky as a gift to the Maasai and now all the cows on earth belong to them. The Maasai I spoke with believe the legend.

It's as though time has simply passed by the Maasai, much like the cars and jeeps that speed by the menfolk herding their cattle. Most Maasai have never ridden in a motorized vehicle. We were in a Land Rover, driving by four high-school-aged teenagers who were waving at us. We stopped and our guide told us the young ladies wanted to know if they could have a ride in the back. He said it would be their first time in a car.

So we drove them down the winding road about five miles and stopped long enough for them to jump off, only to walk back to where we had picked them up. They were very excited. Walking five miles is nothing to them. Maasai are known to walk fifty miles a day.

We were in Tanzania with a missionary named Gary Woods. He is with the US-based, non-denominational organization called Christian Missionary Fellowship. Woods reminded me of a special ops or Delta Force kind of guy. He was in terrific condition, his hair cut short.

He and his wife and been ministering in the bush for twenty-five years. In our interview, Gary described what he found when he first arrived: "I remember one day when I first came here I heard two ladies talking and they said, "Is it an animal or what is it? Look at, he has hair on his arms." They were trying to figure out what I was cause they'd never seen a white man before."

Christian missionaries have proselytized the Maasai for more than 150 years with little success. But within the last two decades, for reasons no one seems to understand, the tribe started converting to Christianity. Now as many as a quarter of the 400,000 Maasai in Tanzania have become Christians.

Woods said when he first arrived, the witch doctors were very influential and feared. "They cursed the church to die," But he said the witch doctors are now in retreat. "They have been defeated." That may be a bit premature.

Woods called his missionary work "planting churches." He explained:

"We empower national Maasai to do the ministry. I didn't start any of these churches. I'm not the leader of any of these churches. But we've trained these people so that they could move out and do it. When a Maasai comes into a community it doesn't quite—it doesn't cause a stir like when I come. When I come everybody is, Oh the white man's here. But when they come, they know the culture, the language, and it's easier to integrate into the community."

Before Joseph Ngida, one of Woods's "planted" pastors, was converted, like all young Maasai men he served as a hunter-warrior for his tribe. It's a longstanding tradition and custom. I asked him if he had ever killed a lion and he said no, but he had killed a leopard with a spear.

When he started as a pastor a year earlier, he had three followers. When we were with him he had fifty eight. Some were helping him build a new schoolhouse. Until it was completed, a group of mothers, many with AIDS, attended classes under an acacia tree. Ngida said it is much better that they come to him than go to the numerous state orphanages where women with AIDS were not treated very well. In fact, they were treated abysmally.

Ngida said his mission includes more than just converting new believers. He explained that he had two missions—one to help people learn to live better and the other to convert them to Christianity. I asked if one was more important than the other. "No," he said. "We normally say it is holistic, so if you treat one side and leave another side, it is like dividing your body, so it is holistic."

Woods said the missionaries wanted people to have a better life, but they also wanted them to learn about the afterlife and about Jesus Christ. Converting to Christianity is a huge step for Maasai and one that can have serious, real life consequences. We met with Jacob Loserian, a Maasai who said he paid a high price when he became a Christian. "You lose friends. They will not come to your house because you already got cursed."

Despite the personal cost, Jacob said Maasai were converting because they think it will make them a better person. "If you're a thief you will not steal anymore. If you were a killer, you will not kill anymore because the church will only teach good things."

Christianity brings them more than changes in their belief system. It brings, for instance, changes to their diet. Over the years, Woods became a student of Maasai beliefs, legends, and culture, which all blend together. He said traditionally the Maasai would eat nothing but meat, no vegetables. "They have a proverb that says that God would be angry with you if you scratch the earth or, you know, did

193

some digging." And then he showed me how the Maasai have scratched the earth and started growing vegetables. "We can see right here, these people have broken that proverb and they planted and now they're taking care of themselves able to feed themselves."

We ran across a group of Maasai young men who were covered in bright paint and attire. We learned their bright coloring indicated they had recently been circumcised. In the Maasai culture, young women must also go through the much more painful process of female circumcision, but among the Christian converts this is no longer true.

It may be the women who have benefited the most from their new religion. Joseph told us about the terrible oppression of women: "Maasai culture, the women are just a possession. It's something that they own like their donkeys or sheep, their goats, cattle. And I asked a man why, how many donkeys he had and he said he didn't have donkeys, cause he had five wives."

Critics of missionary work argue that taking the white man's civilization to indigenous people isn't always a good idea, that it can cause friction between the new and old religions and cultures. There's no question that there has been friction. But Gary Woods believes the positives outweigh the negatives. He said he has seen changes that can only be good. For instance, even young females started going to school and husbands now know it's wrong to beat their wives and they are playing with their kids.

The Maasai worship a volcano, live in constant fear of evil spirits, throw meat at the sky to thank the spirit-God and make animal sacrifices at the base of a fig tree. Jacob said the Maasai are afraid of all sorts of things, even when they're safe at home, especially the owl. "When the owl comes, you know, flying up on the house, then start make the sound, then the Maasai, they are afraid, especially when they have a sick person. Then they'll be afraid that maybe this person is going to die."

And when they die, the Maasai do what they have always done with the dead bodies. They wrap them in a sheet, then place them out in the bush for the hyenas to come and eat them. Christian burials seem far more civilized, to us.

My producer Trent Harris, myself, and some Maasai elders were packed into Gary Woods's Land Rover, headed far out into the bush to visit the mayor of a village who, along with many in the village, had converted to Christianity. At first the road was paved, then gravel, then dirt, and then muddy ruts. Woods drove like a mad man racing death. The Maasai are not particular about guests showing up on time, especially since they have no clocks, so we were crashing forward just because Woods knew "Heavenly Father" was looking out for us.

Then we hit an embankment and our truck tilted over perilously close to falling about six feet into a gulley. That was our secondary problem. The first obstacle was getting the truck upright so we could crash forward.

If we couldn't get out of there, the chances of someone from civilization finding us in the near future were slim to none. We were in a rut far less traveled. Fortunately—or as Woods would have put it, "Thanks be to God"—there were some Maasai herders passing near us with their cattle and they stopped to help push the car upright. But it wasn't budging.

Trent and I decided I should do an on-camera standup explaining our predicament. Just as I began, a donkey brayed and I heard Trent go "Oh-oh!" The Land Rover suddenly slid to within inches of rolling into the gulley.

I will not forget the braying of the donkey. I can hear it now. Finally, in one last attempt I knew was going to fail, Gary jumped into the driver's seat and gunned the engine. The Maasai were pushing with all their might and miraculously the Rover tore up over the side of the mountain and we were free. Hallelujah. I was a believer.

When we finally got to the village I knew I wasn't cut out to be a bush missionary. The mayor, James, lived in the only cement building in the village with one door, no windows and lots of flies and mosquitoes. The entire village was waiting for us to join them for a goat barbeque. First though, the ceremonial toast inside the mayor's home with village elders.

Because there is no electricity, no refrigeration, no modern amenities, the special drink was sour milk. It's a celebratory drink hunters use when they come home with prey. I like buttermilk, but this was nothing like that.

It was sour milk with thumb-sized lumps in it. Remember that everyone in the hut was watching me to see if I liked my drink. It was not the first time I was required to taste local food that made me want to gag. I didn't gag, but when I saw the tape, I sure didn't look like I was enjoying it. You could see the flies congregating on my nose and in my milk.

James told us more about how becoming a Christian had been and still was very difficult. His father had been a witch doctor, something James now regarded as a devil practice. Lifelong friends would no longer talk to him. He was uninvited to their homes and they would never visit him. His family disowned him. He had been banished from the tribe. Fortunately, if misery loves company, he was not alone in this little outcast village.

Then it was time for the barbeque.

Over the years, I've partaken a number of delicacies I would prefer not to think about. In New Zealand I swallowed a tiny live fish that wiggled as it went down. In China I ate crispy fried scorpions, although they were actually quite tasty. The worst were fried sparrows with their feathers still attached. Those I stuffed in my pockets. Unfortunately, there were so many villagers watching me eat the goat delicacy, I had to stuff it in my mouth. It was raw. I had blood on my tongue. I could taste it. I pointed to Trent and everyone looked at him, so I stuffed as much of the goat as I could in my pants pocket.

I had been dreading the long ride back to Moshi but I would have walked back to get out of that village. I'm a fair weather adventurer. I can handle it as long as I can sleep in a nice hotel at the end of the day.

The following night Trent and I joined Gary and his wife for dinner at a café in downtown Moshi. It was a street café and the food was terrific and not at all bloody. First we stopped by their compound, which was a house inside a wall with barbed wire strung across it. Inside the house there was an armed security guard. Even with the armed man living with them, their place had been broken into more than once.

So even when they weren't in the bush they were in danger. But they were dedicated enough to risk their lives to convert people like Jacob who was devoted enough to risk losing his friends for what he believed. And then there was me. I was laughed at by a jackass.

Maasai teenagers after their first ride in an automobile, actually the back of our Land Rover

RELIGIOSITY & JUSTICE

Thinking about individuals and their stories as a reflection of the common traits and truths of a larger group can help us recognize that generalizations often don't work. The world is not black and white. The truth is almost always grey.

ALEX AND HIS WIVES

I met Alex Joseph in a bar in downtown Salt Lake City. I was surprised that he had asked to meet me at a bar inasmuch as I knew he was a polygamist and polygamists are almost always fundamentalist Mormons who don't drink or smoke. But I didn't know Alex.

I had heard about him as I was finishing an hour-long documentary called *Polygamy, Prospering in Exile* for KUTV in Salt Lake City. The title sounds kind of sexy but it was a serious and rare look at a religious lifestyle that I had assumed was underground and quite small. I was wrong. At the time there were as many as 25,000 polygamists living in plain sight in Salt Lake County alone. They weren't flaunting their lifestyle, but it wasn't all that hard to find them in their big houses in the suburbs.

Until Utah became a state in 1890, many—but not a majority of—Mormons had practiced polygamy, under instructions from God to Joseph Smith. As a prophet, Smith could communicate with God, who apparently sanctioned the practice. Smith said it was needed, in part, to keep the Church from dying away because so many of its menfolk and leaders were being murdered by anti-Mormon mobs. This was before the Mormons arrived in the Salt Lake Valley.

Congress wouldn't let Utah become a state until the territory agreed to ban polygamy once and for all. It was the only territory that was required to legislate such a ban. The Republican platform at the time equated polygamy to slavery and barbarism. So the church prophet, Wilford Woodruff, announced a manifesto abolishing the practice of polygamy. That made some members angry enough to leave the Church. They were convinced that polygamy was and always will be ordained by God.

I was familiar with the community in Southern Utah, straddling the border with Arizona, that practiced polygamy openly. The women generally wore their hair in braids and always covered their bodies in neck-to-ankle dresses.

The houses were understandably very large but never looked as though they were completed. They were always in the process of getting larger. The community on the Utah side is called Hildale. On the Arizona side it's known as Colorado City. If this sounds confusing, it was meant to be.

In the early 1950s, authorities from Utah raided the border town (then known as Short Creek), arrested several men and threw them in prison. After that, Short Creek was divided into two towns straddling the border. Then if Utah cops raided Hildale, residents could simply cross over into Colorado City, Arizona, and there wasn't much the state authorities could do.

I had been to Colorado City a few times as a TV reporter and it had never been a pleasant experience. It wasn't a particularly friendly place. Actually it wasn't friendly at all. No one would stop to talk to you. The women would scurry away. The men usually weren't around but when they were, they were hostile. I imagine if I was openly breaking the law I would be a little paranoid myself.

Actually, the first time I visited Colorado City I was a senior at Hurricane High School. It was Senior Sneak Day. Hurricane is only about thirty miles from Colorado City; in fact, we had polygamist kids attending our school. I was not unfamiliar with the lifestyle or the town.

I'm not proud about what we did and my parents practically disowned me for it. Traditionally, Senior Sneak at Hurricane High is when seniors do something daring and stupid, like stealing another school's mascot. We were determined to do something that no other class before us had done. We decided to conduct our own raid on Colorado City in the dark of the night, pretending to be the cops.

It was a beautifully organized hit-and-run operation that almost got us thrown in jail. One of the more technically oriented among us actually broke into the town sheriff's car and disconnected his two-way radio. Then we dropped off tires at several intersections and set them afire. We had a siren and a couple of shotguns loaded with blanks.

As we zoomed through town with our siren blaring, we fired shotguns into the air to make sure no one slept through our escapade. Then someone in our group fired a shot that turned out not to be blank and broke someone's big plate-glass window. I cringe to think about it.

After the raid we hid out in a nearby canyon, which was a good idea because police were looking for us. Actually now that I think about it, if they had looked hard enough they could have found us. I think they must've cut us some slack because we were kids and they were polygamists. I'm not proud of what we did. I've always felt creepy about it and my mom and dad grounded me for two weeks.

Years later as a reporter in Salt Lake City I found myself drawn to stories about this openly secret lifestyle. I felt sorry for the kids. They always looked so unhappy. Polygamist wives worked in the stores at the entrance to Zion National Park not far from Virgin, and they acted like zombies. The men ran construction companies and could outbid the competition because they pooled their earnings and would work for less.

One reason I was drawn to polygamy, I think, is because it was a taboo subject. People didn't talk openly about polygamy. It was usually in whispers. I wanted to know: Why would women go along with it? If the authorities knew about it, why didn't they arrest them? The kids knew people were talking about them behind their backs just as I knew my friends' parents were talking about me when I was growing up in Virgin, although I wasn't ostracized as they were. If anything, I ostracized myself.

I remember one trip to Colorado City as a reporter when we were greeted outside of town by the sheriff. It was the same sheriff whose car we had vandalized on Senior Sneak Day, Sheriff Dan Barlow. He didn't know that I was one of the teenaged culprits but he knew I wanted to do a story he didn't want me to do. I liked the sheriff's dry wit. He kind of chuckled while he talked but he made it quite clear that we weren't welcome. He pointed in the direction of out-of-town and told us we ought to '"head in that direction.

I was there with my cameraman O.C. Budge. O.C. a world class BS-er we thought could sweet-talk the sheriff into letting us stick around. So he said, "You know, Sheriff, my last name is Budge. My uncle was the former attorney general of Utah. Budge—you ever heard of him?" The sheriff replied, "Yeah, we've heard of him. He was the attorney general who prosecuted polygamists. We prayed for him and he died two months later." In one of the rare moments of his life, O.C. was speechless. I said, "You're not going to do that for me are you, Sheriff?" He said, "Can't say." Somehow those two words did more to convince me to get the hell out of there than anything else he could have said.

A few years later, I got reluctant permission from the station manager to do an hour documentary on polygamy. I had made contact with a local attorney connected to a polygamist community in Pinesdale, Montana. I had in mind an exposé revealing the dark side of polygamy, since that's presumably what made it a taboo subject. I discovered it was also taboo because there were people practicing plural marriage who were related to good upstanding church members.

I was introduced to Dr. Rulon Allred, an osteopath and head of the sect that settled Pinesdale. I immediately liked Dr. Allred and the three wives with him when we had our initial meetings. I never met any of the other wives and can no longer remember how many he had altogether.

It was a beautiful Montana day when Dr. Rulon Allred drove us around Pinesdale in his big Oldsmobile with one of his wives sitting in the front seat next to him. She was a pretty woman with a regal bearing and the two held hands even as they drove us around.

It was clear that Dr. Allred was proud of his little community of about 400. It was an idyllic place in the pines, clean and neat. The houses were large, of course, but unlike Colorado City they had a finished look. Pinesdale had its own school, grocery store, and church. It had a park with swings. I imagine most visitors would think it a nice place to live.

I spent some time with a family of six wives and a dozen kids. They lived in a six-bedroom home belonging to a well-known Utah legislator, although it was not known in Utah that he was a polygamist and we agreed not to identify him. With that concession we had the run of the house. The kids seemed like most kids.

The wives acted like wives everywhere, chattering and kidding each other. It would all have looked like any other American home except for their stern hairdos and long dresses. The only arrangement that was difficult for me to wrap my mind around was that the oldest wife, an attractive woman of about fifty-five, was the mother of the

205

youngest wife, who was also attractive. Other than that, it seemed like one big happy family.

Their church was called the Apostolic United Brethren—descended from a group of Mormons who had broken away from the mother church over the polygamy issue. There were several such groups, some larger, some smaller, located throughout the US and Western Canada.

The *Apostolic United Brethren* was conservative, but compared to other groups quite progressive. For instance, if a woman wanted a man to take her as a plural wife, he had no choice. If she went to the elders and asked for his hand, he would have to give it no matter what she looked like. I saw a couple wives that would have caused me to quit the Church and flee.

The only dark side of Pinesdale that I could detect was that armed guards were posted on the outskirts of town each night. I thought that was a bit odd until I learned that some of the extreme polygamist groups practiced something expounded by Brigham Young called "blood atonement."

It has been well documented that the Church's second prophet, Brigham Young, preached that some apostates and church tormentors could only be saved by shedding their blood, involuntarily. A couple years after my time with him, two wives from another splinter polygamist group walked into Dr. Allred's office and shot him dead. The man charged with ordering the killing, Ervil LeBaron, was practicing "blood atonement." He ended up in prison.

I returned to Salt Lake City to spend time with a young polygamist family, a threesome: one young, handsome man with two lovely wives and one little baby. They could have been sent by central casting, if the story was about all-American families. But of course it wasn't. The thing that struck me about this family, and the ones I had met up in Montana, was what a deeply religious lifestyle this was. I couldn't say that sex wasn't one motivation but it certainly wasn't the driving force.

When I set out to do the documentary, I was certain that it would expose a sordid lifestyle with an even darker underbelly. I won't suggest that an hour-long documentary can get much beneath the surface, but I spent several months shooting and researching and I was taken aback at how wholesome the culture seemed, at least among Dr. Rulon's group.

I came to think that his group should be left alone, that their lifestyle wasn't hurting anybody. If the kids suffered it was because of the way they were treated by non-polygamist kids. Ironically, the Mormon Church actively defamed polygamy around Pinesdale. Church attorneys encouraged prosecution and members attempted to discourage locals from doing business with them.

When I was putting the final touches on the film, it occurred to me that what I had was a very candid look at a very religious lifestyle— not a very provocative program but certainly one of the more open and honest looks at polygamy available at the time.

I should have stopped while I was ahead but I had just heard about a renegade ex-Mormon polygamist named Alex Joseph and his gun-toting wives who were in an armed-standoff with the federal government. I figured they could add some spice to my project and make it easier to promote.

Unlike all other polygamists I had tried to locate, Alex was easy. He called me back. We spent the first night together drinking beer and playing pool. His hair was long, shoulder length with an Indian band around his forehead. Alex had attitude. He was a former marine and cop, a Mormon convert who became a bishop until he was excommunicated for practicing polygamy. Alex had a wicked sense of humor and was a pretty good pool player. Over the years we spent several nights shooting the stick. I liked him right away, even before I met his wives.

I think he had about eight wives at the time but he nor his wives would confirm the number. The rather large family settled down in an absolutely stunning part of the world in southeastern Utah near Lake Powell and the Grand Canyon.

The town with a population of under fifty was called Big Water. There was a bar with a pool table but not much else; a few mobile homes and some tiny clapboard houses. It was a blight surrounded by an oasis. On the other hand, the town was so small if you blinked you'd drive right by, so hardly anyone knew it was there.

We were there to film Alex marrying yet another wife. I think it was his ninth, but could never find definitive numbers. There was also a photographer for *USA Today* on hand. Alex was not shy about publicity: he liked it. But as I got to know him, his romance with media was more than simply wanting publicity.

He was proud of his lifestyle and defiant against anyone who condemned it. He was using the media no doubt about it, but he believed deeply in what he was doing. In the beginning I wondered if he wanted the publicity to attract more wives. That may have been true, but Alex told me on several occasions that being the head of a polygamist household was not easy. I know that he took some trips just to get away from his wives.

The marriage took place on top of Brigham Plain, which overlooks Big Water and is especially appropriate since Brigham Young was an enthusiastic proponent of polygamy. Brigham had fifty-five wives and fifty-nine children. On this day, Alex was marrying sixteen-year-old Paulette Combs, recently Miss Teen Kentucky. It was an unforgettable scene. Ms. Combs was gorgeous. It was a beautiful day.

Once again O.C. Budge was my cameraman and he shot the ceremony with a sunburst shining just over the preacher's shoulders. O.C. loved sunbursts and it was just the shot I needed. After the ceremony I spoke with both Alex and his new bride on camera. I remember asking her if she was certain she was doing the right thing. She answered, "I have never felt righter about anything in my life." Bingo.

After the ceremony, I sat around with his other wives eating Navajo bread and drinking red wine and watching out of the corner of my eye as Alex and Paulette hugged and kissed in the background. It seemed to bother me a whole lot more than it bothered the wives.

To someone peering in from the outside it would likely have been a disturbing scene—an older man caressing a beautiful teenage girl with several women sitting around laughing and drinking, apparently happy that their husband had a new child wife. In fact, that's just what it was. But sitting there it all seemed quite natural. If his wives weren't upset, why should we be?

The more I got to know the women, the more I realized this wasn't an ordinary polygamist family. The women didn't dress like polygamists. They wore their hair and dresses both long and short, not all in one style.

They weren't particularly sweet or obsequious. To the contrary, they were strong-willed, independently-minded women. Throw out a cliché and they'd stomp on your tongue. Ask a dumb question and they'd make fun of you. I know from experience. For the most part, I liked them.

Elizabeth became a lawyer while she was married to Alex. Another was a successful real estate broker. She took on the name of Bodicia, meaning "victory." I always called her bodacious because she was, and she knew it. Joanna was also quite pretty, but with a biting sense of humor.

Those three were from Montana. Most wives were quite attractive in a next-door sort of way. And they seemed unaffected by the camera. They made no attempt to be nice to Alex when we were around if they felt he was out of line. But it was very clear that Alex was the boss. When he asked them to do something, he didn't have to ask twice, although I never heard him raise his voice.

About that time, Alex and wives made national headlines as they set about homesteading some federal land near Big Water. The Bureau of Land Management told them to leave, that they were breaking the law. The Josephs said "Make me" and walked around carrying pistols and assault rifles.

Eventually both sides backed away, but it was the authorities that blinked first. The encounter only endeared them to Southern Utahans who hate the federal government a lot more than they dislike polygamy. The family not only spiced up my documentary, life in Southern Utah had suddenly become a lot more interesting.

As the years went by, more wives came and went. Some just didn't like the lifestyle. Others were driven away by existing wives who didn't like the newcomers. They would band together and when they did, it was all over. Alex might lecture them, but when they took a stand together, he would back away.

The core group of eight stayed with Alex for almost twenty years. I asked them on several occasions why they think their marriage lasted as long as it did. Alex was the big factor but I think almost as big were the feelings the wives had for each other. They were like sisters, like one big family of sisters with one lover.

Alex became the mayor of Big Water and Elizabeth, the county attorney. Bodicia sold half the real estate around town. The kids— not as many as you'd think, seventeen in all—seemed remarkably well adjusted They idolized their father and he was never shy about lending them his wisdom. Alex was actually quite a religious man, an amateur scholar of ancient hieroglyphics who would talk your head off about early Mormon doctrine if you let him.

Alex's wives controlled his schedule, and they drew up a new one each week for a little variety. The wives lived in separate homes close to each other and Alex would learn from the schedule which house he was supposed to spend that night in. The women worked it out amongst themselves.

It was like a monogamous marriage, only with a different wife every night. For Alex the pressure was always on, every night, unless he was traveling, which may be why he was always traveling. I always wondered if they had group sex but never dared ask.

When I heard that Alex was dying from stomach cancer I flew out to visit him. He was living on a boat docked at Lake Powell. He said he needed to get away from his caring wives. "Too much care," he told me. Other than growing grey, he looked pretty much the same with the same gentle, biting sense of humor. He said he was going to beat the disease but you could tell he didn't believe it.

A few years after his death, I had lunch with Elizabeth and Joanna. Elizabeth, who'd been in rehab twice, was still a practicing attorney.

When we talked, she was planning on becoming a Methodist minister. She grew up a Methodist. Joanna was doing work with abused kids. And then I ran into Margaret, one of Alex's first wives, who had remarried but to just one man.

She told me it was a difficult adjustment being strapped to just one man with no other wives. Bodicia got married again to a polygamist, but it didn't work out. She had been seeing another polygamist but was calling it off because he gave her a rash. They told me that monogamy had little appeal because with polygamy they had much more independence and freedom. They also didn't think it would work for most women and most men.

PREACHERS I HAVE KNOWN

When I parted company with NBC News after the unfortunate drug incident, I was middle aged and thought my career was over. I was wrong. Since NBC, I've had more fun and satisfaction than ever before. Just at the time of my departure, *Religion and Ethics Newsweekly* was starting up at PBS.

I knew the host, Bob Abernethy, from our international correspondent days with me in NBC in Tokyo and Bob in Moscow, respectively. The show's executive producer was in charge of *Weekend Today* when I worked there. So I had friends in the right place for once. By the time the show folded twenty years later I had reported hundreds of stories, and visited more churches, synagogues, and mosques than I can count. It was another part of my career I would have never imagined.

My very first assignment as a television reporter on my first day on the job at KCPX in Salt Lake City was to take my windup Bell and Howell camera into the tunnel leading from the Mormon temple and take pictures of the new church prophet and president coming out after being chosen by his fellow brethren and, apparently, by God. For some reason we knew the new prophet would be coming through the tunnel.

I cranked the camera and headed out completely intimidated by the task at hand. I had never shot a movie camera. I had no idea how to focus, only how to wind the damn thing up when it ran down. The new president was Joseph Fielding Smith, a descendent of church founder Joseph Smith. Joseph Fielding was not charismatic. He had always been known as the church scholar, not a leader.

So I ventured into the tunnel, which was quite well lit. Like most people in Salt Lake, I had no idea there was a tunnel before this assignment. (Actually there is more than one.) About two minutes after I entered, along comes the new church leader. I stopped, pointed the camera and pressed the button. In that instant, he stuck his hand out and straight-armed me, pushing the camera back into my face.

Miraculously, the picture was in focus although we never used it. Even though KCPX was not the Mormon station we could not be showing pictures of the new president of the Mormon Church ramming a camera down a reporter's throat.

Joseph Fielding turned out to be a little more popular than expectations primarily because of his wife Jenny. She was everyone's favorite. Jenny was grandmotherly (sweet and rotund) and an accomplished singer. She made her stern husband more likeable.

I remember a time during the Church's semiannual general conference when once again I was assigned to take pictures with my wind-up Bell and Howell. It was lunchtime, in between the morning and afternoon sessions. The prophet walked out of the tabernacle with Jenny by his side and they passed right in front of my shaky camera to get into his limo. He was walking behind her as an aide opened her door and he started to get in behind her. I was close enough that I could hear her tell him, "You get out and walk around the car and you wave to everyone." And he promptly did.

I've done stories with dozens of preachers, imams, rabbis. Not all of them were, in my view, admirable. Some of them were world-class con artists. Some went to jail. On more than one occasion I've done stories about TV evangelists who were raking in millions from people who couldn't afford it. I remember one nationally known preacher who tried to hide his new Cadillac. We found it, with him in it. Another tried to hide his mansion in Dallas. We found it, hidden in a suburb of million dollar homes.

James Whittington

One preacher who stands out for all the wrong reasons is James Whittington, pastor of the Fountain of Life ministry based in Greenville, North Carolina. Whittington preached the prosperity gospel—in other words, "If you give me money, God will give back to you." He did it better than anyone I ever met.

Whittington traveled around the South in two luxurious buses, which at the time cost about $250,000 each. He would promote a revival, set up a huge tent, preach prosperity, and watch the money flow in. James felt that the best way to convince his followers to give him money was to show them how God had blessed him.

He owned a Rolls Royce and a mansion with a big pool. I interviewed him by the pool with his beautiful wife looking on. She had been an Alabama beauty queen. He wore two rings he claimed Elvis gave him. What else could a man want?

I was particularly impressed with the preacher's buses that featured every amenity you could desire, including a sound studio. Elvis would have wanted a ride. But the icing on the cake was his Fountain powerboat. The company once sold Fountain powerboats to Iran until the CIA stopped the sales after Iran used the speedboats to harass US ships in the gulf.

Presidents Lyndon Johnson and George H.W. Bush both had Cigarette boats, which were very fast and could easily outrun the Secret Service's boats. But they were as slow as tug boats compared to Whittington's Fountain boat. There were seven of us onboard, plus camera gear, and even with that load the Fountain flew through the water. He used to take his wife for Sunday brunch ninety miles south to Charleston, South Carolina. Whittington was a living billboard for his religion's tenet that God blesses those who bless James Whittington with money.

A few years after I did that story, Whittington's wife called me to say he was in prison, serving two years for defrauding a Florida woman of almost a million dollars.

James and Tammy Faye Bakker

While I never met or did a story on them, I was mesmerized by Jim and Tammy Faye Bakker. Whenever I checked into a hotel room I would turn on the TV and look for the Bakkers' show.

It was more fun than a soap opera and probably raked in as much money. At one point, Jim and Tammy Faye were reportedly taking in a million dollars a week in contributions. They started the Heritage Theme Park in South Carolina, which featured a huge waterslide plunge and a retirement community of believers.

The Bakkers took conspicuous consumption to a new level. I remember one show opening where the camera slowly zooms in past the rear end of a Rolls Royce to reveal their luxurious home in Palm Springs. Then the camera cuts to James with Tammy Faye standing by his side. The two took the viewers on a tour of their very nice home.

At one point Tammy excused herself and the camera closed in on Bakker who said in a hushed voice, "Some of you may have noticed that Tammy Faye hasn't been on the show for several weeks." He said, "It's because she has been suffering mental problems." (The camera pulled back to reveal Tammy back standing next to him.) He continued: "Tammy has been gradually improving but she still needs more therapy, so if you could please contribute to help pay her medical bills, God will bless you for it."

Things went sour for Bakker after he paid $250,000 as hush money to get a young, pretty woman named Jessica Hahn to keep quiet about her charge that he and another preacher raped her. Then he was sentenced to forty-five years in prison for wire and mail fraud. Forty-five years? Murderers rarely get forty-five years.

It seemed that anyone who was anyone in the religious world piled on poor James, including other pastors like Jerry Falwell. After he took over the Bakker ministry in order to save it, he started preaching that Bakker was a liar, embezzler and sexual deviant. Bakker appeared on *Nightline* (the show's highest ratings up to that time) and accused Falwell of attempting to steal his PTL ministry.

I thought Bakker deserved jail time, but forty-five years was outrageous. I think the judge must've felt that was what the public wanted. His trial had been on television every night. *Nightline* anchor Ted Koppel seemed obsessed with the Bakkers, featuring the story night after night.

I learned a long time ago that when there is blood in the water, journalists pack together like piranhas, and God help the victim, guilty or not. It's my biggest complaint against what it is we do. Sometimes when journalists work together it produces good results, sometimes it's very unfair. Bakker's sentence was eventually reduced to eight years and he served five. On his release he started a new ministry.

Tammy Faye and Jim never got back together again. She died of colon cancer in 2007. The documentary about her called *The Eyes of Tammy Faye* revealed a kind-hearted woman. I think I would have liked her. I couldn't imagine her deliberately defrauding believers of millions of dollars. Maybe it was just Jim.

No doubt, publicity about TV evangelicals gone bad has contributed to the decline in membership of mainline churches which has been steady and broad. Charismatic churches, meanwhile, have been flourishing.

I've been to some that made me wonder if I was actually in church. Those, for instance, that feature rock-n-roll bands with lyrics displayed on a big screen as the congregation sings along following the bouncing ball. The music and the lyrics are a lot more fun than the old hymns, almost makes you want to dance. At first I liked them, then it started to feel like church-lite.

The mega churches are particularly fascinating. They're like small cities. McLean Bible Church in Virginia stands out, although it's not the biggest. I've done a story about McLean Bible. It felt like I was in a mall. At one end there's a beautiful sanctuary with plush chairs and the music is supplied not from an organist but from a harpist.

At the other end of the church there's another chapel for the younger set. The services there were conducted by a grunge pastor. Between the two sanctuaries you can find Starbucks in case you're thirsty. The Pastor, Lon Solomon (a Jew who converted to Christianity), told me he doesn't want the biggest church in the country, he wants the most powerful. There are several conservative congressmen and senators who attend McLean Bible.

I've been to many churches where the pastor drives a Mercedes. One in Detroit had two parking spots set aside for the pastor and his wife.

The pastor drove the biggest and most expensive Jaguar. His wife drove a smaller model Jag.

One pastor of a megachurch in Raleigh, North Carolina, I visited was wearing alligator cowboy boots and a suit made by Oxford. (I saw the label on his coat when it was draped over his chair.) Oxford suits usually sell in the range of $4,000 to $6,000. At first I was put off by their ostentatious lifestyle, but then I learned that many congregations, especially black ones, want their pastor to reflect success. It's as much a cultural thing as a religious one.

Yoido Full Gospel Church

I've never been to a megachurch quite like the Yoido Full Gospel in Seoul, South Korea. On a typical Sunday more than 150,000 members will attend one of seven services. The main sanctuary holds 21,000 worshipers, packed to the rafters.

Each service has its own orchestra decked out in formal wear, its own choir in beautiful gowns, its own pastor. There are hundreds of assistant pastors. Each service is translated into sixteen languages. The senior pastor described the church to me as a well-tuned orchestra designed to make perfect harmony. It was very impressive.

Yoido Full Gospel Church has the world's largest congregation, over 800,000 altogether. The church sends missionaries to more than sixty countries. The doctrine places heavy emphasis on prayer and "speaking in tongues."

Each day busloads drive out of the city up to Prayer Mountain, which includes a sacred cemetery. From a distance you can hear the sound of wailing and of people speaking in languages they don't know. There are individual prayer rooms barely big enough to kneel and pray.

Yoido is a prosperity church very much like those within the US, maybe even a little better at it. "The more you give, the more you get"—that's a message that resonates in a country that values material possessions. The church was founded by Reverend David Yonggi Cho, who had become one of the most revered religious leaders in Korea. Sixty years ago there were about 50,000 Christians in South Korea. Now there are more than ten million and almost one in ten were baptized in the Yoido Full Gospel Church.

I was told that it was a great privilege to meet Reverend Cho. I could tell by the obsequious way his underlings constantly bowed to him that he was powerful and revered. He was gracious and supremely self-confident and was attired in a very expensive suit.

Sadly, a couple years after I did a glowing story for PBS about the Yoido church, Pastor Cho was sentenced to three years in prison for embezzling more than twelve million dollars. That would explain the nice suits.

The IRS Bogeyman

We hear loud howls about the threat of the IRS prosecuting churches that preach politics from the pulpit and revoking their tax-exempt status. It's another way to get parishioners riled up but it's baloney and it drives me crazy. Churches preach politics all the time and they don't lose their sacred tax status.

That is because the relevant law, written into an amendment by then-Senator Lyndon Johnson, stipulated that only regional commissioners could approve prosecutions but after the IRS reorganized around 2005, the regional commissioner position was abolished. Marcus Owens, former head of the IRS Exempt Organization Division, told me, "That effectively shut down every IRS church investigation."

So these preachers screaming to high heaven either don't know that they're not going to be prosecuted or they're using the threat to get their congregation riled up.

I think for too many religions, politics end up mattering more than religion. I'll give an example. At the height of the immigration debate during the George W. Bush administration, the Mormon Church pushed comprehensive immigration legislation through the legislature that was lauded throughout the country as reasonable and progressive. Utah legislators, who were good Mormons, went crazy. They yelled and hollered and voted against it because it was against their party's platform, forget their church's position.

Another example, again from Utah since I'm quite familiar with that state: Mormons voted for Donald Trump partly because of his fear-mongering, anti-immigration rhetoric even though it was entirely against church teachings and doctrine. Even more puzzling, many church leaders subtly encouraged members to vote for Trump. As it turned out, the enthusiasm for Trump waned after the president targeted Muslims. Mormons were once targeted by the US government and they've never forgotten it. But they still support Trump. Still, surveys have shown that a higher percentage of Mormons support Donald Trump[than other evangelical churches.

The Mormon vote would be quite different if it were held church wide. That's because the Church as a whole is more liberal than the church inside Utah. It's become that way because over fifty percent of church members live outside the US and outside the country is more moderate than inside.

The Church can't be seen as targeting immigrants if it wants permission to build a tax-free church in Mexico or Tanzania. So the Church worldwide has become more liberal, while its core members in Utah remain quite conservative. This paradox will come to an interesting head one day.

For all the dubious pastors I've met, the majority deserve to be called servants of God. It's a hard job with long hours and little pay and scarce appreciation. I admire those who preach inclusion and hope.

Those who preach damnation and intolerance shouldn't be preaching as far as I'm concerned, not if they claim the New Testament as their guide. These churches have contributed to the great divide in our country. Other pastors have done more to bring us together than any politician ever could. Pope Francis would fit that description.

Dalai Lama

I had never followed the Dalai Lama until I was assigned to go to his home in India to interview him. I knew who he was and admired him from afar but that was about all. But I had never been to India and I wanted to go. So off we went, my producer Ricki Green, her daughter and I. We arranged for a fixer and crew in New Delhi.

When we arrived in New Delhi I thought my clothes had become part of my skin. It was ungodly hot. Fortunately, we were only there twenty-four hours before we took off for Dharamsala in the northern Indian state of Himachal Pradesh. It was a midnight train out of the Delhi station and if I'd have slept that night I'm sure I would have had nightmares. The crush of humanity at the station was like nothing I had ever seen.

We shared a cabin with our fixer, who was big enough to fill the cabin himself. It was a long night's ride. The scenery constantly changed from ugly to spectacular and back again from valley to valley. That's the thing about India: it's a country of extremes, extreme beauty and abysmal ugly, extreme riches and indescribable poverty. I saw the Indian caste system up close. It takes a long time to undo a system 3,000 years old.

We arrived at our destination about five hours from Dharamsala early in the morning and immediately embarked with our van and driver. It was a gorgeous ride as we gradually climbed to the city situated in the shadow of the Himalayas. When we finally got there, Dharamsala stood out from all the other towns we had passed. It was spotlessly clean, bustling with Internet cafes and hostels. This was the de facto capital of the Dalai Lama's government, courtesy of the Indian government after he escaped the Chinese invasion of Tibet.

There was a time when Tibet ruled a good part of the Eastern world. But its military might had long faded by 1950 when Mao Zedong took power in China and wanted to control Tibet. The Chinese wanted a buffer between themselves and India and Tibet was it. By then the Tibetans had only a few thousand soldiers; China, hundreds of thousands. It was no match.

In 1959, the Chinese drove the Dalai Lama out of one of the world's few theocracies. He was forced to sneak out in the dark of the night destined for India. Eventually India's Prime Minister Jawaharlal Nehru offered him Dharamsala to use as his base, much to the chagrin of the Chinese. Gradually over the years, hundreds of Tibetans made it across the barren, stark and brutal terrain to be with their beloved leader. Meanwhile, the Chinese have carried out their strategy to dilute the ethnicity and the religion to the point that it no longer poses any threat.

We were in Dharamsala a couple of days when the Dalai Lama's assistant called to say his Holiness had to leave the country earlier than planned and could we come by and talk about our questions.

My producer had a list of really predictable questions at the ready. She handed it to the assistant who looked at it, smiled and handed it back. Then he said, "I only want to make sure that the questions aren't too easy. His Holiness prefers questions he hasn't been asked before. He prefers more difficult questions." That was the first and only time any interviewee or his or her assistant ever said that to me.

The thing that struck me when we entered his comfortable but not palatial home was his consuming curiosity. Often in situations like this, before the interview begins there is an awkward period of either silence or small talk. Not so with his Holiness. He wanted to know where we were from, what we thought of issues and leaders. It was like speaking to an old friend. There were five of us and he was as curious about each of us as we were about him. He rises before the sun each day prays for hours. Near the end of the interview I asked him what he would be in the next life. He smiled and said, "If I'm a good boy, I'll be the fifteenth Dalai Lama."

The Chinese government must realize what a force the DL has become. They've called him a terrorist. That's insane. Even his most devoted followers believe he has been way too accommodating to the Chinese. His passion for peace is genuine. He has never wavered from that position.

When I told him many of his disciples were getting impatient, he said, "Then they need to learn more patience." Ironically—and the

Chinese love irony—if the Dalai Lama had not been driven out of Tibet, he might not have become the world leader he is today.

When I flew out of New Delhi, the DL was on the plane, actually in the back of the plane. Over the years I've met lots of famous people, movie stars, politics leaders, etc. I've never once asked anyone for an autograph. In fact I far prefer being around regular folk. But I was so taken with his Holiness, I asked him to sign his book and then I gave him one I had just finished about the holocaust. He said he'd been wanting to read it.

Pastor David Brown

Pastor David Brown was a circuit preacher who ministered to seven Baptist churches in Louisiana and Mississippi. It's a tough job with long hours and barely enough in tithes to pay for gas, let alone put food on his table. It was not unusual that he would drive seventy or eighty miles from one church to another and he made the rounds during the week as well as every Sunday.

Brown was a dynamic preacher and could probably have found a single congregation to support him but felt that the Lord called him to minister to the little churches that can't afford a full-time preacher.

Brown was African American, like about ninety-nine percent of the people he preached to. I've been to many, many churches and my favorite will always be African American. The music moves me and the preaching comes from the gut. The church has been especially important to the culture.

When families were falling apart because of ridiculous welfare rules and unjust drug laws, about the only place families could find solace and help was the church—the church and grandmas. The church gave solace and purpose. The grandmas gave a home and protection. Don't get in the way of a black grandma.

We followed Brown around one Sunday to three churches, 50 or 60 miles apart. All of them were quite small. One church had fewer than thirty souls. It didn't matter how big the congregation.

Pastor Brown would get as worked up with a tiny congregation as with the big ones. He would start out slow and gradually build up to a level that demanded attention. It practically rattled the windows. It was a combination of rap and hellfire and brimstone. When he got going he would punctuate his sentences with a staccato grunt as if he was inhaling the Holy Spirit. It was mesmerizing.

He was a big man, probably more than 300 pounds, but he moved with grace. At the end of each sermon, sweat would be pouring off his forehead and he looked too spent to give another sermon, A couple hours later he would start all over again and the next sermon would be as powerful as the last.

Brown carried on a tradition that got its start just after the Civil War when former slaves were allowed to attend churches on plantations. But the congregations were too small and poor to afford full-time preachers.

In movies like *Pale Rider*, Hollywood portrayed the circuit rider as a macho preacher who rode into town, shot dead all the bad guys, and then prayed for the congregation. The reality was much less glamorous. Circuit preachers often traveled thousands of miles in their lifetime on horseback from one small town to another, keeping tiny congregations alive. No one knows how many circuit preachers there are today. Pastor Brown said he was aware of only two or three besides himself in the Deep South.

My producer Phil O'Conner and I rode in the back of his car as we traveled through the Louisiana countryside. He gave us a history of each little community and of the tiny churches where he preached. He was proud of his mission but it was clear that he had a hard time making ends meet.

A few weeks after our story on Pastor Brown aired, we heard from a Pastor Robbins with the Marvin United Methodist Church in Tyler, Texas. Robbins was deeply moved by our story. He said he watched it at least twenty-five times and told his congregation to watch is as well.

Before long, the United Methodist congregation was sending money to the Baptist circuit preacher. How often does that happen—one denomination helping another? We discovered later that Pastor Robbins started to look at Pastor Brown as a mentor, strange as that may seem considering that Pastor Robbins holds a doctorate degree in divinity. He was a very modern preacher, deeply involved in social justice issues, assisted by four pastors and a large staff who helped him supervise several ministries.

Marvin United Methodist is a large, beautiful church in downtown Tyler with a well-heeled congregation. Several members are oil company executives. Because there is a medical center in Tyler, there are a number of doctors and lawyers. Lots of money. It's also a very active congregation in charitable and civic affairs.

Robbins continually tried to enlighten his congregation to the way other people live and what they believe, so it was not unusual when he invited Pastor Brown to come and preach at Marvin United Methodist.

We were there the day Pastor Brown and his wife Gwendolyn drove in from Monroe, Louisiana. He had driven through a horrendous storm to get there in his son's Honda because his own car had broken down. The transmission finally gave out.

Pastor Robbins was there to greet Pastor Brown and took him on a tour of his magnificent church. When they finally arrived at the sanctuary where he was to speak later that evening, it was apparent that Brown had never seen anything quite like it. It was one of the most beautiful sanctuaries I have ever visited, surrounded with marvelous stained glass windows. One of the members said the church had just spent $500,000 reconditioning the stained glass.

I interviewed Brown again before he left to take a rest before his preaching. He figured that the prim and proper congregation might be taken aback by his manner of speaking but he didn't seem at all nervous. When I spoke with Pastor Robbins, he talked about how there were still too many congregations that remain segregated. He wanted his to understand the fiery kind of preaching that goes on in black churches throughout the South.

The special service Pastor Brown was to address was at six on a Wednesday evening, not a good time for many businessmen or their families. Nevertheless there wasn't an empty seat in the large sanctuary, which was filled with hundreds of white faces and two or three that were African American.

After a couple of renditions from the choir, Pastor Robbins got up and gave a short introduction to the guest speaker. Pastor Brown didn't use the podium. He did something I had never seen him do before. He grabbed a couple of folding chairs and set them across from each other.

Then for about half an hour Brown, with his massive frame, would move from one chair to the other. In one chair he would act as Jesus Christ, using quotes from the bible. In the other chair he would be a wayward disciple. I was very concerned, and I'm sure the audience was, that one of the chairs might give way under his ample carriage and I think it might have happened if not for divine intervention.

I kept looking at the faces in the audience for their reaction. I saw some who sort of rolled their eyes and looked around. Most were attentive, straining to figure out what this black man was saying and what his message was. By the end of the speech he sat down, dripping with sweat, they knew the message was that excuses don't work with the Almighty.

When Pastor Robbins stood to introduce the circuit preacher he suggested in a very persuasive way that his parishioners should be generous. They heard him. The collection plates passed around before his speech totaled over $14,000, probably about half as much as Pastor Brown collected from tithes on the circuit in one year.

When he got back to his home in Monroe, Louisiana, the first thing he did was get his transmission fixed. He then learned that his car needed a whole new engine. That would cost several thousand dollars. The Marvin United Methodist congregation heard about his plight and raised enough money to buy the Baptist circuit preacher of a different church a brand new car.

Pastor Brown died two years after our second story aired. His heart just could not keep up with the pace and that rich Louisiana food.

Father Michael Doyle

I first met Father Michael Doyle when he was conducting a Mass for the dead at Sacred Heart Catholic Church in downtown Camden, New Jersey. Each time he would read out the name of a victim of violence, a person wearing that name would join the line that gradually encircled the large sanctuary. This was something he'd been doing once a year for nearly twenty years. In 2013 there were fifty-five murders in Camden, almost all of them caused by guns. Father Doyle takes these deaths personally.

Beneath his calm, measured manner, Father Doyle is deeply angry at what he sees as a deliberate injustice in the world's richest country. He says Camden is a "terrible, terrible place for kids to grow up in," even in a "very generous country, but one that has made a decision to sacrifice the poor." He explained, "Look around, the poor are concentrated in places like Camden, and that concentration is deadly."

It would be difficult to find any place in the US where the poor are more concentrated than Camden. When we were there, nearly half the population of 77,000 lived in poverty. Unemployment was about twenty percent. You could still buy a house there for as little as $15,000, not fancy but not falling down. Across the Delaware River in the shiny city of Philadelphia, houses sold for as much as $15 million.

It's not just poverty. The neighborhoods looks like they've been bombed out. In 2012 there were 266 shootings, 67 of which were homicides, making Camden at the time, according to the FBI, the most dangerous city per-capita in the US. Father Doyle counted 788 murders in seventeen years.

He said he heard kids say they're not afraid of terrorism because "if the terrorists fly over to bomb Camden they will think they have already done it." I spoke with one seventeen-year-old whose God-brother was blinded by a gunshot. He said as he was growing up he wasn't allowed to play with friends on the street where he lived because it was too dangerous.

Father Doyle said ninety percent of crime comes out of drug wars and of the prevalence of guns. He thinks the US love affair with guns is partly responsible for what he calls the "slaughter of Camden". He thinks it's even worse today than when he first moved there about four decades years earlier.

Doyle is not a hellfire and brimstone preacher. He speaks slowly, softly, and sincerely. You just know the man does not embellish. He does not try to impress. He will engage a homeless person on the street with the same attention as he would an enquiring reporter. In his view, we are all equal. I rarely encountered anyone quite like Father Doyle who looks at us all as "God's children," none above the other.

Father Doyle was not above breaking the law to serve what he sees as God's purpose. During the Vietnam War, he was arrested along with Father Daniel Berrigan, his close friend, as part of the famous—or infamous—"Camden 28" charged with breaking into a government building to destroy draft records. It was seen by many as a referendum on the Vietnam War.

Sacred Heart funds food kitchens and sponsors a primary school for 200 kids, many of whom are not Catholic. Father Doyle created a sponsorship program where members would give $300 each year to fund the school.

Each month members get letters written by Doyle containing homilies and poetry and a request for financial help. He has raised over $900,000 in a single year. The city's mayor Dana Redd, a Baptist, attended Sacred Heart School after her parents died from gun violence. She told me Father Doyle helped shape her life.

Then there's the Heart of Camden project founded by Father Doyle. It has purchased hundreds of homes and refurbished and resold most of them at reduced rates for those who could never afford a house before. We were there when Cristya Rodriguez and her two boys moved into the first home she ever owned. Cristya would be paying $600 a month from her job at the police department.

Doyle has a farm in Ireland that he visits for a month each year. I asked him if it was hard coming back to Camden, which he has called a "peopleflll," a landfill for people. He said that he sees beauty in the people of Camden that is deep and wonderful, sometimes tragic. He said there are "burdens and wrinkles but the beauty just jumps out at you."

If Camden survives and actually becomes a place where families can live, it will be in no small part because of the soft-spoken, big-hearted, steel-willed pastor from Ireland.

Father Doyle of the Sacred Heart Catholic church in Camden, New Jersey. He's been a force against violence and poverty in Camden for many years. He thinks there is a deliberate attempt to isolate poverty in cities like Camden and he's not shy about sharing his views. He's the earned the right. Camden is a much more hopeful place than it would be without this soft spoken man of God.

Sallie the Voodoo Priestess

When I was asked to do a story on a voodoo priestess in New Orleans on the Day of the Dead, I couldn't think of anything I would more rather not do. I'm not into magic and spirits, good or bad. I never saw *Poltergeist*. I never saw *Nightmare on Elm Street*. My kids rebelled and refused to go to anymore Disney movies, which was about as much magic as I could handle. I was sincerely hoping the story would go away and the show would come to its senses. Voodoo was not the kind of story we did.

I was right that the story would haunt me, but not the way I thought it would.

I liked Sallie the voodoo priestess. Her background was not at all what I thought it would be, although she was somehow what I expected a priestess to be. Sallie was a Jew from Maine. There was a serenity about her that calmed the anxieties of a reporter who wanted to get the hell out of there. She had a nice sense of humor and kidded me about my qualms.

Sallie was keenly aware of how most Americans feel about voodoo and voodoo priestesses. She wasn't defensive or apologetic. If you didn't buy what she believed that was fine. She wasn't selling. She wasn't acting. Sallie was comfortable in her skin.

I've included a copy of my script in this book, but as always there are things that just don't fit in a TV script. In the story that aired on *Religion & Ethics*, I mentioned how the people in the neighborhood seemed to like and respect her. What doesn't come through in the piece is the deference they showed her, actually more like reverence, believers and non-believers. What is not in the script was how the dogs bowed down to her.

We were walking in her middle-of-the-road neighborhood. The yards along the street all seemed populated with barking, growling dogs. I like dogs and can usually get them to come up to me. These I didn't even try. They were vicious—that is, until Sallie walked by and then they went quiet. They started whimpering and put their heads on the ground almost as if bowing down to her.

This didn't just happen with some dogs. It was every dog. The whole street went quiet. Unfortunately, the camera crew was concentrating more on the pictures and sound of our interview as we walked along so they missed the dogs, although you could barely hear the interview for the cacophony in the beginning.

After a couple of days with Sallie, including midnight on the Night of the Dead in a New Orleans cemetery, I felt I had been in the presence of one of the more spiritual persons I've ever met. It was a wholesome experience. That doesn't mean I plan to participate in any more Day of the Dead ceremonies.

Revival

I did three stories about the so-called Brownsville Revival for two networks: for NBC News and the PBS program *Religion & Ethics Newsweekly*. Obviously there was something about the story I liked. There have been very few times in my life I've come even close to what I consider a manifestation of "the spirit." Brownsville was one of those.

I was there when people from all over the world were lined up for blocks, many spending the night before the service on church grounds. They were there to hear the preachers preach until the spirit descended and overwhelmed. The next five years as many as four and a half million people attended the church. It became a destination for religious pilgrimages.

When the spirit first blew through the Brownsville church in Pensacola, Florida, in 1995, it was described as like a train rushing through a station. What followed was a phenomenon that has been documented in this country only three times before.

The church's pastor John Kilpatrick was preaching that a revival was coming for two years. Interestingly, he heard about the revival from Dr. David Yonggi Cho, the pastor of the Yoido Full Gospel church in Seoul. Cho said God told him he was going to create a revival in the seaside city of Pensacola that "will spread like fire" until all of America is consumed by it.

The First Great Awakening occurred in the early 1700s. It was a spirit of religious enthusiasm that swept the young country. The Second Great Awakening occurred in the early 1800s and resulted in new religions we know as the Mormons and Seventh Day Adventists. The third awakening, around the turn of the twentieth century, gave us the Pentecostals. The jury is still out on the fourth great awakening, if indeed there was one.

What fascinated me most was the process that led to—even prompted—the great release of the spirit. The services would begin around seven in the evening and not let out until two or three in the morning. And by the time the services ended, you were too high to go to sleep.

As the night wore on, the music continued to build in intensity. And when it reached the crescendo, we were all ready for something. At a given moment, church elders would put their hands on a visitor's forehead and then he or she would either crumble or fall-over backwards. Fortunately there was someone standing behind to break their fall. By the end of the evening, we were all spent, even those of us who were not showered with the spirit.

When I asked Pastor John Kilpatrick if the music wasn't contrived to get the congregation in the mood to accept a miracle he was righteously indignant. He told me he would not let a man whip up people's emotions. He said, "I hate that." But there's no denying that the music built you up for something big.

So many people besieged Brownsville that church leaders decided to build a huge new sanctuary. Along with the crowds there were claims of miracles and faith healing. The bills started coming due about the time people lost interest. In 2012 the church was eleven million dollars in debt.

Pastor Steve Hill, who was preaching when the spirit swept people off their feet, eventually moved to Dallas and started his own church there. I liked him. He seemed genuinely humble, though he was not a particularly inspiring speaker and I could never figure out why the spirit would arrive when he was at the podium. He died of colon cancer.

The *Pensacola News Journal* did an award-winning investigation into complaints that Hill and Kilpatrick enriched themselves. They both moved into big new homes. The story cited financial irregularities, and incomplete bookkeeping.

Pastor Kilpatrick went on to form Kilpatrick Ministries. I watched a couple of his sermons on YouTube. In one, he seemed to be saying that God wanted him to support Donald Trump for president. Now I'm starting to wonder if I didn't let that glorious music get to me a little too much.

I've included a copy of my last Brownsville script.

Nadia Bolz Weber

I assumed when I attended the House for All Sinners and Saints in Denver that it would be a little different from most mainline churches. It was, even though the preacher was an ordained pastor in the Evangelical Lutheran Church in America.

Her name is Nadia Bolz-Weber. Oh yes, she has tattoos over most of her exposed body. And she sometimes swore, from the podium, like

237

a steelworker. I almost forgot, she was once a standup comedian. That was after she survived Graves' Disease, an autoimmune disorder that caused her eyes to bulge.

Now Nadia looks like a weightlifter in training. Her muscles were bigger than mine. Not sure how I feel about the tattoos. I always wanted one but could never find a good reason. Now I'm kind of glad. Anyway, the package of tattoos and foul language isn't what you would expect from behind the podium.

What is most appealing about Nadia is that she is remarkable genuine and straightforward. No phony baloney. If you say something she doesn't agree with she won't hesitate to let you know. I learned this personally.

Her church, with about 500 members, met in the borrowed sanctuary of the Saint Thomas Episcopal Church. It was unique because the seating was configured in a circle, with members facing each other. That allowed the service to be much more intimate.

It was unique also because so many members were gay and transgender. Many would be considered sinners and unwelcome in many churches. I particularly liked Stuart Sanks, known as the Minister of Fabulousness. He was gay and he came to the House For All Sinners because his previous church didn't want him teaching children. I wonder what God would have said. In the beginning hardly anyone in the congregation was straight. That's changing.

Pastor Weber's message is that too many churches are all about what you shouldn't do. She calls it "sin management". She suggests we look at the bible and see who Jesus hung out with. They were sinners, very much like her followers and most of us.

I was a little reluctant about doing this story. I thought Pastor Weber had found a schtick different enough that it was attracting attention and not only in the US. But the feeling within the congregation was one that we are all brothers and sisters. I've been to lots of churches and few have left me feeling like I want to go back. If I lived in Denver I would attend the House for All Sinners and Saints.

The script for this piece is also included in the appendix.

What Would Jesus Do?

We found Vincent Pannizzo on the corner of Foothill and Coolidge in a very low-rent neighborhood of Oakland, California. He was preaching to a couple dozen homeless people, men and women. He was preaching salvation, not damnation. "And God will wipe away every tear from our eyes. This is what John says."

Vincent was a good looking guy, reminded me in his bearing and looks of a college professor. He had a beard. I like men with beards. I seem to trust them more. Maybe that's because I've had a beard for almost all my adult life. My mom told me I went to hell when I grew a beard. She was only partly kidding.

When I pitched a story about Vincent, my superiors had serious misgivings, which was kind of unusual given that Vincent was a street preacher and our program was about religion and ethics.

They were concerned that he was a religious zealot who had gone off the deep end. I confess I had my own misgivings. Because Vincent didn't own a phone and we couldn't get in touch with him, we went to Oakland not knowing if he would be willing to talk with us. We finally located him late at night in a dark vacant lot.

When I asked him if he would do an interview, he told me that he didn't want what he was doing "glorified." But he said he didn't like to be ridiculed either, by folks who believe he's taken his religion too far. So he agreed that we could speak to him the next day at his home—or should I say, his designated space in a little homeless camp hidden in the trees next to a noisy freeway.

For someone singing the praises of Jesus, Vincent was not a happy camper. "I despair every single day." I repeated, "Every day?" He said, "Yeah, how would you like to be homeless, living on the street? You'll say, Well you chose homelessness.' I don't choose anything. God chooses everything for us."

Being a street preacher wasn't Vincent's childhood dream. Religion was not an important part of his upbringing. He was an honors student in ancient history at Rutgers University. Then when he was in his fourth year of a doctorate program at U C Berkeley, he started casually reading the bible and came across a verse that changed his life in a profound way. It was in Luke chapter six and said, "Give to all who ask."

He decided he would give it a try, more as an experiment than anything. He began giving things away and the more he gave away, the more his faith increased in Jesus.

Vincent started inviting the homeless to his apartment. He had been kicked out of three apartments for boarding homeless people and his wife had finally gotten fed up and left him. I can't imagine many wives who would be willing to share their apartment with street people. After the third eviction he decided he might as well live on the streets himself.

That's how and why he ended up in the camp near a freeway. It was like no other home for the homeless I'd ever seen. It was spotlessly clean and neat. Next to his sleeping bag, Vincent kept about ten very thick books.

His fellow boarders told me about how the camp had changed since Vincent moved in. Melvin Bear told me he felt safe since Vincent moved in. I couldn't figure out why, because Vincent is not a big man. Donna Little Moon said he taught them to treat everyone, outsiders and other homeless alike, with respect and dignity. They used to chase people away. Now they welcomed them.

Vincent preached on the same corner every night at ten-thirty. He always started with a prayer.

"Heavenly Father, we pray for the Holy Spirit to enter our hearts and to guide us, to strengthen us, to set us on the right path."

In the dark, this was not a safe neighborhood. Vincent had been robbed six times, sometimes at gunpoint. He told me it wasn't as bad as getting slapped in the face, which had happened a couple times. "Just people who felt that they needed to get their aggressions out on a homeless guy."

After the sermon, he gave away blankets, loaves of bread, and small amounts of money. He knew that some of the folks he gave money to would head straight for an all-night liquor store but he didn't care. He said he's doing what God told him to do. I guess God didn't say anything about being ripped off. He got the money to buy the food and bedding and to dole out from doing odd jobs. Sometimes he pumped gas. Most days he found work as a carpenter.

I talked to Louise Hill who had retired from the EPA; she hired him for small jobs quite regularly. Here's what she told me: "He keeps nothing for himself at all. He buys food for people, and he keeps nothing for himself." When I asked Vincent about giving almost all

241

of his money away, he said, "Not some of it, all of it. I have no use for money at all. I know that God takes care of me. He provides me with everything that I need so I can take care of people, people who essentially can't take care of themselves."

"You don't do drugs?" No. "You don't drink?" No. "You don't smoke?" No. So I asked him, "What do you do?" Vincent said, "Suffer. Jesus says pick up your cross and follow me and deny yourself every day. And that's what I'm doing. What did Jesus say? 'He who seeks his life will lose it, but he who loses his life for my sake will gain it everlastingly.'"

What annoys Vincent more than anything is that people think he's crazy. He said what he's doing on the street is no different from the many stories of personal sacrifice in the bible and he can't understand why people today consider it so unusual. He kept looking at me to see my reaction, to see if I thought he was off his rocker.

"I mean, it's painful. I don't like people to think that I'm nuts. I like to be treated with respect and dignity. I mean, for crying out loud, I once desired a career in academia. Now I'm a homeless guy having nothing, being a servant to everybody on the street and people thinking I'm nuts or on drugs."

My producer Trent Harris and I kept looking for signs that he had lost touch with reality but we couldn't spot them and we're both about as cynical as they get. The fact that he wasn't thrilled with his calling suggested he wasn't insane.

Vincent has now been out on the streets late at night, preaching and giving away all he earns and living with the homeless for almost twenty years. I'm thinking he's the real deal.

MY LIFE BEHIND BARS

I don't know many reporters who have spent more time in prisons than I have. I've had producers tell me that if I did one more prison story they weren't going to work with me anymore. I can count twenty states where I've done prison stories. I've done stories in Sing Sing, San Quentin, and Angola.

Once when I was interviewing a convicted murderer in Folsom State Prison in California, I apparently asked him a question he found annoying because he suddenly leaped from his chair to mine and grabbed me by the neck. Fortunately, there were two guards in the room who grabbed him and pinned him down. I had argued against guards being in the same room during the interview. I don't argue anymore.

I can't quite explain my fascination. I know of no one in my family who was a convict, although way back in the mid 1800s, there was apparently an ancestor who was a horse thief. I think he bypassed prison, though, and was hung from a tree.

Maybe it's because I'm fascinated about what causes people just like me to step over the line and break the law. I've always wondered if "there but for the grace of God go I." Maybe it's because I like underdogs and I know that too many folks behind bars started out as underdogs. Maybe it's because I don't like authority.

I've noticed that as I get older, rather than getting mellower I resent authority more every day. It's all I can do to not talk back to the cop who's writing me a ticket. While I'm accusing him of operating a speed trap, my wife Karyn is digging into my leg with her fingernails to get me to shut up. I think the main reason prison fascinates me is because there are far too many people locked up who don't belong behind bars. There's no shortage of stories about injustice.

The first inmate story I ever did was when I was working in Salt Lake City. It was about a swindler who had served most of his sentence of five years in the state pen and was trying to get an early discharge for good behavior.

Jon Nichols had owned the coolest restaurant in town. He ended up in prison after it was discovered his investors owned about fifteen hundred percent of the business: he had oversold his enterprise and pocketed the change. Everything went along fine until several of his investors asked for their share of the profit at the same time.

Jon was not a typical prisoner. He was educated, articulate, lacked tattoos, and seemed repentant. I read several letters he had written to people he had swindled, apologizing and promising to pay the money back. Even though he had served his minimum sentence and was a model prisoner, the sheriff and the warden seemed determined to make him serve his entire sentence. It didn't seem like justice to me.

I started doing stories about Jon. At the time, I hosted a weekend half-hour program on KCPX-TV about community issues and I invited Salt Lake County Sheriff Pete Hayward on as my guest and asked him to explain why he was keeping this guy behind bars. I was pretty tough on the sheriff and he didn't have good answers.

At the end of the half hour, the sheriff started to stutter and back away from his resolve to keep Jon in the state prison. But I also got the impression that I better not get into any trouble or the sheriff would throw away the key.

Because of my noble efforts, Jon Nichols was released within a few weeks. We had lunch at a Salt Lake hot spot and he told me of his plans to start a new restaurant, better than anything in the West. He was looking for investors, and they were lined up. Of course there would be no repeat of his previous venture.

About a year later, Jon Nichols was on his way back to prison. This time he had swindled investors out of more than a million dollars, thanks in part to me. It was a good lesson about being conned and I like to hope that I became a little bit less righteously indignant when I heard tales from "reformed" inmates. Most convicts I got to know seem smarter than the average guy.

Angola

I've been to the Louisiana State Penitentiary Angola three times. For me, going there the first time was a thrill. I'd heard about it for years. It's located north of Baton Rouge, one of my least favorite cities. When I first saw Angola, I was disappointed. From a nearby hill, it looked kind of nice, like a country club not far from the Mississippi River.

When you get inside, it has quite a different look although still not nearly as foreboding as some less secure prisons. People rarely escaped from Angola. It had a reputation as the biggest and baddest the country had to offer. Ninety percent of the 5,000 inmates sentenced there died there. In Louisiana, there is no parole for most crimes including those that are non-violent.

Good behavior doesn't count. Even if the inmate is only 18 when he (usually he) was arrested, he knew Angola was going to be home for the remainder of his days. Most of the inmates I met were black, many serving life sentences for nonviolent drug crimes. Outside the prison walls very few Louisianans seem to give a damn. Some did and do but they're a voice crying in the wilderness. The bad guys were out of sight and that was good.

I went to Angola a couple of years after the prison got a new warden named Burl Cain. If there was ever a good old boy, it was Burl. He looked like a used car salesman or an over-the-hill reporter. He was compared to Boss Hogg on the *Dukes of Hazzard*. Burl had a huge gut, and he had a good heart.

When he arrived at Angola, inmates who died—often from execution—were put in a cardboard box and carried by pickup truck to the cemetery. There was no ceremony to speak of, certainly no dignity in the process. Burl changed that. He had the prison carpenters construct pine coffins and a horse-drawn carriage to transport the "dearly departed" to their burial grounds.

He educated guards to treat inmates with a modicum of respect and, surprisingly, inmates started treating the guards better. I should mention that right next to the inmate cemetery there's a firing range where the guards practice their marksmanship. They no longer practice during burials.

One of Warden Cain's most enlightened ideas was to start a hospice at Angola for inmates who were terminally ill, a hospice where inmates cared for inmates. I don't think I've ever seen anything more touching.

The tenderness of these lifers toward each other was very moving. I remember, in particular, a doctor who was dying from emphysema. He ended up at Angola after his wife got cancer and he was arrested for cultivating marijuana to help ease her pain. His sentence was thirty years. She recovered. He died not long after our visit.

Warden Cain was a devout Christian who started a branch of the New Orleans Baptist Theological Seminary at Angola, which housed eight chapels. He actually sent inmate missionaries to other Louisiana institutions.

 It was probably not legal for a state-funded institution to sponsor missionaries, but who was going to complain? It was better than institutional violence and it did seem to curb inmate-on-inmate aggression. The warden also did a brilliant job promoting the annual Angola Prison Rodeo and transformed it into a financial windfall.

Cain was accused of a shady real estate deal involving Angola prisoners, and of using inmates to work on his private home. He says it was his being "creative and thinking out of the box" that got him in trouble. He said, "I should be rewarded rather than condemned." The jury is out on that, but Cain deserves credit for making Angola a little less bad.

Texas State Penitentiary at Huntsville

Texas has long been ground zero for capital punishment The state executes five times more inmates than the next closest state, which is Oklahoma. One reason is that Texas appellate judges are elected, not appointed, and if they want to be re-elected they need to be seen as strict enforcers of the law. Also, in Texas mitigating circumstances are not allowed in initial jury consideration and the public defender system is barely funded.

I can't forget death row at the Texas prison in Huntsville. This place has executed more convicts (most recently by lethal injection) than any other institution. The number, since 1976, is over 540. Almost 150 of those executions were when George W. Bush was governor of Texas. I'm sure the governor must've lost some sleep over at least

247

some of these executions, although he certainly didn't convey that impression. He said he trusted the judge or jury who did the sentencing and if the Board Of Corrections he appointed thought the execution should go ahead, it was the right thing to do.

When I was at Huntsville, there were 438 men and eight women on death row, out of a Texas prison population of 150,000. The population on death row was so huge it required not one, but four full-time chaplains.

I'll never forget a private conversation I had with the chief chaplain after our interview and after the crew had put away the camera. The chaplain came up to me, grabbed my hand with both of his, looked me in the eye and said, "I know for a fact that innocent men have been executed here." He couldn't say that on the record because in Texas chaplains are on the state payroll and because the injustice had already been done. That's just one reason I do so many prison stories.

There is nothing that gets me angrier than the public demand to imprison so many of our own people. We have a greater percentage of our citizens behind bars than any other society in modern times, including Communist China, Stalin's Soviet Union, and Hitler's Germany. What in the hell does this say about us? About 650,000 federal and state inmates are released back to their communities each year. Two-thirds of those will be back in prison in three years.

 We spend so much money incarcerating people, there's only a dribble left over to rehabilitate them. Chances are ex-cons are coming home more bitter and more likely to commit another crime than when they were sentenced. They're in your community.

Talking to an inmate in some prison but I have no idea which one

Mandatory Sentencing

I've thought many time about my story at the Alderson Federal Prison for women in West Virginia. It was the same place Martha Stewart served her time. As prisons go, it was not a bad place, more like dorms with fences and guards around them. I spoke with three young inmates, all of them mothers.

None had been convicted or even accused of using or dealing in drugs. But because their boyfriend or husband did deal and the wives knew about it and didn't turn them in, they and their kids were the ones serving mandatory minimum sentences of five to ten years. The men usually got their time reduced because they had information they could trade for lighter sentences.

Mandatory sentencing, as we know it today, was approved by Congress in the early 1970s and strengthened in the eighties. It was because of repeated headlines about judges delivering sentences many thought were too lenient. Senators, eager to show the voters back home how tough they were, enacted mandatory sentences— taking sentencing discretion away from federal judges and giving it to senators, who knew nothing about the convict, the crime, or the case. I've always thought if these lawmakers had kids of their own in similar predicaments there would've been no such legislation.

I was talking with Utah Senator Orrin Hatch at Dulles Airport one time and he told me that he knew a young black singer who was a tremendous talent, and whom Hatch would like to get out of prison early, if only it weren't for those mandatory minimum sentences. Hatch must've forgotten he was one of the original sponsors.

I said, "Senator, if he's in prison longer than he should be, it's because you and other senators wrote this awful legislation." We went way back to when Hatch first became a senator and we've had always had frank conversations. He did not disagree. But the injustice of his legislation only came home when it was someone he knew personally.

After I visited the Alderson prison, I went to Florida, which at the time imprisoned more of its people than any other state. What a distinction. I spoke with a federal judge who was outraged and quitting the bench because of mandatory sentencing. A number of federal judges around the country got fed up and quit. This judge told me he was forced to release inmates who were hardened criminals early to make room for mandatory sentence inmates, a majority of whom were in for the first time, for drug sales.

Then I went with another judge to a state prison near Orlando where I spoke with a man who was in prison for battery and was being released early to make room for nonviolent offenders. He told me he wasn't ready to live on the outside, but he was being evicted to make way for new mandatory sentenced inmates.

While I was in that prison I rode up the elevator with a woman inmate who was clearly not a candidate for early release. Her real name was Blanche Taylor Moore but she was known as the "Black Widow," thusly named because her lovers kept dying.

She was convicted of killing a boyfriend and suspected of doing-in three husbands, all with rat poison, also known as arsenic. There was another intended victim but he survived. The Black Widow totally spooked me. The woman was truly evil looking and she kept looking at me. I couldn't get off the elevator quick enough.

I always chuckle when I think of the first time I saw Elaine Bartlett. We were supposed to meet her outside the subway stop at Columbus Circle in Manhattan. When we got there we discovered there were three subway exits and because Elaine didn't have a cell phone, we didn't know which exit she would be taking. If we missed her, we would be screwed because we had no backup plans to meet her someplace else, and we were already committed to the camera crew and they don't come cheap.

Elaine had told my producer she would be easy to recognize and not to worry. Inasmuch as worry and paranoia are the basic traits of a good producer, she worried. Then Elaine emerged from the subway exit and we knew instantly that she was Elaine. She was wearing four-inch red pumps that matched a bright red dress and the red ribbon in her hair. Elaine was a sight to see.

Elaine's dress was almost as bright as the purple outfit she wore when she walked out of Bedford Hills Correctional Facility in 2000 after serving sixteen years of a twenty-year mandatory sentence for transporting a four-ounce package of cocaine to Upstate New York. She makes no excuse for what she did. It was easy money— $2,500— and she and her four kids desperately needed it. Elaine's story was not that unusual for someone who lived in her public housing neighborhood on Manhattan's south side. One brother had been murdered, another died of AIDS, a third was in prison.

Elaine was a victim of the so-called Rockefeller mandatory minimum sentencing, the first and some of the harshest state sentences in the country. Who would have thought such an unjust law would come from such a moderate governor? Nelson Rockefeller's aides had advised against it, but he was running for re-election and needed something to improve his bona fides with the state's conservative Republicans who were always suspicious of Rockefeller's liberal tendencies. The mandatory sentences were a huge hit and Rockefeller was easily re-elected.

The court record shows that Elaine was set up by an acquaintance. She didn't know he was negotiating a lighter drug sentence for himself by becoming a snitch for drug agents. It went beyond snitching. He knew she needed money and approached her to carry a brick of cocaine two and a half hours by rail to Albany. Elaine had never been in trouble before, never even received a parking ticket, according to her. She pleaded guilty and they threw the book at her.

Even though Elaine had no record whatsoever, the Rockefeller law required that she be sentenced to twenty years in prison. The judge had no choice. It mattered not that she had four children. During sentencing, she was asked if she had anything to say. Elaine said she felt she was being railroaded out of her life and that it wouldn't take her twenty years to learn her lesson.

Fortunately, Elaine had a mother who would look after the kids. Yvonne was a remarkable woman who was hooked on drugs herself when Elaine was growing up. But Yvonne beat down her addiction, mostly so she could keep her family. Once when the state welfare department threatened to take away the kids, Yvonne said she would jump off the George Washington Bridge. Yvonne brought the kids to prison to see Elaine every single weekend. Hardly ever missed a visit until she was stricken with a severe form of diabetes that eventually took her life.

After Yvonne died, the family started to fall apart. Elaine's youngest son Jamel got involved in drugs and was frequently in and out of prison. One daughter attempted suicide. Another simply moved away. Only the oldest son, Apache, stayed out of trouble. He was determined not to add any more sadness to his mom's life. Apache is a tall, very handsome kid who was teaching kids in the tenements how to play basketball, trying to be a role model in a place where they are scarce.

By the time Elaine walked out of prison, her family was in shambles. Jamel was in prison. One daughter was gone. The only place she could stay was with Apache, and that meant sleeping in the same bed with him. They are both big people—not fat, but big and solid, and for eighteen months, mom and son were forced to sleep together. She said that she had moved from one prison to another one without bars.

When I met with Elaine, she was living in public housing on Manhattan's lower East side. She had little money and no job but the outlook was improving. A *Village Voice* reporter, Jennifer Gonnerman, wrote a very good book about Elaine called *Life on the Outside*. Elaine was in demand on the lecture circuit. She became an articulate and convincing voice against unjust mandatory sentencing laws.

Jails and the Mentally Ill

Consider these statistics: The Los Angeles County jail system is the largest institution for the mentally ill in this country. The second largest is the Cook County jail system in Chicago. It's because people with mental disorders have precious few other places to go. What few mental health care institutions we have are seriously overbooked.

When President Reagan closed down the mental hospitals in the 1980s, he promised to build community outpatient centers to fill the void. Many hospitals needed to be closed and were. At about the same time, the US was going through a prison boom. Communities bid for them because they represented steady jobs, although low paying.

Private prisons were springing up like weeds. Unfortunately, politicians forgot about the other part of the deal—building community-centered facilities for the mentally challenged.

Taxpayers weren't complaining. Who wants to spend money on people we'd rather not think about? So wardens and deputies became the de facto caregivers for America's mentally ill.

Most are locked in jails instead of prisons because jails are usually the first stop for petty lawbreakers. Sometimes it's because the mentally ill don't comprehend that they've committed a crime. Sometimes it's because they try to get arrested so they can get some help, or at least some pills.

Cook County Sheriff Tom Dart, who I found to be one of the most progressive cops I ever met, told me about a man who had been in his jail as long as authorities could legally keep him. The man didn't want to leave but there was no choice. So when deputies let him out, he walked down the street to a department store, threw a brick through the window, cut up his hands, walked back to the jail and turned himself in.

All this wouldn't be so bad if we were a poor country and didn't know any better. But we're learning there's a price to pay. American taxpayers spend almost $80 billion a year locking up our citizens. There has been a small shift in attitudes and actually more emphasis on rehabilitation. But it's not because politicians have come to realize that our incarceration spree was immoral, it's because jails and prisons are more expensive than education.

Even though incarceration officials have spoken out forcefully against it, as I am writing this book Attorney General Jeff Sessions, with apparently no evidence in hand, is pressuring authorities to once again vigorously enforce antiquated, unjust mandatory sentencing laws. That in itself is a crime worthy of incarceration.

ISSUES THAT DRIVE ME CRAZY

I don't understand why people believe some of the absurd things they do. I think most often it suits their outlook on life. I know for certain that when I tell a story, if I don't give both sides a fair hearing, even the absurd one, I've wasted my time and polarized people even more than they were.

ATOMIC VIRGIN

My mom was very superstitious. She was darkly afraid of black cats and would walk around the block before she would walk under a ladder. We really hated lightning and thunder storms when we were forced to crawl under a table or under the bed. "And stay away from the phone."

Mom, however, had no concern when it came to above-ground atomic testing in the Nevada desert about one hundred miles southwest of Virgin. On those mornings in the late 1950s and early 1960s—and they were quite frequent—Mom would get us out of bed before sunup and we would stand in the highway that ran past our house and watch for the sky to light up and then wait for the boom.

Virgin only had a couple lamp posts so it was very dark and then suddenly the town lit up. The boom reverberated through the mountains around us. We were excited and proud because we knew we were near the front lines of the cold war. We knew the testing was safe and would keep us safe from communism.

We knew this because there were lots of news stories about Soviet advances in atomic warfare. It was the hot topic of the day. There were also a number of public service announcements telling us to be afraid of the Soviets but not of the testing in our backyard. One I remember in particular showed a milkman in the predawn hours delivering milk and eggs and stopping to watch the sky light up. The narrator said, "Nothing to worry about."

The films would instruct Americans what to do if the bombs fell. We were to get under the bed or in the basement or somewhere well protected. Bomb shelters were the rage. In elementary school, I remember drills where we would be instructed to get under our desks. In some schools there were buckets filled with sand to put out the embers after the bomb fell. Somehow I don't think the desks offered much shelter from radiation and if there were embers, we would all be fried anyway.

So when we saw the sky light up in Virgin, we knew that America was going to be prepared to respond to an attack with bombs of our own. I don't think we thought much further than that. Certainly not in Virgin. If anyone had a question about the safety of the testing it wasn't expressed openly. To question would have been considered unpatriotic. Those were the good old days.

I didn't think anything about the testing until I was a reporter for KUTV in Salt Lake City several years later. KUTV was an unusual TV station. It was owned by a very prominent Democrat who took his responsibility to enlighten the public seriously.

I don't think there was a station in the country at the time that was spending more money making documentaries and public service programs, which were huge drains on the budget and didn't do much for the ratings. Consultants were just introducing "happy news" as a way to make the news go down easier and viewers were happy to watch it.

About that time I started hearing from relatives and friends in Southern Utah about what seemed to be a high incidence of cancer. I drove down to my old stomping grounds to see if there was anything to the rumors. It's important to remember that even by 1980, there had been very few stories suggesting that there was any kind of causal link between cancer and radiation. Very few people were drawing that connection, myself included. But everywhere I went people knew someone who had cancer or had died from it.

A few were suspicious that the testing might have caused what seemed to be a cancer epidemic, but only a few. Certainly no one suspected that the government deliberately tested on days the wind was blowing toward Virgin and the surrounding area because there were more jackrabbits than people. The official population of Virgin at the time was 104.

I started talking about Southern Utah's cancer rate with my colleagues at KUTV. The station may have been local TV, but they were as good as any journalists I ever met at the network and they took their jobs seriously. Looking back it's difficult to relay how much more people believed the news then than now.

As a lifelong journalist, I am deeply troubled that President Trump has succeeded in convincing so many Americans that genuine news is "fake news." It is a very scary development. Back then, as now, people believed what the mainstream news media told them. At the time, Salt Lake was an especially good news market because there were a number of excellent journalists who could have moved to much larger markets but they loved the mountains and the culture.

We started making phone calls. Remember, we didn't have Google to rely on for research back then. We only had a few newspaper accounts about how successful the testing had been. It took weeks, but eventually we tracked down scientists who had worked at the Mercury test site in Nevada. Some were nuclear pioneers.

Most wouldn't talk but enough did that we started to realize we were onto something. We started getting secret documents in the mail, phone calls in the middle of the night. Eventually we pieced together a story that colored my view of government and almost everything sacred for the rest of my life.

What we found was that the Atomic Energy Commission knew there would be harmful effects from radiation fallout. There was enough science to confirm that. Above-ground tests were deliberately conducted on days the wind was blowing northeast toward less populated places like Virgin. There would be no tests if the wind was blowing southerly toward Las Vegas and Southern California. It was a cold calculation, and we had the documents.

We knew we had a solid, explosive story. I remember booze-filled all-nighters going through documents and transcripts. We just sat there and got more and more pissed and drunk. When we started our research, we never imagined what we ended up finding.

I think we even got a little paranoid that the government was watching us although we never had any proof. Knowing what I know about government today, I wouldn't be surprised. It's difficult today to understand what a blow it was to discover that we couldn't trust our government, and that not trusting the government was not unpatriotic.

Eventually we cobbled together an hour-long documentary called *Clouds of Doubt*. When I look at that documentary today, I'm astounded at how choppy and amateurish it was. For some inexplicable reason I had my hair permed, the first and last time in my life. As a viewer, I wouldn't have believed a damned thing I said. Despite my appearance, the jerky edits and the bad lighting, the documentary left little room for doubt. It was convincing and very powerful.

Clouds of Doubt won several prestigious awards, including the Chicago International Film Festival, DuPont-Columbia, Radio Television Digital News Association's Edward R. Murrow, and National Headliners.

I remember accepting an award in the company of Mike Wallace and Dan Rather. I thanked the Atomic Energy Commission for providing us with such good material. More important than the awards, though, was the attention the documentary focused on the issue of atomic testing and American victims. The government continued to deny vigorously, and with righteous indignation that there was a connection for several years.

When *Clouds of Doubt* aired, the Democratic governor of Utah, who happened to grow up in Southern Utah, asked to see the documentary and then became a powerful voice for the victims. Governor Scott Matheson was joined by an unlikely bedfellow, the conservative Republican senator from Utah, Orrin Hatch.

I watched hearing after hearing in Washington where Matheson would testify or Hatch would use his judiciary committee to interrogate government scientists who would flatly deny everything. I must have attended a hundred hearings over the years. My stories did not treat government officials gently, because I knew the truth.

Finally government officials admitted there "could be," and then after a few more hearings, "probably was" a connection between the fallout and the incidence of cancer. After several more hearings, Congress passed what was known as "Down winders" legislation, compensating victims who suffered specific types of cancer, or their survivors who were in the path of atomic fallout. That included not only Southern Utah but also hot spots as far away as upstate New York. It was officially called the "Radiation Exposure Compensation Act."

Several years later, my mom died of gallbladder cancer, one of the kinds covered by the legislation. I think my sister and I were awarded $25,000. Years earlier my sister had survived uterine cancer. I never checked to see if it would have been covered.

Never in a million years as I covered the story did I imagine that the legislation would actually impact me. A few months after Mom died, Governor Matheson died of stomach cancer, which was also covered by the legislation he helped bring about. What continues to trouble me is that in the name of national security, seemingly decent men—and they were all men—deliberately put innocent Americans, like my mom, at risk.

The people of Southern Utah have not forgotten the deception. On almost any other issue, the solidly Republican residents of what is known as Dixie would walk off a plank if the party asked them to. In recent years there has been growing pressure, mostly from Republicans, to resume testing in Nevada. The military wants what are called "nuclear bunker busters" to get at those deeply imbedded bunkers the enemy is said to have.

There continues to be a rationale that somehow we need to keep building and refining atomic weapons as a deterrent. For the life of me, I can't understand how more nuclear bombs will make us safer, and it's undeniable that testing doesn't make people feel safer.

The absurdness of the argument that more bombs is better always makes me think of *Dr. Strangelove*. Most of the new testing would be underground which is safer, although there are always radiation releases into the atmosphere.

It will be a hard sell in a place where people would otherwise buy almost anything the government is selling, especially if it has to do with national security. This is a very conservative area, even more than when I grew up. But a poll taken when word got out that the defense department was developing nuclear 'bunker busters' concluded that the people of Southern Utah who once welcomed atomic testing, were overwhelmingly opposed to testing aboveground or underground.

GUNS, GUNS, GUNS

I've always had a premonition I was going to die from a gunshot. I don't know why. I'm not fond of guns, but I don't hate them. What troubles me is that they've become more sacred than God to some people, and that drives me crazy. It's a short drive. What really makes me angry is the NRA, the National Rifle Association. I have friends who disagree with the fear-mongering of the organization but still belong to it and I can't understand that.

I imagine it will happen this way. I'll be out west and I'll complain to some Harley Davidson owner that the Gawd-awful noise from his beloved motorcycle is invading my space as it has throughout my career. I cannot tell you how many on-camera standups or how many interviews have been ruined because of a Harley driving somewhere in the vicinity.

I remember once in Billings, Montana, on a quiet Sunday afternoon, a Harley struck up clear across town and invaded the peace. Harleys don't come out of the factory obnoxious. They come out quiet. To make them loud requires a special $400 muffler. So I'll be complaining and the Harley owner will get pissed, pull out his .357 Magnum and shoot me dead.

Or else, I'll ask the stranger sitting next to me at the bar why he's wearing a gun and he'll turn around and ask me if I have a problem. I'll say, "Yes I do," and he'll shoot me dead.

My dad had a .32-caliber pistol in his chest of drawers. I think the only time he ever used it was late one night when Mom thought she heard someone outside, maybe an intruder or a peeping-tom. My dad walked outside with my cousin, who was staying with us. Fortunately they never found anyone.

The way my cousin describes it, Dad held the pistol by the handle with his thumb and index finger, as if he was holding a dirty diaper. The barrel was pointing down. If he could have found the trigger, Dad was more likely to shoot his own toe than any intruder.

It was a joke around town: don't get around Jack, he doesn't know which end of a gun to shoot. Actually he didn't even know which end to hold. Dad would grin. He didn't mind what they said because he wasn't particularly fond of guns. He didn't see that as an affront to his manliness. Mom didn't like them either even though all the menfolk in her family owned several. I was obsessed with them.

There was a tiny green shack at the far end of our property and it was my very own green shack. It was where I hid my guns. I had .22s, over-and-under shotguns, sawed-off shotguns, and a pistol. I could walk down the hill and fire them without Mom or Dad hearing. For a while it was all I cared about. It was my only hobby even though my parents didn't know about it.

I also had knives and learned how to throw them pretty well. I was convinced I was going to be in the military. I could see myself, after serving a long military career, walking along a rocky beach in Maine, with my trusty black lab running in front of me. I walked with a cane and a limp and wore a patch over my eye from some war wound. I would be thinking deep thoughts because I had seen it all.

I think I first started to question guns when I nearly shot Wallace Stout, one of my closest friends. It was horrifying. We were both sixteen.

His father had a Winchester .30-30 hanging on the wall and I asked if it was ok if I took it down. Wallace said, "Sure, it's empty." So I lifted it off the rack and cranked the lever a couple times. A .30-30 is the kind of rifle John Wayne and all the cowboys used so I knew how to work it.

After a few minutes I pointed it at Wallace, actually not directly at his forehead, sort of above it, and pulled the trigger. The gun went off. Words will never describe the shock when the rifle exploded in my ear and jerked me off balance. It was a few seconds before I realized and Wallace realized that he was still alive. I'd missed him. The experience still scares me. Whenever I think of it, I get sick.

Because my dad and I were considered city slickers, and because the locals were concerned for us and wondered how we could possibly get along in the world without some gun knowledge, my friends invited me to join them for the first day of deer hunting season. They lent me a powerful .30-06 hunting rifle. I was excited and nervous and wondering what in the hell I'd gotten myself into.

By ten in the morning, we had bagged a four-point buck. That's a big one. Most of the excitement went away when I got up close and saw the glassy eyes staring back at me, or at least staring somewhere. My friends said I was the one who shot it, even though we all fired at the same time. That was fine by me. I was ready to go home. But then we had to skin and butcher the deer. Right then I swore to myself that I would never ever go hunting again. I started getting rid of the stash of guns in the green shack. We carved almost the whole deer into jerky strips and let it dry. I do like jerky.

My mom let me own a BB gun when I turned twelve. She monitored me closely but she never saw me knock the sparrows or robins out of the tree. In Virgin there was not always a lot to do. So I used to have BB gun fights with my friend Danny Christie. He was the oldest son of a down and out family my folks helped out from time to time.

One day Danny and I were having a battle that went on for hours throughout the whole town of Virgin, which wasn't much of a town but it covered a lot of territory. When you get hit with a BB, it hurts like hell. The force is powerful enough to kill small birds. It hurts more than the sting from getting hit by a paint gun.

By late afternoon, we had shot each other several times but always in the back and legs. Neither one of us was the bravest of warriors. We'd hide behind trees and old cars. We had been shooting at each other for a couple of hours. Finally at dusk, Danny was behind the green pickup drawing a bead on me, and I popped off a lucky shot. Lucky because I didn't shoot out one of his eyes, but I did hit right between them. He jumped, grabbed his head and yelled, "I'm blind, I'm blind!" then he swore he was going to kill me. He chased me from one end of town to the other end, into the night.

My mom and dad came out looking for me. I was glad when they said I had to come home. What was I to do? By the next morning Danny and I were friends again, but that was our last BB gun fight.

I can't believe I shot all those pretty birds. I didn't dare tell Mom and I couldn't tell my wife. She would never forgive me. Red robins, yellow sparrows. But what I'll never figure about myself is how I could join my friends for midnight massacres of jackrabbits. There was a desert area about fifty miles north of Virgin that was rabbit-infested at certain times of the year. We would drive around in pickup trucks with spotlights. When the jacks would stop and stare into the lights, we'd shoot them. There was no sport to it. It was as if the grass and the sagebrush was alive with rabbits. Most people I know would be repulsed to know that about me. At least I hope they would.

My target practicing obviously helped when I was in basic training at Fort Bragg, North Carolina. It was my favorite part. My only favorite part. Most of my time in basic was spent doing kitchen patrol and pushups; I did more pushups than anyone in my squad. Out on the range I was a sharpshooter. I could hit those targets, although I'm sure if they turned into real people I'd be running the other way.

I don't know when it happened that I turned against guns. I don't think it was so much guns as the lobbying effort behind them, that they are a God-given right. Think about that. Guns from God. I'm not going to get into an argument about the Second Amendment because it's a waste of time to argue with ideologues.

 The Roberts court is the first and only Supreme Court to say private gun ownership is protected by the Second Amendment. The others have ruled that it applies only to militias. When Supreme Court Chief Justice Warren Burger retired, he wrote that the battle over the Second Amendment was a waste of the court's time, that the argument that guns should be protected by the constitution is a fraud.   And Justice Burger was a conservative.

The National Rifle Association is often considered one of the most powerful lobbying groups in the country. But until the late 1970s it was quite a different organization—one for hunters and sportsmen, one that taught Boy Scouts the safe use of firearms (training I could have used that would have saved me the trauma from almost shooting my friend in the head with a loaded .30-30).

Originally the gun rights group thought guns should be licensed. The NRA was then against exploding bullets, plastic guns, and assault rifles. Problem was the NRA was losing its membership and its contributions so the association became much more about scaring people about crime and spreading fear that the government wanted to take away people's guns. Lo and behold, membership and contributions increased dramatically.

I remember interviewing a pastor who was also a Kentucky legislator and was proposing legislation that made it legal for pastors to carry firearms in church. He lived in a very rural area. I remember asking him if he had ever been threatened or if there had been an incident that caused him to take such an unusual position for a preacher. He said no, he couldn't think of one.

I remember asking him if a law requiring a trigger locks would save even one child's life, would he support such legislation. He said, "No, it would be an abridgement of the Second Amendment." That, he said, would lead to "anarchy."

Watching the video of the interview back in the control room in Chicago you could see, as the editor pointed out, that I was ready to leap across this man's living room and strangle him. Imagine a mindset that God would prefer that you keep firearms free of regulation such as trigger guards, even if that freedom meant risking a child's life. And this jerk was a preacher.

I was not unhappy when NBC assigned me to do an hour primetime special for NBC News called *Guns, Guns, Guns*. I was to be the host. One location we chose for one of the four segments was Jackson Memorial Hospital in Miami, because it treated more gunshot victims than any hospital in America at the time. First we went to the emergency room to check in with the doctors who are usually not very cooperative with journalists—but there are all kinds of reasons for wanting or not wanting your story told. These doctors did amazing work and they saved lots of lives. Ours was a national program. The doctors didn't like guns. We were going to show them saving lives. It was a win-win situation.

We stationed one crew in the emergency room and two others out with patrols in Liberty City, which was the roughest neighborhoods in Miami. We rode around and listened to cop-calls for hours. There were domestic problems, assaults, small crimes, but no shootings. We had been out on patrol for six hours and nothing.

I went back to the emergency room and the doctors weren't happy. They were there to fix bloody people and there were none to fix. Seriously, they were unhappy. They thought it was because of our cameras. I thought the same. It always happens. Bring along a camera and the story goes away.

I went back out on patrol and was about ready to call it a night. It was three in the morning. I was just getting out of the police car when there was a transmission about a double shooting. I'm saying to myself, "Thank you Lord." The cops are saying, "Thank you Lord." The doctors were saying, "Thank you Lord." We weren't happy someone got shot, we just wanted to get our story. Our patrol car took off with lights flashing and siren screaming. We got to the hospital before the ambulances carrying the victims.

The first victim wheeled into the emergency room was an attractive black woman who was in serious condition. She had been shot in the stomach and was unconscious when they took her into surgery. Next, the paramedics wheeled in a rather handsome, well-dressed Cuban gentleman who had the most perfect bullet hole through his upper right arm. A Hollywood makeup artist couldn't have created a more perfect bullet hole. Fortunately the bullet hadn't hit a bone, so the Cuban was going to be fine.

We had our cameras in the operating room while doctors worked on the woman. She would live but wouldn't be applying her trade for a while, and was certainly not up for an interview. The Cuban with a bullet hole in his arm agreed to be interviewed but only on the condition that we didn't identify him.

We did the interview with his back to the camera. He said he was parked in his car when two men came up, banged on his window and demanded money. Apparently the car was running so he slammed it in gear, stood on the pedal and squealed away. As he did so the assailants fired into the car and he was hit in the arm. I figured the woman was shot in a separate incident.

On my way out of the hospital, I asked the paramedics what happened. Here is what they said: The well-dressed man had gone out for a night of fun and picked up the attractive prostitute. He pulled into a vacant lot with the intention of getting some nookie. But before he could get any, the two would-be robbers showed up. He wasn't anxious to get held up while getting nookie so he sped away. That was when the assailants fired a gun through the window. The bullet went through his arm and into her belly.

That may have been why he was so shy about having his face on camera. I'm thinking to myself, Here's a man who has had a bad day. He started out with high hopes, picks up a prostitute for fun, gets held up and then shot and then when he arrives at the hospital, NBC News is there waiting for him with cameras rolling.

I lived in Japan in the mid-1990s and while I was there I did a story about Japan's gun laws. They do allow guns in Japan but it would almost be easier to win the lottery than to get official permission to own one.

First and foremost you cannot own a gun if a neighbor or anyone you know doesn't want you to own a gun. If they say no, that's it. If no one vetoes the idea, you can own a gun, providing it is kept in a vault more secure than Fort Knox. So hardly anyone outside of law enforcement and organized crime owns a gun in Japan.

Most years I was living in Japan, an average of about fifty people would die from gun violence. That's out of a population of around 140 million and most of those were committed by organized crime known as Yakuza, fighting among themselves. Meanwhile in the US, with a population about twice that of Japan, approximately 30 thousand Americans die each year from gunshots. Most are suicides, some are homicides, too many were accidental. Please don't tell me that's not a huge price to pay and a moral price.

I have nothing against people who own guns. That would include most of my family on my mom's side and many of my friends out west. My brother-in-law kept several rifles in a locked closet and taught his three sons the correct and safe way to use them. I also understand that guns are much more a part of life in rural America, particularly in the West. I respect that. It's the fear mongering that 'Uncle Sam is coming to take away your guns' that drives me nuts.

What I don't like about guns is that they are dangerous if the shooter doesn't know what they're doing. Guns are dangerous when kids get hold of them, when drunks get hold of them. I'll never understand why we need a license to drive a car but almost anyone can own a gun, even individuals who have been diagnosed with mental disease.

How ideologically ridiculous can you get. For the answer to that, go to states like Texas and Utah where the legislatures forced guns on university campuses even though the faculty and most of the students didn't want them. Can you imagine: Give the kid an "F" and if he's unstable or in a bad mood, he can simply pull out a gun and blow you away, or miss and hit an innocent student.

Surveys show that a majority of Americans think some sort of gun control is necessary and good for society. But the National Rifle Association is so feared by lawmakers that it has more influence than the voters. It's a disgrace and it's true of almost all so-called red states. "We need those guns to keep the evil government from taking over." It is the most blatant, obvious kind of fear-mongering. And these politicians do it with a straight face. Even after the horrific Las Vegas massacre congress did nothing. Gutless wonders.

I've interviewed a lot of religious leaders and almost always when the interview is over, just for my own information I ask these leaders why they don't think guns should be a moral issue. Isn't 30,000 deaths a year a moral issue? The answer almost always is, there are just too many moral issues and guns are not a priority: "If we were to talk about the problem it would upset our members."

In my view, too many churches have become too beholden to the gun lobby. They prefer to take on superficial issues that show themselves as good guys and get their congregation riled up. You can't go wrong with same-sex marriage or abortion and, of course, the Second Amendment, which all seem to have become more important than the First Amendment, the one that gives churches the right to preach whatever they want. It also gives me the right to say that guns have become way too important no matter how much that irritates my gun-toting friends.

Here's the cruelest blow of all and I first read the story in the *London Times*. My hometown of Virgin passed an ordinance requiring that all homeowners own guns. In other words, if you want to own a home in Virgin, you *must* own a gun. If that had been the law when I was there growing up (before the friend, the Winchester, and the deer hunt), it would have made me very happy.

I wondered if there had been a crime wave in Virgin, but when I spoke to the mayor, Jay Lee, he wasn't aware of any crime wave. He wasn't aware of any crime, period. So even if I wanted to go home, I couldn't, cause I don't own a gun. But I think if I moved to Virgin, I'd probably end up buying one, because I'm sure I would want to shoot someone, or defend myself.

One last, last thing. I'm tired of gun owners whining that they don't have any rights. Give me a break. If some guy is carrying a gun in a restaurant where I take my grandkids for lunch or dinner, and if I don't like it, that's my tough luck. I can leave. He can stay. If I don't like fully automatic weapons being shot near my cabin on US Forest Service property, I can leave. He or she can shoot away. It's the non-gun owners who could use some rights. I'm thinking I'm going to start a non-profit for non-gun owners.

And finally, what troubles me most about guns is the attitude that we need them or we won't survive. Studies have shown that people who own guns are more likely to become gunshot victims, usually from an accident. I may end up getting shot because I don't have a gun, but I'd rather take the chance than go through life looking over my shoulder in a state of paranoia.

VOTER FRAUD

I've done three lengthy stories about voter fraud, in North and South Carolina and in Texas. I went to those states expecting to find voter fraud. At first I was convinced that I must be looking for fraud in all the wrong places because I couldn't find any.

I couldn't understand how it could be such a big story and how come I didn't see any reports refuting it. The answer, apparently, is that most news organizations no longer have the budget to delve into such subjects. By election time in 2016, voter fraud was accepted by many as fact, or as an "alternative fact."

When President Donald Trump tweeted that he would have also won the popular vote if not for three to five million illegal voters, many Americans believed him. It didn't seem to matter that every single state election official, Democrat and Republican, said there was no such evidence.

The president based his accusation on a statement from a right wing activist named Gregg Phillips. He was on the board of a group called True the Vote, created to root out massive voter fraud. The group had been unable to find even a few fraudulent votes let alone three to five million.

The president also based his claim on a German golfer friend who told him about voters "who did not look as if they should be allowed to vote." The *Washington Post* and the *Boston Globe* reported in February of 2017 that they found no evidence to support Trump's claim that thousands of Massachusetts residents were bused into New Hampshire to vote.

Trump is right, there is a conspiracy—but it's on the part of politicians who want to limit those who might vote against them. It is a very callous, cynical, and deliberate effort to take away a citizen's most precious right: the right to vote. There is absolutely no evidence of voter fraud, but thirty-three states have passed or are considering restrictive voter ID legislation. In every one of those states, the legislation is sponsored and supported by Republicans.

In Wisconsin, a Republican lobbyist who was worried about a close election for the State Supreme Court wrote, in a document leaked to *The Guardian* six weeks before the 2016 election: "Do we need to start messaging widespread reports of election fraud so we are positively set up for the recount regardless of the final numbers? I obviously think we should."

In 2012, a Florida Republican Party chairman was quoted in *The Palm Beach Post* as saying that voter ID laws and cutbacks in early voting are "done for one reason and one reason only, to suppress Democratic vote."

I learned many years ago that a story that didn't give both sides equal play only succeeded in further polarizing people and diminishing my credibility. That's especially true when it's stories that appear too partisan, and I'm sure that's the way this one appears. But the truth is voter fraud is a fraudulent issue. If folks want to say we need safeguards so there won't be voter fraud in the future, I can understand that. But the voter fraud laws on the books and under consideration target particular voters, especially minorities, and it really burns me.

This is a fact. It is more likely that an American "will be struck by lightning than he or she will be impersonated by another voter at the polls." That's the conclusion of a Brennan Center report that reviewed several elections that had been meticulously studied.

A study by the *Washington Post* in 2014 found thirty-one credible instances of impersonation fraud from 2000 to 2014 out of more than one billion ballots cast. That number is probably high because it was based on claims only, not convictions.

A five-year study commissioned by the George W. Bush administration found similar results. A 2012 survey of election fraud in every state found the overall fraud rate to be infinitesimal: ten cases in twelve years. Investigations into voter fraud almost always reveal clerical and administrative errors and that's about it.

One of the rare cases where voter fraud impacted an election was in a state senate race in Pennsylvania in 1993. Democrat William Stinson had won the election until a judge found he had engaged in election fraud and declared him the loser. The judge gave the election to the Republican, which shifted control of the state senate to the GOP.

In the piece I did in South Carolina, I spent some time with Dr. Brenda Williams, a five-foot tall African American who has registered hundreds of minorities to vote in that state. Whatever the battle, I would want her on my side. She wore me out. Dr. Brenda had fire in her eyes when she talked about South Carolina's voter ID law and compared it to the Jim Crow laws that legalized discrimination against African Americans at polling places. "There were poll taxes back there in those days. African Americans had to pay a tax.

African Americans were penalized when they went to even register to vote at the courthouse. They were given literacy tests that included guessing how many marbles were in a jar." The newer voter ID laws are not so blatant, but serve the same purpose.

Barbara Zia is the former head of the South Carolina League of Women Voters. She said the state's law makes it more difficult for the elderly, the disabled, and students, but will definitely impede minorities the most. "Many South Carolinians, especially citizens of color, were born at home and lack birth certificates and so to obtain these birth certificates is a very costly endeavor and also an administrative nightmare.

Donna Suggs, a nurse's aide, told me she "never had the opportunity to vote," and cried because "I didn't have the papers to vote." Donna couldn't vote because she couldn't prove who she was because she never had a birth certificate.

For many years, in the South in particular, births among blacks were not recorded in courthouses. They were born with the help of midwives and their births were recorded in family bibles. These births were never publically recorded. Donna was finally able to get a photo ID after an attorney helped her get a birth certificate free of charge. Attorney fees to produce a birth certificate or an accepted substitute usually run about $1,800.

Many people don't know to go to an attorney and if they did, don't have that kind of money. Donna had tears in her eyes when she talked about having the privilege to vote for the first time. Dr. Brenda said the first hurdle she has to overcome is convincing blacks who have never voted that it's not a privilege but a right.

I spoke with African Americans who have voted all their lives without a valid driver's license because it wasn't needed. Suddenly they were not allowed to vote because a new law required a picture ID that was impossible to get without a birth certificate. I spoke with students from out of state who couldn't vote because they didn't have the proper ID and their student ID card was unacceptable. In

Texas, other state and student IDs are not acceptable, but a license to carry a handgun is.

When I spoke with the former head of the Sumter County, South Carolina Republican Party Braden Brunch, he told me requiring a photo ID to vote is just common sense. He said, "It's a pragmatic step in order to fix—whether the possibility of irregularity or even just getting rid of these old wives tales out there that all kinds of fraud and deceit is going on. If you have this in place those stories go away." Who is spreading these "old wives tales" anyway? Could it be Braden Brunch?

Barbara Zia told me, "There are no documented cases of voter fraud by impersonating somebody else to vote for decades in South Carolina. We've talked to the state Elections Commission. They know of none and they've gone on record saying that there is none. So we say it's a solution in search of a problem." My producer and I checked with the Elections Commission, and double-checked, and found no fraud.

State Senator Chip Campsen was one of the South Carolina bill's sponsors in 2011. He said it would be contrary to human nature for there not to be voter fraud. "Human nature, being what it is, will steal. I lock my house—my house has never been broken into, but I lock it and I don't have to have a thief break into my house and steal something before I'm justified in locking my front door, and so human beings will steal my car, they'll steal my money, and they'll steal my vote too." He told me this with a straight face. I've always wondered if politicians like Senator Campsen think reporters are stupid.

So we should have a voter ID law that denies certain people the right to vote because those kind of people are likely going to steal something sometime anyway. By the time I left the senator's office, I wanted to kick his ass.

In the 2016 North Carolina governor's race, Republican Governor Pat McCrory repeatedly claimed there was going to be voter fraud even before the election. Then when he lost narrowly, he blamed illegal voters. I saw several actual 'fake news' sites linked on Facebook that reported huge irregularities in North Carolina. Six months after the election, The North Carolina State Board of Elections completed a comprehensive investigation that found 0.01 percent of the 4.8 million votes cast were suspicious. Point-zero-one percent.

When President Trump created the Presidential Advisory Commission on Election Integrity, he chose the Kansas Secretary of State Kris Kobach to run it, under Vice President Pence, the titular head. Kobach likes to refer to himself as the "ACLU's worst nightmare." Battles between Kobach and the ACLU have mostly pertained to immigration.

As Secretary of State Kobach made illegal immigration his primary cause. He also sponsored the Secure and Fair Election Act that required a passport, birth certificate, or naturalization papers to vote. The ACLU argued first that there is no voter fraud and then that the real purpose of the law was to stop the existing electorate from expanding and shifting demographically.

The law has been compared to the grandfather clause in Jim Crow laws because it allows those who no longer qualify but who have voted in the past to continue voting. Those who have voted in the past are almost exclusively white.

Kobach has degrees from Harvard, Oxford, and Yale. He is no dummy and has helped craft anti-immigrant laws in several states.

He worked closely with Arizona's Maricopa County sheriff Joe Arpaio who was allowed to arrest 33,000 undocumented immigrants because of Kobach-inspired legislation. Arpaio campaigned for Kobach when he ran for Kansas Secretary of State.

In 2010 Kobach held a press conference to announce that at least 2,000 dead Kansans were still listed on voting rolls. He singled out Alfred K. Brewer, born in 1900, and obviously dead. Turned out that Kobach was looking at Alfred's father's birth certificate. The real Alfred was actually seventy-eight and very much alive when the *Wichita Eagle* found him mowing his lawn. "This ain't heaven," he said.

Kobach hosted his own radio show even while he was secretary of state. He agreed with a caller that the "rise in Latino immigration could lead to ethnic cleansing of whites." This is the man the president chose to lead his Commission on Election Integrity. Sleep soundly America.

Turns out the president's commission ran into all sorts of early problems. When the group requested details on actual and registered voters, forty-four states and the District of Columbia refused to turn over their information. That included deep red states like Mississippi.

So we had a commission that is a fraud investigating a fraud that isn't. I've been looking to see if I can find a phrase in George Orwell's *1984* that adequately describes the situation. Anyway, occasionally justice prevails. The commission was disbanded. The official reason was that not enough states were cooperating. The real reason is that there was no fraud to investigate.

ISLAMOPHOBIA & JIHAD

About a billion Muslims around the world answer the call to prayer each day. So when Duke University, founded by Methodists and Quakers, announced that it would broadcast the call once each Friday from its gothic church bell tower, it was hailed as a positive step toward religious and cultural tolerance and diversity. The university put out a video promoting its new enlightened policy. Then Duke suddenly cancelled its plan. Here's the way the school explained its reversal in a press release:

"Initially the call to prayer was to occur from the top of the chapel. That announcement generated questions and concerns from the Duke community. That led the university to rethink its original plans."

Coincidentally or not, the "original plans" were cancelled one day after the Reverend Franklin Graham posted this message on his website:

"As Christianity is being excluded from the public square and followers of Islam are raping, butchering, and beheading Christians, Jews, and anyone who doesn't submit to their Sharia Islamic law, Duke is promoting this in the name of religious pluralism."

Someone should explain to Franklin that the vast majority of victims of Islamic extremists are Muslims themselves, not Christians or Jews. When I asked Duke's public relations representatives to explain the university's sudden reversal, they declined to answer.

Then I found out that Duke refused permission for any employee to speak with us. That's not what I call enlightenment. Duke has always had a strong reputation as a place of higher learning. That reputation took a hit, at least with me, when Duke allowed the Reverend Franklin Graham to cow this institution of higher learning to submit to Islamophobia.

I know Franklin Graham. I've interviewed him three times and I can tell you he is not his father, Billy Graham; not even a faint shadow of his father. Franklin Graham is a bigot, which is defined as a "prejudiced and intolerant" person. Here's an excerpt of an interview I did with him thirteen years earlier, shortly after 9/11. "The God of Islam is not the same God of the Christian or the Judeo-Christian faith. It is a different God, and I believe a very evil and a very wicked religion."

At about the same time, the Reverend Jerry Falwell, founder of the "Moral Majority," referred to Muhammad, the founder of Islam, as "a terrorist." Comparing Muhammad to a terrorist was an ultimate insult and it caused riots worldwide.

Falwell later retracted his remarks but the damage had been done. Over the years Falwell and I became pretty good friends. He took me on a tour of Liberty University. As with Franklin, Falwell's son Jerry Junior makes his father look like a pillar of enlightenment.

After he took over Liberty University, Junior recommended that students buy guns and said he was going to build a target practice range on the campus. Here's what he said in a widely covered 2015 chapel talk: "If more good people had concealed-carry permits, then we could end those Muslims before they walked in." There's a religious leader for you.

I'm not suggesting that Islamic terrorists aren't "evil." I can't imagine how anyone could descend to such depravity, especially in the name of religion. But the biggest threat in the US comes not from Islamic terrorists but from homegrown non-Islamic terrorists.

A study by the Center for Investigative Reporting looked at 201 terrorism incidents in the US between 2008 and 2016 and found that right-wing extremists were behind nearly twice as many incidents as Islamic terrorists.

We know about the Islamic terrorists' role in the Boston Marathon bombings and the San Bernardino mass shootings, but we rarely hear about the murder of three Muslim students at the University of North Carolina by a right-wing extremist.

We forget about the mass shootings in Sandy Hook, in Las Vegas and the Planned Parenthood Clinic in Colorado. We have so many mass shootings domestically, they rarely make the front page.

The Southern Poverty Law Center said the upsurge in hate crimes was greater following the election of Donald Trump than it was immediately after 9/11. In the first ten days after his election there were 300 hate incidents targeting Muslims in the US.

What seems to scare Americans more than anything about Islam are Sharia law and what they think might be the true intention of Muslims embracing it in the US. Even though there exists no evidence that Sharia endangers the US, at least sixteen states have passed legislation banning the practice and others are considering it.

This is how Imam Khalid Griggs, the Muslim Chaplain of Wake Forest University, described Sharia to me: "It's a Muslim code of conduct that encompasses, from the time a Muslim wakes up, what they should do, what they should say, and praising God and those kinds of things. But it's for Muslims."

That's a very kind view of Sharia compared to the one held by Donald Woodsmall, who believes that American Muslims place Sharia law above the constitution and that Sharia calls for jihad against non-Muslims or infidels.

Woodsmall is a Wake Forest-educated lawyer who emailed 24,000 alumni asking them to withhold donations to the university because of Imam Griggs' public endorsement of Sharia and personal jihad for Muslims.

He claimed he didn't want Imam Griggs fired, he simply people to consider the threat. "How many people have to die around the world at the hands of Sharia supremacists before you would feel comfortable debating this subject on the Wake Forest campus?"

Woodsmall said all he was asking for was a debate on Sharia and whether it was compatible with American constitutional principles. Unlike at Duke, the president of Wake Forest, Nathan Hatch, did not run away. Instead, he took a stand firmly behind Imam Griggs and against Donald Woodsmall's demand. Here's what he said in defense of Griggs: "He has been in this community for thirty years. We know that he is a man of peace...We know the influence, the positive influence on students, so we think those criticisms are deeply unfair."

Woodsmall didn't buy it. He saw something dark and calculated in Imam Griggs: "He has an underlying ideology that if he wore it on his sleeve he wouldn't be at Wake Forest, he'd be gone. He has a place of recruitment, he has a position of authority and a lot of influence to recruit more, you know, I'll call them confused students."

Safyah Usmani said she is definitely not confused. She was a Pakistani Master's student in documentary film at Wake Forest.

Safyah is a Fulbright Scholar and a Muslim. While we were there with *Religion & Ethics*, she was working on a film about jihad. She told me, "The idea is to educate the people about the real meaning behind jihad. It is to struggle. It is to look within and struggle to make life better. I feel like I really need to do this. It's my attempt to sort of reclaim the word jihad."

Woodsmall's deepest concern is the "true" meaning of the word "jihad." "You don't have to dig very deep before you understand what jihad is and I think America wakes up, has woken up, and understands what jihad is." Woodsmall thinks it is a threat. Safyah thinks it's an answer: "It's not just my jihad or just your jihad alone but as a society, a collective jihad to make this world a much healthier, happier, and safer place for our kids to come."

Hamtramck, Michigan, may be the best case study of Sharia and jihad in America. It was the first city with a Muslim-majority city council. Hamtramck is a small incorporated community of about 22,000 within the city of Detroit.

During the heady days of the big three automakers, Hamtramck employed 45,000 autoworkers. It was Polish Catholic back then. Today it's fifty-one percent Muslim. Mayor Majewski is Polish Catholic. She said, "We roll our eyes when we hear" about the fear of Muslims within Hamtramck. She said the biggest concern is that the potholes won't be filled.

Saad Almasmari was elected to the city council, he said, because he knocked on every door in Hamtramck. "I was married to an American citizen. She brought me here. I got my citizenship. I'm going to school. She's going to school. My kids going to schools. We're doing fine. We found ourselves American. Here we are. Now we have to serve this country as American."

Greg Kowalski is the director of the Hamtramck Historical Museum. He said, "A hundred years ago, we would be talking not about the Muslims moving in here, but about the Polish people moving here, and we would be German because they were original settlers here."

Today, less than fifteen percent of Hamtramck is Catholic, but the Archbishop of Detroit, Allen Vigneron, reminded his priests that they need to stand against those who would restrict Muslim immigrants because of their religion. "This is one of the great foundation stones of American life: the First Amendment, religious liberty. We speak for it. We need to stand for it for one another."

When I asked Saad Almasmari about Sharia and the widespread concern that it will always be supreme to American Muslims, he answered, "I'm telling you here. I'm American. My rule is going to be the US Constitution and the state and the city law." It's possible that Saad could be a secret terrorist, but I'd be willing to bet he's not. I would be willing to bet he'll get those potholes fixed.

I find the level of ignorance toward Muslims appalling and it is an ignorance nurtured by fear-mongering politicians. I love the political cartoon that shows Texans lined up behind a barbed wire fence pointing their automatic rifles at a Syrian family of eight that the US government wanted to settle in the Lone Star state. As if this family poses a serious threat. Texas was vigorously fighting through the courts against the immigration of even one Syrian.

I would rather Syrians live next door than many Texans. No Syrian or any other nationality that have gone through the refugee program, have ended up committing terrorism in the US. They have been vetted for two years, and are almost certainly better educated than a majority of American citizens.

Education is vitally important to refugees. I've been introduced to many families who were educated back home or clamor for education when they get here. In Hamtramck I spent time with a Syrian family with seven children. The parents spent their entire day taking their kids to and from school. It was by far the most important part of their new life.

At least thirty governors refused to take in Syrian refugees in 2016 through 2017. Conservative red state Utah, however, not only welcomed refugees during a political push against them, but also through the years resettled over 60,000. It's not only Mormons. Catholics and dozens of nonprofit organizations from all faith groups support refugees.

Mormons have a history of welcoming refugees partly because of their history. When they arrived in Utah, they were fleeing persecution. In Utah all refugees work four hours each weekday sorting out clothing to be sent around the world. They get paid for this work. In the afternoons, they learn English and how to get a job. After they get a job, they're required to pay back their airfare.

In 2016, Mormon leaders launched a campaign called "I Was a Stranger," based on the biblical mandate to welcome the stranger, asking members to donate their time and effort to the refugee cause. There was a huge response and the Church deserves a "courage in the midst of ignorance" award.

Over the years I've met a few individuals that really stand above. Some are famous, like the Dalai Lama; some you'll never hear about, like Chinese dissident Wang Dan. Most are regular folk who are doing good things for their fellow man. Several are Muslims.

One in particular is the Aga Khan, the leader of about fifteen million Muslims scattered around the world known as Ismailis. They believe he is the only living hereditary Imam in direct descent from the Prophet Muhammad.

The Aga Khan presides over one of the world's richest charitable organizations, although Ismailis don't see it as charity. They see it as their moral duty. The Aga Khan Development Network is huge. It operates around the world, but primarily in the poorest regions of Africa and Asia. The network has a simple mandate: to relieve disease, deprivation, and ignorance for the people they serve, no matter their faith. The same is true of the network's many thousand employees, who come from all different faiths.

The Aga Khan was a twenty-year-old student at Harvard when his grandfather bequeathed the title Aga Khan to him, bypassing his father who was known as a rich playboy who was once married to the actress Rita Hayworth. The Aga Khan is a billionaire who owns private jets and yachts and is welcomed internationally as a spiritual leader and for his work in social justice.

I was fortunate to have a rare interview with him in Toronto. He had recently addressed a joint session of the Canadian Parliament. I was very curious to meet him, particularly after spending time with his followers who clearly revered him.

I expected a garrulous, charismatic man. He was charismatic but with a very quiet, understated manner. I actually had a difficult time hearing everything he said. He spoke about the environment, that it is Muslims' duty to leave it in better condition than they found it. He spoke about pluralism in a very different way from Franklin Graham.

"The empires which functioned best, you have intellectual pluralism, not only ethnic pluralism. You have intellectual pluralism. That is, the best qualified people in society, in medicine, in law, in space sciences, whatever it may be—they came together for the benefit of the community."

I interviewed the Aga Khan in Toronto because he was there for the opening of a beautiful new Ismaili art center. His main home is in France. I've been around presidents and world leaders and so I'm familiar with the security necessary to keep them as safe as possible, but I've never seen tighter security than that for the Aga Khan. There was clearly great concern that he was a target for assassination by Islamic terrorists. I asked him if he was optimistic about the future.

"No, frankly. No. I would hope that we would see a greater tolerance and greater acceptance of the divisions in society, because I think we are seeing forms of polarization which are very, very unhealthy, indeed."

I consider the Aga Khan one of the great men I have met and I can't really explain why. He was so quiet and unassuming but wise and compassionate. I thought I was in the presence of an extraordinary man.

THE WALL

When they build the wall, I hope it won't be so high I can't make it over it on my way into Mexico. The notion of a wall around my country rattles me to the core. It's not who we are or at least who we've always been: a country of immigrants.

We've gone through periods when there has been an influx of immigrants, like the Irish, followed by an anti-immigrant outcry that they are taking our jobs and committing crimes. But we never built a wall. We know it won't keep people who really want to get in, out. For some Americans, the wall is an excuse for bigotry and racism. Not everyone, but, unfortunately, too many.

Donald Trump kept referring to the Israeli so-called barrier as an example of what a wall can accomplish. I've been there. It's big. I've seen the wall that surrounds the holy city of Jerusalem—"City of Peace"—that has withstood endless bloody battles. I've walked along the Great Wall of China. Now that's a real wall. I've also been to several sections of wall or fence that already exist along the US-Mexican border. I've been on our side and theirs. I've been there when it's dark and foreboding.

My view about the wall comes from somewhere inside me. Every story I've reported about immigration and the wall has only increased the intensity of that view. I remember one night along a section of the wall made of corrugated metal panels south of Tucson, Arizona. We were riding along in a pickup shining a spotlight against the wall when we spotted a man and a woman.

Without the spotlight we'd have never seen them. They didn't know each other. The woman was from Southern Mexico. She was a mother of four. The man was from the highlands of Guatemala, father of four. Behind them was a wall with razor wire along the top. Behind it you could see flashes from the lights of the border patrol vehicles. You could hear the dogs baying.

It was the last place on earth they wanted to be but somehow they had to get on the other side. They were scared to death but they had children at home they couldn't feed. They needed a job. On the way back across the border I kept asking myself, "What would I do?"

A few months later I was with the mayor of Eagle Pass, Texas, just across the Rio Grande from the Mexican city of Piedras Negras. The Department of Homeland Security wanted to build a wall separating the two cities and had filed a suit against Eagle Pass to force the city to give up land for the wall. The city and it's Mayor, Chad Foster, were resisting. I liked the mayor and his lack of BS. He wore a ten-gallon cowboy hat, shit-kicking boots, an oversized silver belt buckle, and a handlebar mustache. He could have come straight out of central casting, but he was the real deal.

Mayor Foster told me that ninety-five percent of the residents of Eagle Pass opposed the wall. He said the two cities had grown up together and a wall would divide them. Piedras Negras, population 170,000, is about five times larger than Eagle Pass. It has universities, including a medical school, and the world's largest brewery of its kind.

When there's a fire in Eagle Pass the fire department from Piedras Negras sends their firemen and firetrucks across the border to help put it out. The Eagle Pass fire department does the same. Once every year during the celebration of Abrazo (which means an affectionate greeting), people from both sides of the river meet on one of the bridges and embrace each other.

The proposed wall would cut through the city's golf course and the city park, which may be the greenest piece of land in the whole county. That alone is reason enough to stop the wall. Green is gold in this part of Texas. The wall would also eliminate a planned development along the Rio Grande River. DHS was oblivious to these considerations in 2008.

Mayor Foster said the wall would separate families. "I guess that's the best description. It's as if I were to put a wall up between my house and my brother's house."

Father James Loiacono of Our Lady of Refuge told me when he thinks of a wall, he thinks of the Berlin Wall. When locals found a statue of Christ floating in the Rio Grande River, Father Loiacono placed the statue in his church and called it "the undocumented Christ." He offered sanctuary to many undocumented aliens going or coming across the border.

Father Loiacono had lost members of his congregation who objected to using the church as a sanctuary. One I talked with, a former border patrol agent, told me what we need are more detention camps. He favored a wall even though he said it "won't stop illegals." He thought it might slow them down.

There is crime along the border, but according to the FBI it's far less than exists in cities like Dallas and Houston. Locals I spoke with favor cameras with night vision but they don't always work and they cost about $65,000 apiece. Border patrol officers I spoke with who didn't want to be identified estimated it would take two to four minutes to breach the wall. No one seems to think a wall will actually keep people out. That includes those who are most in favor of a wall. There is universal agreement that the folks in Washington don't really understand what's going on.

Consider these figures. In the last twenty-five or so years, spending on border security has increased fourteen times, the number of agents increased 500 percent and the number of people apprehended trying to cross the border decreased by eighty percent.

We're spending about $4 billion dollars a year on border security. There are now 21,000 agents working the border. In 2000, 1.6 million illegal immigrants were arrested coming across. In 2010, only 463,000. These are FBI statistics. The reality does not square with the fear.

Mayor Foster lived a quarter of a mile from the border and said he wasn't afraid. He reminded me that there's never been a known terrorist caught coming in from Mexico and that's true. The only terrorist caught coming into the US by land was coming from Canada.

When Donald Trump flew into Laredo to underscore immigrant crime, he got out of his black SUV and said to the breathlessly awaiting journalists, "I know this is not a safe place to be." Wrong. The FBI has said none of the cities along the Mexico border are even among the top ten most violent cities in the US.

El Paso, Texas, for instance, is considered one of the safest cities in the country and it sits directly across the river from Ciudad Juárez, which had the second highest murder rate in the world. Nineteen people were beheaded one weekend I was there.

I've spoken with authorities all along the border and they all say immigrant crime is less than it is among the general population. Government statistics confirm that.

You'll get a different answer from the National Border Patrol Council, the union for border agents. They'll say they are overworked and understaffed and maybe they are. I wonder, though, if they're not like the various unions for corrections officials who need a growing prison population to justify their existence. They are among the loudest critics of legalizing marijuana because it will reduce the prison population and prison jobs.

When I hear politicians talking about what a crime scene it is near the border, many have never been there and when they have it's on a tour arranged by the union to show the world how scary it is and how understaffed the border patrol is. I know they've got a hard job. I know most are trying to be humane. It's gotta be a tough job. Unfortunately, the wall has become militarized and the enemy, too often, are people just like us, desperate to escape poverty and to feed their family.

Many walls have been built to keep invaders and bad guys out. Australia actually built a 1,200-mile long wall to keep jackrabbits out. The US wants one to keep immigrants out. All the while we love to beat our chests about being a Christian nation with Christian values.

In my humble view, the most fundamental of all Christian values is to care for the least among us and to love thy neighbor as thyself. There is nothing Christian about our immigration policy. It divides families, sends parents home while allowing kids born here to stay, and now we want to build a wall.

Walls have been constructed all over the world and they have produced mixed results. The most famous is the Great Wall of China. Actually it should be called the Great Walls of China because different sections were built at different times beginning in the third century BC. I've been to several sections of the wall. The first time, when I was with NBC News, the climb was so steep the soundman had to stop halfway up and stay there. The view for those of us who made it to the top was extraordinary. The wall is actually visible to astronauts circling the globe.

The Great Wall was built mostly to keep invaders out. It eventually failed. Manchurian troops broke through in the seventeenth century, which led to the demise of the Ming Dynasty. It's been said that the wall is about as useful to China as a bible on a battlefield: it can give comfort but won't stop the enemy. Still, the wall has more value today than ever before, as a tourist destination.

The Berlin Wall was built not to keep people out but to keep them in. It stood, a symbol of oppression, for twenty-eight years, coming down in 1989. The barrier had guard towers situated along the way with a good view of an area known as the "death strip," which included anti-vehicle trenches and beds of nails known as "fakir beds." The Soviets called it the Anti-Fascist Protective Wall. Over 5,000 East Berliners attempted to escape over the wall. As many as 200 were shot trying.

And then there is the Israeli wall. The Israelis call it a "barrier" against terrorism. The Palestinians call it an "apartheid wall." As planned, upon completion it would stretch 440 miles, with the bulk of it cutting through Palestinian territory.

Construction began during a very violent time known as the Second Intifada. There's no question that what has been constructed has reduced the number of suicide bombings, like the one at the El Al Café that blew up several friends of Gerald Steinberg, who was next door at the time. He told me, when I interviewed him for PBS, how unnerving it was to live in constant fear of terrorism. It's also true that about the time construction on the wall began, Palestinian leaders determined the suicide bombings were counterproductive, so the wall is a factor but not the only one. There is little doubt that it has greatly increased tensions between the two peoples.

I spoke with Dr. Sari Nusseibeh, president of al-Quds University. He said, "Going along to visit Palestinians, you find anger, frustration, poverty—in a sense, surrender and inner surrender to the inevitability of the darkness both of the hour and the hours to come." Even liberal Israelis were beside themselves with frustration. Hirsch Goodman. a former journalist and military expert said, "It's like an act of desperation. If this is going to help, okay, let's try it. I mean, people can't see peace on the horizon."

The wall in some sections is twenty-four feet high, with guard towers and roads running alongside with built-in sensors that can detect movement. The bulk of the wall is actually a six foot high electric fence. Palestinians say they would not object to the wall if it stuck to the established borders between the two countries, but it does not. In reality, eighty-five percent of the wall dips into Palestinian lands, effectively isolating 25,000 Palestinians, and confiscating seventeen percent of their territory.

I saw a stretch of the wall in the West Bank, a twenty-four-foot high stretch that cut right in front of a farmer's house. He told me that before the wall he could simply walk across the road to work his farm, which was quite large, at least several acres.

Now he has to drive a few kilometers down the road through an Israeli checkpoint where he and his car are searched and then drive back the few kilometers to get across the street from where he started. So what had taken him about a minute now takes him about an hour each way. Imagine what American farmers would do if the government built a wall through their property.

Dr. Sari Nusseibeh told me: "It is going to end up looking like a set of cages. In other words, with walls surrounding populations living in areas very often cut off one from the other and needing permits to visit one another. There is a lot of anger and frustration, yes, but you should never lose hope."

When the wall was first designed it was intended to run right through the middle of al-Quds University, the largest in the region, with approximately 5,000 Muslim students. It would have meant that students couldn't simply walk from one building to another. They would have to go to a checkpoint. After strong resistance from Muslims and Israelis, the wall now runs adjacent to al-Quds, so students only have to go through the checkpoint to get to their homes. It was heart-wrenching to watch the elderly mothers with children and the disabled, waiting in line to go across the street.

I've been in Israel when suicide bombers were killing innocent people, young and old, when I didn't dare take a bus and didn't want my taxi driver stopped next to a bus, when men with Uzi machine guns stood guard at food markets. I could understand how the Israelis felt. I felt very vulnerable. Then I went to the West Bank where several ambulances were lined up waiting for Israeli guards to conduct a security check before the ambulances could take their patients to the hospital. I could understand the Palestinian's frustration.

I was there during the Second Intifada when Palestinian teenagers were lighting tires on fires in intersections and throwing rocks at Israeli soldiers. The soldiers were supposed to fire guns with rubber bullets but that didn't always happen. I walked up to a house where a youngster who had been shot with a real bullet was lying in the living room.

The father, a handsome man wearing a keffiyeh, greeted me at the door. He pointed to the middle of his forehead and said, "There, that's where they shot my son." Inside people were sitting around the casket, wailing and swearing revenge. I knew there would be yet another generation of hatred. I'm not sure whether a wall stops or causes hatred. So far it hasn't brought peace.

STORYTELLING

Some stories I couldn't really tell because higher-ups didn't want them told. Some I didn't want to tell because they misrepresented the big picture. Sometimes the process of telling them was ridiculous, like the assignment for the *Today* show to tell about the huge increase in visitors to national parks while I was in Yellowstone and it was burning down.

INSIDE THE HERMIT KINGDOM

I've looked in on North Korea from the outside, wondering what it must be like inside the world's most closed and oppressive country. That's why it's called the "Hermit Kingdom." I've also spent some time inside the North and concluded that it is both a prison and a kind of Disneyesque Magic Kingdom where nothing is real but no one is happy.

My first exposure to North Korea was sponsored by the American and South Korean military. It was yet another crisis at the so-called Demilitarized Zone.

We were looking down on the village called Panmunjom at the heart of the DMZ. It's a surreal place of rectangular buildings surrounded twenty-four hours a day by armed soldiers who act as though shooting is going to break out any minute. Negotiators from North and South Korea have met in these buildings on several occasions to negotiate peace, with hardly anything to show for it. The two countries are still technically in a state of war.

We were escorted by US soldiers and from our vantage point you could see US and South Korean soldiers on one side and North Korean troops at the other. It seemed very tense, at least from the US and South Korea side. The soldiers would poke their heads around the corner of the buildings as if they were afraid of getting shot. At the other end, North Korean soldiers were meandering around as if they didn't have a care in the world. It seemed odd that our soldiers were far more worried about the enemy than the enemy was about them.

This scene has been replayed daily since July 1953 when the Korean war wound down to a stalemate along the thirty-eighth parallel. This after a three-year war that resulted in half a million South Korean and 36,000 American deaths.

The war started when the North invaded the South in 1950. But if you talk to the citizens of the North they'll tell you that the war started when the South invaded their country. It is a fiction but it's very unlikely you would find a single person in the North who doesn't believe it. It's Propaganda 101 in a society whose reality is propaganda.

Pyongyang is the capital city. As a rule, only the elite live there. Citizens from other parts of the country are required to have a special permit to even enter the city—it's considered a great honor. Many North Koreans will never have that honor. If they are invited to live in Pyongyang it means they are in good stead with the regime. When they are ordered to move out of the city it usually means they're life is going to take a serious turn for the worse. It might be that the picture of the current leader has dust on it or has been hung in an inconspicuous place, or someone heard you questioning official economic estimates. Thousands have been sentenced to one of the many gulags for crimes no more serious than these.

The North remains the poorest country in Asia. Fly over it and the countries surrounding it at night and you'll see only a black hole where the North is supposed to be. Even in Pyongyang there are blackouts almost every day. In other parts of the country the electricity only works a couple of hours a day.

For a country that has nuclear bombs, there are few paved roads in between cities. Several major roads are not even blacktopped. Outside Pyongyang, poverty is widespread. In the mid-1990s as many as two million citizens died from starvation. They were not living in Pyongyang.

The country is run by a dynasty. The current ruler, Kim Jong Un, is the grandson of the founding ruler, Kim Il Sung. Kim looks a lot like his grandfather and reportedly does everything he can to further that look, including gaining weight and keeping his hair in his grandfather's style.

The grandfather and father lived like kings and were treated like gods. Each had several villas, always fully staffed even if they were rarely visited. The few citizens who got to see these leaders often broke into tears because they were so revered. The citizens now gather and pay homage at the statues of their "Dear" and "Great" leaders. There are statues everywhere. Now Kim Jong Un receives the same reverence. Whether it is out of love or out of fear may never be known.

Just across the DMZ there's a little farming village that appeared to be in working condition even though we never saw anyone working the fields. The farm is ringed with loudspeakers that periodically blare out propaganda.

The DMZ is said to be the most heavily mined border in the world. Over the years there have been several violent but isolated encounters along the border, usually provoked by the North.

For over sixty years the stretch of land known as the DMZ has been off limits to humans, and especially humans with firearms. As an unintended result, this untouched landscape has become a sanctuary, a nature preserve for migratory birds, wild pigs, lynx, antelope, black bears, leopards, and other wild things.

Species that have disappeared in other parts of Korea and Asia have reappeared inside the DMZ. There is a wonderful and perceptible difference between the tension surrounding the DMZ and the tranquility inside it. We were not allowed private tours but it was like driving through unspoiled nature, and we could hear the birds singing.

The North has succeeded in several assassination attempts of enemies in South Korea and other countries. In 1968 North Korean agents came within a breath of assassinating the South's president. The assassins were stopped at the last minute in a wild gunfight.

The current leader's half-brother was assassinated in Malaysia after having a toxic poison rubbed in his face. The poison was so toxic it's considered a weapon of mass destruction, which was probably created in North Korea. If NK is brewing this particular kind of poison, that could be an even greater danger to mankind than atomic bombs.

Analysts say the assassination of his sibling probably indicates that Kim Jong Un is afraid of a coup attempt. The reality is analysts and experts don't know much more than we do. The regime is totally unpredictable partly because its citizens will do whatever they're told.

I'm always surprised that U.S. and South Korean intelligence agencies have so little information on the innards of the North. Obviously it's such a tightly controlled country it would be very difficult to sneak in a spy.

I've done stories with missionaries who have ventured inside the North from China and who are in contact with NK citizens who sneak across the Yalu river regularly. It's dangerous but it has happened thousands of times. If they can do it I don't understand why trained spies can't do it.

Pictures of Kim Jong Un (always surrounded by fawning generals taking notes) suggest he must be worried about something or he has an eating disorder. He's ballooned in size since he first assumed power. Fascinating that citizens are proud that their leader is fat, even though the average North Korean often looks starved. Studies have shown that because of generations of hunger, the people of the North are significantly smaller than those of the South.

The US Army public affairs officer who oversaw the news media at the DMZ made us feel that an invasion was imminent. At one point, he cuffed my cameraman Yashiro at the side of the head because he wasn't crouching low enough. On our trip to the DMZ from Seoul we stopped for a briefing from a US captain who explained the situation to us. Jimmy Carter, perhaps our best ex-president, was inside North Korea negotiating a deal over their nuclear program. He was there on behalf of President Bill Clinton.

 I was there when he came out and said North Korea had agreed to freeze its nuclear program. I was there when New Mexico's then-Congressman Bill Richardson came out with an American helicopter pilot who had flown into a no-fly zone and was captured by North Korean soldiers. Not long after, the pilot killed himself. Richardson has spent more time in the North than any other American official.

The DMZ is only about forty miles from downtown Seoul, a straight shot along a modern four-lane highway. It is the most heavily fortified border in the world. South Korea and the US have thousands of troops present and the North is said to have over a million soldiers who are constantly on high alert.

If North Korea chose, it could roll tanks down the road and be in the northern suburbs of Seoul in a couple hours. That's what happened in the Korean war, and why so many thousands of Seoul citizens were killed in its first few days.

I once visited a Raytheon Patriot missile battery north of Seoul and the commander admitted that they could not launch missiles fast enough to stop North Korean projectiles, or at least most of them, from hitting Seoul in a surprise attack. Then there are the tunnels the North has dug underneath the DMZ, big enough to accommodate two tanks side by side. Four major tunnels have been discovered and it's presumed there are more. Then there's the poison gas the North has in abundance

The US knew for years that Kim Il Sung had serous weapons of mass destruction and didn't do anything militarily about it, partly because there's no way we could attack the North without the North attacking the South with conventional weapons and inflicting huge casualties. Now that we know that the North has more nuclear weapons than we thought and surprisingly sophisticated intercontinental missile technology that can deliver them to the U.S., what can we do?   Pray.

US history shows we rarely invade countries unless it's in our national security interest, and that usually means they've got oil. If that sounds cynical, there's plenty of evidence to back it up. There are other realities that strain my patriotism.

We're much more likely to invade a country if it's close and easy. Consider Grenada, a very tiny country. We invaded Grenada because the Cubans were building a long runway on the island. That, and because the leader was a socialist Marxist. I've flown over that runway and I can vouch that it was very long. But Grenada and

Panama were both invasions necessary only to make the president in power look tough.

Grenada was actually quite a clean invasion with not many casualties. No so Panama. We invaded Panama to get rid of its dictator, Manuel Noriega, a former paid informant for the CIA.

What never made the news except for a few publications like *Rolling Stone*, was what a poorly managed invasion that was. US forces killed hundreds of innocent Panamanians when they mistook the poorest ghetto in Panama City for an insurgent stronghold. The death toll was reportedly close to 2,000.

We don't invade Cuba because that country has a proficient armed service and the casualties would be too high for the American public. At the same time we punish the Cuban people because of the human rights record of Fidel Castro, but we turn a blind eye to the human rights abuses of countries like China because it's in our interest to do business with them.

Why didn't I learn more about the ugly underbelly of US foreign policy when I was in college? Maybe it's because I wasn't listening. Maybe it's because it takes time for the truth to filter through the education system. I was constantly surprised at how little my executive producers knew and understood about what was going on in the Western US, let alone beyond our borders.

When we were informed that my NBC News crew and I could join a Japanese tour to North Korea, I was more excited than if the tour was going for a sunbaked vacation in Hawaii. How we slipped through the cracks I'll never know. The North Korean authorities must have known we were journalists representing a major US network. Maybe they figured we would only see the bright side of North Korea since we were accompanying a tour group.

If such an opportunity were offered today I would turn it down flat. Americans, journalists in particular, have become pawns the North uses against the West. The tenser the situation, the greater the danger for visiting journalists. Besides, they won't let you see anything anyway.

We hooked up with the tour, after a long train ride, in northern Japan where we boarded a North Korean jet for Pyongyang. It was one of the old Soviet-built jets that were copied from our Boeing 707s with a slight miscalculation. The plane tended to scrape its rear end on takeoffs and landings so engineers had to add an extra rear wheel.

From the minute we boarded the plane we were in another world. The Muzak was straight out of Disney World with melodies that were eerily similar to "It's A Small World After All." Lawrence Welk would have been very popular in North Korea. The flight attendants were dressed in flowery velvety uniforms. They were pretty, sweet, and friendly. The food was tasty and there was plenty of it which surprised me because I had thought North Koreans were starving.

It was only about an hour flight. That's how close and dangerous North Korea is to Japan. As we taxied to the terminal outside Pyongyang, it seemed that most of the ground personnel were uniformed young women. They smiled, as did the immigration and custom officials (again mostly women), but they were not particularly friendly. I can't image what they were thinking inasmuch much as they are taught from when they're kids that Americans are evil baby killers.

It seemed we were all alone on our ride into the city. There were hardly any cars on the highway, hardly any people walking around. We later learned that only the state owns cars. Downtown

Pyongyang, the boulevards were very wide and spotless. They were also deserted of both cars and people. The city has an odd feel to it.

The best way I can describe it is as a Potemkin village. It didn't feel real. It didn't feel inhabited. There are dozens of high-rise apartment buildings and a few genuine skyscrapers. I stayed in one, which had a twin. The other one, I'm quite sure, was empty at least on the lower floors. I never saw any lights in the building. Driving through Pyongyang at night was a dark experience. There was no neon, no bars or cafés. Where did all the people go? What we were experiencing was a city with a power outage.

One gets the impression it's a city with not that many people. It feels like the people were painted into the landscape to give it a semblance of life. I can't adequately describe how surreal it is. But according to the most recent statistics available, in 2008, Pyongyang had a population of over three million citizens, far and away the biggest city in North Korea.

On the second day we were there, we were taken to a huge stadium that could hold 90,000 people for sporting events. The World Games were held there two years before. From the outside, the structure was very impressive. Up close it looked ready to fall down.

I walked into the men's room in the stadium. There was only one and it was on the main floor. It was the most attractive lavatory I've ever seen. The walls were marble. It was also the largest by far. I counted sixty urinals. Only problem was, there was only one dangling lightbulb in the entire lavatory. Only one.

Most of the buildings downtown are populated by government workers. They look very similar to government buildings in Washington, which look similar to government buildings in Europe.

I didn't see a single café as we drove along the wide, empty boulevards. What we did see were lots of twenty-something traffic girls directing traffic at all the major intersections. They must get excited when they see a car. I think they were there just to add a little color to an otherwise colorless landscape.

We didn't see any car dealerships, although we were taken to a showroom featuring a car built in North Korea. Our hosts were obviously very proud. The car bore a striking resemblance to a Mercedes Benz 190E. It was a yellow beauty. I'd seen just about every knockoff you can imagine in China, but this took the cake. It was not an attempt to make the car similar to the Mercedes, it was meant to be an exact replica—except for the hood ornament, which was close but no cigar. I know because my wife owned this car only it was made in Germany.

 I knew it wasn't the real thing when I opened the door and it practically fell off. The leather was fake. The clutch went all the way down to the floor. I couldn't imagine the car surviving a Washington pothole.

When I asked why it looked so much like a Mercedes, the response was unapologetic: Mercedes is the world's best car. All the official cars are Mercedes. Why wouldn't we make a Mercedes? I don't think North Korea exported even one of their "Mercedes" and I'd be willing to bet a buck that NK officials did not ride in home grown Mercedes.

Because we were on an official tour, we had an official guide. The truth is there are no tours of North Korea that are not officially guided. Because we were the media, we also had our own media guide, along with the guide for the Japanese tour. His name was Mr. Hung, a short stocky fellow with thick black hair and thick black glasses. I'm not really sure he did anything for us, but he was with us everywhere we went and often that included the bathroom. It wasn't only Mr. Hung.

We were shadowed by shady looking men in black suits driving black cars everywhere we went. I kept asking Mr. Hung if he could arrange an interview for us with a North Korean official. He kept promising me "maybe tomorrow."

Every night we were entertained at wonderful variety shows, huge stage events very much like those that were so popular in the US in the 1950s and 60s. These were extravagant affairs. Many of the performers were big stars within North Korea. The dances had a patriotic fervor to them, more like military marches.

What was most surprising about these grand galas was the amount of food at each table, and there would usually be at least fifty tables. The food was excellent and abundant for any country, let alone one where so many were hungry. The wine left a lot to be desired but the beer was good.

The first morning we were there my wake-up call was in stereo. At 6:30 a.m. both my console radio and the TV popped on, both with martial music. The TV featured troops goose-stepping on parade. I felt like I should be marching around my bed. I wondered if a hidden camera would reveal that I wore Mickey Mouse boxer shorts. Anyway, if the intent was to wake me up, it worked.

We thought we'd try to get outside without our guide to catch some interviews with people on their way to work. We did manage to escape for about an hour one early morning and actually found a few people who could speak broken English. Every answer was almost verbatim the same as the one before it. There was a deer-in-the-headlights quality to everyone we spoke with. Old folks and youngsters would get tears in their eyes when speaking of the "Dear

319

Leader." They spoke as if they believed that North Korea is an island of peace in a world at war.

North Korean kids are brought up hating the Japanese and the Americans even more. From when they first start their schooling they are taught that America is evil and wants to invade their country. There are dreadful depictions of American soldiers bayoneting young children during the Korean war. I was surprised we didn't encounter more hostility, considering the propaganda these people live with day after day.

One reason for the hostility was that during the war, US warplanes so completely ruled the skies, they bombed without interference. It was unusual to find a two-story building still standing undamaged. No wonder the animosity. Americans may have won that horrible "stalemate," but we created a country of deep hatred toward us.

We were taken on a tour of what we were told was a typical North Korean apartment. If it was indeed typical we might all move to Pyongyang. The apartment was beautiful and spacious. What was most striking were the floors heated by hot water pipes. Our guide assured me it wasn't a special apartment just for foreigners to see. I asked him if he had heated floors in his apartment and he said, "Yes, but they're not working." Truth is, they don't work in any apartment when there's no electricity and there are seldom days when electricity is available even half a day.

Every day we were there I would ask our guide to arrange an interview with a government official. No one ever interviewed the Dear Leader so I didn't ask for him. When our time in the North was running out, I realized we probably weren't going to get an interview if I didn't get more demanding.

I pushed Mr. Hung to do the interview himself. He said he didn't want to and I couldn't blame him. If he said something the government didn't like he would either be shot or end up in one of the gulags that exist near the Chinese border. I persisted, grabbed a mic and told Yashi the cameraman to roll while we were standing next to our car.

Most of what Mr. Hung had to say was unintelligible. I think I ended up using about ten seconds in my story. If I were there today, I'm not sure I would push anyone for an interview.

The fact that I virtually twisted his arm did not sit very well with Mr. Hung. He became quite hostile and would hardly speak to me. I knew I was in trouble when at the performance that night I was not allowed to sit at the usual table very close to the stage with my colleagues. My colleagues included my producer, cameraman, and soundman, along with Julie McCarthy with NPR.

Mr. Hung sentenced me to a table at the back of the large hall right next door to the kitchen, with the waiters walking in and out. I remember watching the table where I would normally sit. I could see Mr. Hung staring back at me with a mocking expression on his face as if saying, "Now you know who is in charge here." He wouldn't let me sit up front for the remainder of our stay.

It was so cold—twenty-four degrees below zero to be precise—the morning we headed south out of Pyongyang toward the DMZ. I was anxious to see what it looked like from the North, but even more anxious to get my feet warm. Our vans did not have heaters that worked or window defrosters.

We had to scrape the van's windows from the inside to see where we were going. It was about a two-hour drive along a divided highway directly south. They didn't need a divided highway because there were no cars. They just needed cars with heaters.

North Korea gets bitterly cold during the winter. I was based in Chicago where it was so cold my reporter's notebook cracked in half, but I don't remember being as cold as when I was in North Korea.

When we first got to the DMZ, we were granted a briefing by a four-star North Korean general. He explained the fortifications surrounding the area and it was pretty apparent that it wouldn't be a good idea to go wandering off the main trails.

What was different in this briefing, as compared to the ones I had received from US officers in the South, was that the general seemed to have a good sense of humor and if anything, he played down the danger of war breaking out. Despite the official line, the general didn't seem to be very worried.

What was most astounding to me was that when we actually got to the Panmunjom village, the atmosphere was totally casual, almost as if the village was off limits to war. Not only were the US and UN soldiers on the other side not hiding behind buildings as they were when we visited from the South—they were walking about, talking with one another and occasionally waving to the North Korean soldiers at our end of the village. Did that mean US and South Korean troops were just putting on a show for the media when we visited the DMZ? Yes.

The night before we were to return to Japan, I called Mr. Hung up to my room and gave him a $200 tip for being our guide. That was quite generous, considering the way he had been treating me. He looked around my room then led me into the bathroom, turned on the tap, and said we should speak softly because people were listening.

He did condescend to take the $200, but said he was still mad at me because I had embarrassed him in front of his peers. The only peers around were the surveillance guys always hanging in the background. He stuffed the money in his pocket and walked out of the room. I calculated that the $200 would pay his rent for about a year.

The most remarkable thing about North Korea is how little the people understand about what is going on in their country, let alone in the world. There are people in one part of the country who think another part is currently under attack. The regime is always decreeing national alerts.

It's also extraordinary how little we know about the North. To my knowledge, there have never been any revelations about spies inside the Hermit Kingdom. Of course that doesn't mean there haven't been any, but certainly they're rare.

Over the past forty years, about 30,000 North Koreans have made it out of the country and eventually into South Korea. They tell horror stories of starvation and of brutality against anyone who even appears to cross the regime. People have been executed or sentenced to gulags for embracing Christianity. The young leader Kim Jong Un has reportedly ordered the execution of several underlings for corruption—although we don't know for sure.

Word from the most recent defectors is that the average North Korean is learning more about the world from radios that have been smuggled in from China. South Koreans often released Hydrogen-filled balloons near the DMZ when the wind is blowing north that carry news and show pictures of the prosperity 40 miles south.

The regime shot these balloons out of the sky when they saw them. A launching in 2014 sparked an exchange of gunfire. Apparently there is nothing that would anger the North more than sneaking a copy of the 2014 American comedy called *The Interview* into the country. It's about Kim Jong Un. North Korean officials said it would precipitate war. American critics didn't like the movie either.

MY WALK WITH A MAN-EATING TIGER

It was a beautiful morning. I remember the birds chirping. The abbot was serving breakfast to the monks in a giant outdoor pagoda. I wasn't invited to join in and I wasn't unhappy about it.

We were in Western Thailand near the Burma border, a long drive from Bangkok but not far from the site where Allied prisoners constructed the bridge that became the subject of the movie *Bridge on the River Kwai*. We were at a Buddhist monastery and the monks had just returned from collecting alms.

For those who may not be familiar with alms, they are offerings (in this case, food) the monks collect each morning from families living within walking distance of the monastery. Almost anywhere in Thailand, which is a seriously Buddhist country, you'll see long lines of monks heading out each morning to collect alms.

When the monks returned with their bounty, I was instantly hungry. It was a wonderful collection of Thai food, which is my favorite— fried rice and other delicacies such as ginger chicken, shredded pork, and sticky, sweet, mango rice.

What I never realized before is that the abbot, the monk in charge, takes all these wonderful dishes and mixes them up in one large bowl. Can you imagine? He had turned something delectable into something inedible. But the monks dove in as if it tasted wonderful, or they didn't know better.

The concoction made me want to upchuck. Buddhists believe that food should not be eaten for pleasure but only for sustenance. I tried to explain to the abbot that the food could provide both sustenance and pleasure if he wouldn't scramble it. He didn't seem to understand. I think he was pretending.

While we were filming the monks eating and praying inside a giant open pagoda, a couple of cub tigers were playing with my shoestrings. They were cuddly cute, but big enough to get my attention. Here I was sitting in a pagoda on a beautiful morning, watching what should have been a delectable meal turned into hash, all the while gingerly pushing tiger cubs away from my ankles. And I don't have a picture to show my grandkids.

The pagoda was situated in the middle of what could have been a safari park in Southern California. There were wild animals grazing peacefully everywhere. There were deer, water buffalo, antelope, monkeys, wild boar, peacocks, and full-grown tigers.

The tigers were in individual cages in the morning, but later in the day they would be let out and chaperoned by monks. I had mixed feelings about being there when the tigers were not in a cage. I was there to shoot a story about why it's important for Buddhists to care for wild animals, not about wild animals eating Buddhists, or me.

The story about how this collection of animals came to be located in a monastery says a lot about the Buddhist philosophy of reincarnation and about how behavior in this life will impact who you are in the next life.

In 2002, the monks found a wounded tiger near their pagoda that appeared to be recuperating from a gunshot wound. Although Thailand has become a modern country, the folks living near the monastery were quite poor and hunted wild animals not only for the meat, but also for their skins and body parts which are in great demand throughout Asia, often as aphrodisiacs. The wounded tiger seemed to understand that he would be safer at the monastery.

At first the monks left the tiger alone, which was probably wise. But eventually they started to leave water and then food. Slowly the tiger healed and then disappeared. Before long, more wounded tigers showed up as well as a variety of other wild animals, and the monks felt they had no choice but to care for them. The grounds started looking like the staging area for Noah's ark.

What attracted me to this story when I read it in the *Bangkok Post* was how the Buddhist belief in reincarnation played a role in the way the tigers and other animals are treated. Buddhists believe that not long after we die we are reincarnated to another life, hopefully one better and more enlightened than the one before. That depends, of course, on how good we are in the current life.

The monks believe if they don't take good care of the tigers and other animals, they could be downgraded in the next incarnation. They could, for instance, come back as a tiger or something further down the food chain if they don't take good care of the animals in their midst. As a result, the animals ate even better than the monks. A number of those that showed up appeared perfectly healthy.

The abbot, Pra Acharn Chan, felt he had a calling to care for these animals. A quarter century earlier, he had been diagnosed with leukemia and told he would die from the disease. The abbot seemed to have a perpetual smile on his face. He told me that in the beginning he could only understand the animal's body language. But eventually he came to understand what they were thinking. He said he could communicate with them. After watching him for a couple of days I got the impression that he might be right.

The abbot named the tigers for their personalities. Cloud, for instance, was a leader because he had a strong personality. Cloud hated perfume. Fortunately I don't even wear aftershave. Sunshine was so named because she always seemed happy.

When was the last time you saw a happy tiger? Chan thought Rainbow was a diva who "thinks she is beautiful." Now how would he know that if she didn't tell him?

Abbot Chan tried to assign certain monks to care for certain tigers because he thought they had similar personalities. One young man known as "Boy" told me the animals congregated at the monastery because they knew it was a place of peace. They knew it was safe from hunters. He said the tigers knew they could trust the monks. If you can't trust a monk whom can you trust?

Word about the sanctuary started getting out and tourists started showing up. While we were there, visitors from France, Canada, and the US had driven all the way from Bangkok to take a look. A French Canadian told me the sanctuary caused him to question Christian views toward animals—that is, that they were created for the pleasure and sustenance of humans. He said that people in the West should learn from people in the East.

The approach to conservation in this remote part of Thailand is quite different than the approach in the West. Here it begins with the spiritual. In the West, the focus is on preserving wild places and the animals that inhabit them. Here the land is not so significant. What is more important is protecting the spirit within the animals, and protecting the spirit within the animals has its own reward.

Dr. Visasmongkolchai, a veterinarian who managed the monastery, explained it this way: "If you save the animal life, it in turn saves your life." He said if you improve the quality of life for the animals, the quality of your life will improve. The sanctuary, it seemed, had become as important to the vet as to the abbot.

Dr. Visasmongkolchai was raising funds to build a place he called Tiger Island. He wanted it to be a rescue center as well as a place to educate the public about the dire future tigers are facing. He said it is an emergency. Tigers have been disappearing at an alarming rate. They are now one of the world's most endangered species. The World Wildlife Fund says there are fewer than 4,000 remaining in the wild, worldwide.

The pinnacle, or the nadir, of my first day at the sanctuary occurred toward dusk. That was when the monks let the tigers out of their cages, under close supervision, though not nearly close enough to suit me.

My producer Trent Harris took a picture of me kneeling next to what seemed to be a giant tiger with my hand resting on his back. I keep the picture in my office and every time I look at it I shudder. You could see from the expression on my face that I was not a happy reporter. All it would take is one wrong look on my part and I would be dinner. Tigers are known to eat more than eighty pounds of meat in a sitting.

What worried me even more, though, was that there were several smaller animals roaming around that would normally serve as a tasty meal for any one of the tigers. If a tiger decided it wanted the deer for a snack, for instance, there's not much we could do to stop it. And then things could really get out of control.

As I stood up to move to safer ground, the abbot appeared and motioned for me to walk with him. Apparently at about that time each day he would take three or four tigers for a stroll and he wanted me to walk alongside the tiger I had been kneeling beside. The video we took made it quite clear from the frown on my face that I was not going to be doing any happy talk with the tiger.

When I say I "rested my hand" on the tiger's back, it's not entirely accurate. The back of this fellow was as high as my chest. I had to reach up to place my hand ever so gingerly on his back. Along the way you could hear the peculiar howls and sounds of the various smaller animals within striking distance and one of the tigers ahead of me veered toward a deer before the abbot stopped it.

I finally settled down and figured if I was going to die, I was going to die. And then we came upon a tree, not a large tree, more like an apple tree. Everyone and every animal around me scattered, and I soon found out why. Just then I felt warm and wet spray all over; the tiger had pissed on me.

Actually, he was pissing on the tree and either missed or I was the victim of a ricochet because from my waist down I was wet all over. It turns out that tigers, like dogs, like to leave their scent on trees and things. I wish the abbot had explained that to me before the walk.

The abbot told me that it is good luck to be pissed on by a tiger, though I've not been able to find his source

A few years after we were there, which was when the Tiger Temple was just being discovered, authorities raided the place and arrested three monks for trafficking in animal parts and animal abuse. The extent of the abuse was horrible. Tiger parts were sold as aphrodisiacs.

Authorities found tiger skin amulets, and other wildlife products as well as forty dead baby tigers in a freezer. By then, Tiger Temple had become the fourth most popular tourist destination in Thailand. It had also become a money-making corporation run by a few monks. Visitors were charged an entrance fee and the place was raking in over $3 million a year.

Officials closed the place and removed 137 tigers. A spokesman for the temple said that Abbot Pra Acharn did not participate and was not aware of the criminal activities by some monks. The abbot was not charged, nor has he been exonerated. To date no monk has been found guilty but court proceedings are ongoing under a cloud of suspicion that the fix is in.

In 2017, Tiger Temple was allowed to reopen, operated by pretty much the same cast of characters as those when it was shut down. Only the name has been changed to Golden Tiger. I saw a tour brochure that promoted "Breakfast with monks and tigers" for $300. Golden Tiger has requested approval to house 500 tigers.

Inasmuch as ours was one of the earliest international stories extolling the "wonder" of the place, I have to wonder if we didn't contribute to its popularity and ultimately to the financial value of those endangered Bengal tigers.

The tiger and I went for a walk and he pissed on me. The Abbot told me it's good luck to get pissed on by a tiger.

TO HELL AND BACK

I've flown about five million miles in my life and only once heard the pilot say, "Ok everybody, lean forward so we can get this plane in the air." It was not confidence-building. I'm thinking, what in the hell have I got myself into. We were rolling down the runway at Salt Lake International on our way to Guatemala, providing we could get the damn plane off the ground.

Our pilot was an oral surgeon. His name was Dan Bluth and he was a good guy for a dentist, not rolling in humor but could chuckle and occasionally crack a smile. He was a Mormon. First he went to church leaders and asked if they had a mission in Central America that needed a clinic.

Bluth had been a Mormon missionary in Mexico and spoke Spanish fluently. The Church had no need at the moment so Bluth started his own charity operating in Spanish-speaking countries.

He formed a group of doctors and dentists called Ayuda, fashioned not after the Mormon model, but instead after the Seventh Day Adventist medical missions that operate around the world. Ayuda means "help" in Spanish. For the past four years Bluth had been flying to a clinic in the highlands of Guatemala. It seemed to me like a good story for *Extra*, the weekly magazine program I produced and hosted.

I'd be lying if I didn't say that the story also intrigued me because I had never been to Guatemala. Besides, I could use a positive story involving the Church because I had done so many stories questioning church doctrine.

About that time, my station KUTV commissioned a survey that found a majority of Utahans perceived our station as anti-Mormon, which was not a good thing. As I recall, KUTV immediately launched a huge anti-smoking campaign, and other more obvious attempts to display our Mormon-friendly credentials.

Bluth was happy to have us come along, not because he wanted the attention for himself—he was too shy for that. He wanted the publicity and the contributions that would follow. At first he said we would be flying to Guatemala in the comfort of his twin-engine Piper Comanche.

Then the Comanche had to go in for maintenance so he said we would go down on a 747 out of Los Angeles. That sounded much better. Then he called to say he had found a single engine Cessna 206 that cruised about 150 miles an hour with a tail wind. This was not good news. I'd flown in a number of small, single-engine planes and I didn't like them.

The Cessna carried six passengers. There were five of us, counting Bluth and the clinic's volunteer director. Larry Roberts was my producer. His films had earned a cult following. Larry was one of the most gentle, mellow people I ever met but when he wanted something he usually got it. Larry died of AIDS a few years later.

My photographer was O.C. Budge. He was a buddy and photographer who I worked with quite regularly at KUTV. Compared to the equipment required for a news production today, we were traveling light, but our gear still weighed about 200 pounds. Bluth took the sixth seat out of the plane and that's where we stored our equipment. There wasn't much wiggle room in the cabin.

It seemed to take forever for the Cessna to get off the runway. I had been timing take-offs for years and if you are still on the runway thirty seconds after the plane starts to roll you are justified in getting nervous. Our take-off took forty seconds. And when we got in the air it took what seemed like forever to get high enough to fly over the Wasatch Mountains. Half an hour later I could still see the Salt Lake International Airport. It was going to be a long ride.

Dr. Bluth had calculated our trip so that we would stay in the air each leg about five hours. That's a long time. I have a condition called "nervous leg syndrome," which can drive me crazy in a big jet airliner let alone stuffed in a tiny cute little red and white single-engine so-called airplane.

The doctor had a solution that worked wonderfully. Each leg before we took off he would give us each a Valium. I have no idea how strong the tablets were but none of us was feeling pain. We sat there five hours at a time like zombies.

The only good part was that the drone of a prop-engine usually puts me to sleep. We spent the first night in Midland-Odessa, Texas, near where George H.W. Bush made his millions. It's a good thing there's oil there because there's not much else except snakes. That night we had a large Tex-Mex meal and too many margaritas.

The next morning, almost to the second as we crossed the border into Mexico, O.C. threw up. I've never seen anything like it. You could barely see out the front window, and the stench was awful. If not for the Valium, I'd have thrown up with him. It was disgusting. Dr. Bluth thought it was because O.C. had too much to drink the night before. I didn't think so. I thought O.C. had "Montezuma's revenge" and the fact that he got sick even before he had a chance to drink the water was not a good omen. An hour and a half of this torture and we finally touched down at the Tampico International Airport to refuel.

Tampico is a fairly big city with a total population of almost a million, so the airport was active. As our plane taxied to a stop on the runway, the engine stopped as well. We sat there trying to start the damn thing on an active runway.

At first the flight controllers were sympathetic, asking pleasantly that we please get off the runway. Unfortunately, Tampico only had one runway and we were blocking it and the two commercial airliners full of passengers circling overhead.

Before long our friends in the control tower were yelling at us in very understandable English. "Get that plane off the runway now!" with a few expletives tossed in. Eventually the dire situation we were causing got through our collective Valium-addled consciousness and we crawled out and pushed our cute little red and white plane off the active runway.

It turns out the battery was dead and could not be revived. For reasons I cannot explain, we didn't acquire a new battery. Instead, after four of us got in the plane, the fifth would stand next to the propeller and crank it. Dr. Bluth, our pilot, manned the throttle. I've often thought about the sinking feeling one gets when one's plane can only be started by hand-cranking it. It was the Valium that saw us through.

You don't need the battery to fly so there wasn't too much to worry about unless the engine stopped while we were in the air. There was one other problem. Flying at night can be dicey because the gauges in the cockpit weren't lit, so it's difficult to read the altimeter or the fuel gauge, little things like that.

We ended up flying not only in the dark but also during an intense lightning storm. Our pilot couldn't eyeball where we were from the ground because of the thick cumulus clouds we were flying through, so we needed the gauges. Fortunately, between the brilliant flashes of light from the lightning and the tiny flame from my cigarette lighter we made our way. Thank God for the Valium.

That evening, after another pill and five more hours in the air, we landed at Veracruz, the beautiful historic town on the Gulf of Mexico. For some odd reason, we left our 16-millimeter camera in the baggage compartment of the plane. Then we checked into a nice hotel.

After dinner, O.C. went back to his room to find that someone had kicked in his door and stolen his very expensive still camera, along with most everything else in his room. Our mistake was going to the local constabulary.

They treated us as if we were the criminals. After we stood in line for two hours at the police station to report the crime, they would not leave us alone. Every half hour a new set of police would knock on our hotel room doors wanting to question us. We left Veracruz without the still camera. We were happy not to be in jail.

By this time, our expectations were not what they were when we embarked.

We were alive and that was good. We were like zombies. If we weren't sedated we might have asked why we didn't buy a new battery. Instead, one of us cranked the propeller and we took off. The next morning we flew five hours into Guatemala City. It was like awakening from a long nightmare.

Our ground transportation was far from comfortable but we didn't require Valium. It was a day-long, bone-jarring ride into the Guatemalan Highlands. We were worried about running into the feared Guatemala National Guard, notorious for indiscriminate killings. A few months earlier the Guard was accused of a massacre very close to where we were going. We could see trucks full of soldiers on the dirt road on the other side of the valley. We knew they could see us, but we lost them.

We arrived at the clinic relieved, but not in good spirits. Both O.C. and Larry were suffering with terrible diarrhea. I wasn't sick but felt it was close at hand. Larry and O.C. spent the first night running back and forth to the well in the middle of the courtyard to fetch another bucket of water to fill the toilet so they could flush it and run back to the well to get more water. It was a circular thing. They didn't think it was funny but I spent the night giggling and hoping I wasn't next.

The clinic was indeed in a very poverty stricken area, even for a very poor country. Not even the bottled water was trustworthy. On one of Dr. Bluth's house calls, we walked in on a patient just as he breathed his last breath. We saw him die. That will get you thinking. Medical care for the villagers was absolutely primitive. I was willing to forgive Dr. Bluth for what he had put us through. He was a genuine humanitarian.

While we were there Bluth helped dozens of people, really poor people who had never seen a doctor before. The locals trusted him completely. He toiled as long as we had daylight. Electricity was still a luxury that worked only a few hours a day. We shot lots of good stuff, although when we got back much of it was overexposed. We hadn't understood the difference in the quality and intensity of the sunlight that close to the equator.

When we had shot enough pictures and interviews to put together a fifteen-minute film, we realized we still had three more days before we were scheduled to go home, three more days of misery. I said to Larry, the mellowest person I've ever known, "If you can convince

Dr. Bluth to go home earlier I'll give you two hundred dollars." Larry came back a half-hour later and said we would be leaving that afternoon.

I wouldn't be surprised if gentle Larry had threatened the good doctor. That's how miserable we all were. As I write this, it dawns on me now that there's nothing like a few nights of Montezuma's revenge to forget the death and real suffering we had just filmed. If we hadn't rushed Dr. Bluth out of there he could have helped more people. I regret to say that I'm sure this was not the only time in my career our coverage of the story got in the way of the story itself.

When we finally made it back to Guatemala City, we were in the mood to celebrate. We deserved it. That night three of us—sans Dr. Bluth—hailed a cab for a night on the town. None of us spoke Spanish but it seemed that the cabbie understood what I meant when I said we wanted to go see a burlesque show.

I tried to make it clear that we weren't looking for a whorehouse; we only wanted to watch pretty girls. The driver replied "Si Si," which we took to mean yes, yes. It was immediately apparent as we entered the first place that it was a whorehouse. Thinking fast, I said to the madam, "We are looking for a Maria Rodriquez." Where I got that name, I'll never know. The woman said in passable English something like, "We don't have one of those but we can name any of these pretty young ladies Maria Rodriguez if you'd like."

When we got back in the cab I told the driver we did not want a whorehouse, we wanted burlesque. He nodded his head and said Si Si. The next place he took us was a teenybopper whorehouse, with jukeboxes and extremely loud noise. I asked again about "Maria Rodriguez."

When we got back in the cab I said we wanted to go back to our hotel but the driver insisted he knew what we were talking about. Our last stop was a castle with a long winding driveway. There was a butler and classical music and beautiful women in long evening gowns and it was not burlesque. Again and finally, no Maria Rodriguez. We went back to the hotel without ever finding Maria or burlesque.

The next morning we headed home. When we got to the airport and saw our tiny red and white Cessna parked in the shadow of a 747 destined for Los Angeles, I had a mutiny on my hands. Larry and O.C. were adamant that they were going home on the 747. Adamant doesn't quite describe it. They were gritting their teeth.

I told them they could but they would have to pay for it out of their pocket. I don't know what possessed me. I wanted the big plane as much as they did. Neither one of them spoke to me for the next five hours, especially after we had to hand crank the Cessna to get it started. I quickly forgot my admiration for Dr. Bluth. He could have purchased a damn battery. We were all depressed, even after our dose of Valium.

We stopped that night in Mazatlán, Mexico, a resort town on the Pacific coast. At last a fun place. That night we went to Senior Frogs, where the margaritas are too large to hold with one hand. We staggered out of Frogs, caught a taxi, and said we wanted burlesque. This time the driver understood and took us to a wonderful nightclub with dozens of beautiful dancers.

In his drunken stupor Larry fell in love with one of the girls. In my drunken stupor I asked him to go outside where I told him it was impossible for him to love a girl because he was gay. Larry took a punch at me. I think he missed. I don't remember. I know he was madder than I thought he could get. We went back to our hotel and eventually talked things through. Then I went for a swim in the hotel pool and dove into the shallow end and bloodied my nose.

The next day we staggered into the plane in terrible condition. I had taken all the skin off my poor nose. We knew we were going to be spending the night in a desolate part of northern Mexico in the state of Chihuahua. After we were in the air longer than the usual five hours, we suspected we were lost. Of course our pilot never let on that we were running out of gas. Why are pilots that way?

My wife and I were on a shuttle to New York that got hit by lightning. The doors in the luggage bins flew open. The lights went off. You could hear the flight attendants gasping. My wife and I were squeezing each other's hand as if it was the last squeeze. Eventually the pilot came on the intercom and said, "You may have noticed a little jolt a few minutes ago. It was just lightning, nothing to worry about." I wonder what he would have said if we were going down.

Even with our daily dose of Valium, after more than five long hours the average guy has just got to go. Larry was getting desperate so he reached in the back of the plane and pulled out one of his cowboy boots. It seemed the perfect receptacle. Finally just as the fuel gauge indicated we were out, Dr. Bluth found the airport. Well, actually it wasn't an airport. It was a piece of relatively flat land in the middle of a plowed field. By then, we didn't care where we landed so long as we did.

It was dusk when we taxied to a stop. Off in the distance we could see a small shack with the sunset tinting the sky behind it. When Bluth shut down the engine we could hear mariachi music apparently coming out of the shack. It was like landing in a Mel Gibson movie. Then we saw several figures walking slowly toward us. It was a little spooky at first and then scary when we realized that the figures were carrying M16 military-issue assault rifles.

It dawned on us that these men were regular army on the lookout for drug runners. They were going to want to search the plane. We had no drugs, but we did have Larry's boot. What if a soldier put his hand in the boot and pulled it out covered in pee. They would shoot us for sure. So we were frantically trying to open a window to empty the boot. We made it but only barely.

The next morning we flew across the border into the US. I remember feeling dazed as I stared down on the barren, flat wasteland that is western Texas. It looked beautiful. I was genuinely surprised that we were still alive. I was sure we wouldn't be. I had a smile on my face. I was still riding high on Valium.

OF MACHO AND MEN

The most embarrassing episode of my career was a one-hour prime time NBC special I co-hosted called *Of Macho and Men*. My co-anchor was Deborah Norville. I thought it was only fitting that we should be working together. After all, I was certain that it was my recommendation that convinced NBC to hire Deborah. Later I learned that I was among several who had talked her up.

I had watched her work as a reporter and part-time anchor for the NBC-owned station in Chicago, which was in the Merchandise Mart where the NBC News bureau was located, and I thought she was very good. I also thought she had the most incredible lips, and that was pre-Botox. Maybe that's what influenced the other recommendations.

 It wasn't long before Deborah was working for NBC News at Rockefeller Center and filling in for the *Today* show anchor Jane Pauley. Her rise was meteoric, as it was for several female reporters during my time at NBC. The publicity and pressure was so intense that many of these talented women burned out.

There was the story that during a meeting of NBC News brass who were looking at Deborah's on-air work, the president of the news division walked over to the monitor, pointed and said, "There gentlemen is the future of NBC News."

Before long there were rumors that Jane was on her way out and Deborah was going to replace her. It became fodder for national tabloids: "Pretty young thing replaces Jane Pauley." People went crazy. Jane became popular all over again.

It was difficult for Deborah to recover. She was a good anchor, but too many people thought of her as a home-wrecker. Deborah couldn't get over the stigma. Working on a primetime special was a good consolation prize.

Before I go any further, let me say that I had reservations about the project from the very beginning. If I had any guts I would have respectfully declined. Unfortunately, I didn't. By then I had anchored and co-anchored a few hour-long specials and they always began with an agreed-upon topic and then an assigned executive producer, two field producers, and a couple of researchers. From there we would scope the subject and work-up an outline, and then a script.

This one was different. This idea was personally approved by NBC News President Larry Grossman. He probably approved all my specials, but this one came during an invite to his office where he handed me a very detailed outline of the show's structure. It was the first outline I had ever been given and it included the title *Of Macho and Men*. Someone had clearly put a lot of work into it before it was assigned to me.

The premise of *Of Macho and Men* was described by the *Chicago Sun-Times* this way: "Just when men were getting the hang of opening car doors, lighting cigarettes, and getting in touch with their feelings, all the rules of social behavior and sexual interrelationships have turned the male self-image inside out." I wish the *Chicago Sun-Times* had done our story.

Fortunately, we did clarify upfront that our special was not about equality, it was about "quality of life." On the surface it didn't seem like such a bad idea. I had been divorced and though I didn't fight the outcome, it didn't seem fair.

Then there were the statistics we used within the special that an American man's lifespan was seven years less than a woman's. Men were four times more likely to commit suicide. More men were institutionalized than women.

Of course, the more I thought about it, the more misgivings I had. For instance, if you're not getting paid what you deserve, that can certainly impact your quality of life. My stories about pay discrimination in the workplace always made me feel like a hypocrite because I knew what my female and male producers were making at NBC and it was far from equal or fair.

As a whole, my favorite producers were women and on average they earned about two-thirds what their male counterparts were making. I've never asked any producer how much he or she earns but some told me anyway and word gets around.

Our special had four parts. Two of them were mine. Deborah had two. She had already moved way past me in name recognition and poise. We had met each other a couple of times but that was all. We never discussed the project until we sat down to do our first shoot, lambs to the slaughter.

The opening of the program took place in a New York nightclub with the Chippendale dancers performing behind us. If you're not familiar with Chippendale dancers, they are all men in every sense of the word.

Their costume, such as it was, consists of bowties and shirt cuffs and a loincloth. This is not a church choir, although there might be more females attending church if the Chippendales were performing behind the pastor.

So the show opened on the near-naked dancers and panned to Deborah and myself explaining that *Of Macho and Men* was about a neglected species, the modern American male. We did it with a straight face, although I don't think anybody was paying attention to the two of us. The program went downhill from there.

My first shoot was in Orange County. It was with a five-foot tall redheaded woman named Robin who was a counselor with United Fathers of America. At the time it was one of four non-profits in the US dedicated to males abused by their wives.

Robin was a reformed husband beater—actually, she beat up both her first and second husbands. I asked, "Did you just slap them?" She said, "No, I beat the hell out of them with my fists." She said she "butchered" the face of one of her husbands. Remember, this is a tiny woman, although I knew sitting there that I would not want to be on her bad side.

She told me spousal abuse of husbands was a big problem but didn't get much attention because men were too embarrassed to report it. What made the interview even more awkward for me was that Robin had recently had her right leg amputated at the knee. So during the interview her knee kept jerking involuntarily and I couldn't think about anything else.

My second interview was with a man who was one of Robin's clients. His name was Ken and his beautiful wife Elaine had beat him up several times. Elaine was in her late thirties and was so put off by her husband that she had moved out of the house and into their Cadillac.

She was living like a homeless person even though she and her husband owned quite a lovely home. Elaine moved out, she said, because one day she came home unexpectedly and found her husband dressed in her lingerie. She beat him up and eventually moved out. It wasn't the first time.

One time she ran into him with the Cadillac and sent him sprawling. Another time their daughter had to pull her off Ken. Yet another time Elaine, who was a pitcher in school, hit him in the face with a baseball. Elaine was quite attractive and very charming. When she got mad, there was an ugly side. I got a glimpse of it and it wasn't pretty. I was struck by how her face changed.

After I left Elaine in her Caddy, I interviewed Ken outside their home. He was quite handsome and seemed like a nice guy. Then when I interviewed him, I found myself wanting to hit him myself. It wasn't because he had worn his wife's lingerie. He was just someone you wanted to punch. I guess the world needs people like that.

I also interviewed comedian Roseanne Barr, who was at the pinnacle of her career. The sitcom *Roseanne* was at the top of the ratings. One of her favorite targets was men. She called them "Lumps, and they just sit there and that's how it is." I don't think her thing about men was just a shtick. It was pretty clear that she genuinely did not like men, and me in particular.

I can only remember one other time when the interviewee clearly couldn't stand me. It was a jerk attorney who called me a "phlegmatic dreg." That's pretty low. I was surprised Rosanne didn't get up and walk away. I think she stuck around so she could continue to be rude to me. Had she known that my wife had already beat feminism into me, she might have treated me better.

I never watched *Of Macho and Men* when it aired. I never saw Deborah's part at all. Mine was enough. I know we had pictures of women working out, and of men "dancing to discover the primal roots of their masculinity." One of the Chippendale dancers revealed that he thought men should be a "little less macho and a little more giving."

Of Macho and Men was doomed from start to finish. My executive producer was an excellent journalist and documentary maker, but he had never produced a program quite like this one. Of course, none of us had. Considering what a cautious, straight arrow he was, I couldn't understand why he didn't shut the project down. It just had this forward momentum going you couldn't stop.

He also wasn't up to snuff on the latest wizardry of production. That was a time when there were lots of technical developments, electronic gimmickry you could add in the control room. You could literally turn a purse into a sow's ear. As I recall, our closing credits had snowflakes falling in the background for no apparent reason.

I found an old review of the documentary in the *Los Angeles Times*. It referred to *Of Macho and Men* as an "alleged documentary." Looking back, I don't understand why I didn't go into hiding.

THE DAMNED PICKUP

The day we blew up the pickup was bittersweet for me. Bitter because I despised the pickup. Sweet, because I was damn glad to be rid of it, even though it was blown up only digitally. It symbolized the end of a two-year long series of reports on the *Today* show in which the pickup was literally and figuratively the vehicle for the story. I don't know how anyone who watched any of my pickup stories could ever take me seriously as a journalist. I'm confident I could find plenty who would agree.

It was a shitty lime green 1953 Chevy. I'm sure they don't make the color anymore. I never liked it from the start to the end. I imagine most people who knew I was from a very small town that claimed more trucks than cars figured I would be especially comfortable driving around in a pickup.

In my experience, pickups were used more to haul dirty, grimy and smelly things, never pretty young girls. So there was nothing about the pickup that said "cool" to me. The pickup was old and clunky and hard to drive. You could hold the steering wheel straight and the pickup would go left or right.

There was no air conditioning. It took all my strength just to crank the window up or down. The steering wheel was so big it felt as though I was driving a tractor. The only thing that would have made the ending of the pickup any better was if we had actually, physically blown it up.

The first time I saw the pickup was in Austin, Texas. We were there to interview Jim Hightower, the state agriculture commissioner— who was also a popular populist, columnist, and author. My producer was Ned Judge and it was his idea to rent the pickup and do the interview with Hightower as we drove around Austin. I suppose it was symbolic because Hightower was agriculture commissioner. I wasn't too excited about the idea but I could tell Ned liked it, and after the story aired so did the *Today* show producers.

So Ned decided, and the show agreed, that we would lease the pickup from the Austenite who owned it and we would use it as a prop for our stories. I couldn't figure out why we didn't rent a different car wherever we went. It would've been simpler.

We could have rented convertibles, sports cars, any kind of actually cool vehicle. Instead we leased the piece of crap pickup. Then we rented a trailer and a Winnebago RV to pull it. We needed a driver, so NBC News hired the brother of Ned's wife to drive the Winnebago from one story to the next. He brought along his wife and their little boy.

As soon as we found out where the next story would be, they would take off from the last one, pulling the pickup on the trailer, and be at the next location before we got there. We would then fly in, rent a car, and hook up with the brother-in-law Dennis and family.

Ned would arrange for a freelance camera crew from the nearest city large enough to supply one. We would shoot the story, usually in two days, drive back to the airport in our rental, and fly home. He lived in Los Angeles. I lived in Arlington, Virginia.

Ned loved gadgets and owned most of them. One was a little mini playback machine. At the end of our shoot he would download the big tapes onto smaller ones that I could insert into the playback machine and watch what we'd shot on the plane home. It was a great idea. With the machine I was able to log the material and start writing while everything was still fresh in my mind.

After writing the script, I would go into the NBC Washington bureau and record the narration. A technician would feed it by satellite to the Burbank bureau, where Ned and a tape editor would edit it. By then we had decided what our next story would be and we were on our way.

One of the many reasons I hated the pickup was that it meant we had to include it in our stories. In other words, we would do interviews sitting in the cab, or leaning against it, or driving along in it. We would use its shadow in our shots when it was possible.

It reminded me of the days when television stations first discovered helicopters which were so expensive it was required that they or their shadow appear in most stories. That became very problematic, considering the loud noise a helicopter makes and the dust clouds it stirs up. Anyway, all this posing took at least an extra half a day to shoot.

Most of that time I found myself waiting while Ned got everything synchronized. He put gel on the cab windows to balance the inside light with the light outside. He had mics installed in the dashboard and tiny cameras the size of my little finger positioned to take pictures of both me and my interviewee. These devices were called "lipstick" cameras because they were small enough to fit easily inside a lipstick tube. Today's cameras like the GoPros can be even smaller.

When I was driving along doing an interview, the crew would be riding in the back of the pickup monitoring the sound. One thing I liked about doing the interviews inside the pickup was that it felt more like a conversation.

Formal interviews where the interviewee is sitting across from the interviewer always drove me crazy and the format has never changed over the years. They weren't natural and they often made the interviewee uneasy. If you're interviewing a government official that's one thing, but I wasn't. On the other hand, including the pickup in the interviews drastically tempted Murphy's Law, which is always in play on shoots.

Something invariably goes wrong and with the pickup it was a certainty. The shadows were wrong, the background was wrong, the eighteen-wheeler passing us honked its horn at entirely the wrong time, or we hit a bump in the road and so on. The pickup lurched even when everything was smooth. And of course the heater didn't work and air conditioning in a 1953 Chevy was a thing of the future.

There's another point I would like to make here and I've made it many, many times to my cameramen and producers. When it comes to setting up an interview, there's almost always a tension between the cameraman and myself.

We both want the best. The cameraman wants a good picture, wants to make me look good. Meanwhile the interviewee watches all these preparations and gets more and more nervous while he or she is waiting. And the nervouser they get, the worse they do in the interview.

I was interviewing an elderly man in Boston one evening. I had worked with the cameraman before and he was one of the best lighters I had ever worked with. My theory has always been if you left a cameraman to his or her own devices, they would light themselves to death. Anyway, after the cameraman had set up eight lights, my interviewee fainted. I really liked the cameraman but never used him again.

So while the camera crew sets the stage, I'm stuck with a person who wants desperately to know what I'm going to ask. Most of the time, I don't have precise questions anyway. I prefer to listen to what they have to say and follow on from there. That's when you usually get the best answers. And the best answers are almost always the first answers.

If you go over them before the camera rolls they're never as good. The interviewee keeps thinking "What was it I said the first time that was so brilliant?" I never—I repeat never—tell the interviewees what I want them to say. If I do an interview that lasts over thirty minutes, it's a rarity. Cameramen have told me of interviews that go on for hours until the producer is satisfied.

I won't forget shooting an interview inside the pickup in downtown Manhattan during a heavy rain. Ned wasn't there for some reason, so I had a fill-in producer. My subject's name was Anne. She sold blinds on the seventh floor of Bloomingdales on sixty-first and Lexington.

Anne was in her mid-sixties and had always wanted to be a standup comedian. She had performed in a few New York and Long Island nightclubs, apparently with some good reviews. We had a camera crew shoot one of her performances and were shocked to discover that most of it was unusable on morning TV. It was too risqué, too dirty. I was shocked to hear such crudeness coming out of this grandmother's mouth.

I interviewed her first at her work. I liked Anne. It was fun to see how excited she was. How many sixty-somethings find themselves with a new exciting life making people laugh and featured on national TV? She was one of those touchy-feely kinds of people— touching my leg or my arm even while I interviewed her. I didn't think anything of it.

We did the bulk of the interview with me driving round and round the block in Midtown in a heavy rain. Because the windows were covered in gel it was impossible to open them to stick my hand out to make a right turn. So we kept going round and round to the left. I was sweating so hard I could barely see through the windows and of course the windshield wipers were useless. The crew was monitoring our interview in the rain from the back of the pickup.

It seemed that the longer the damn interview went, the closer the woman moved toward me until she was practically sitting on my lap. I couldn't scoot any closer to the door without falling out. Then she kissed me, a big wet kiss. I was struck dumb. I couldn't say anything. The crew didn't know what was going on or at least pretended not to know. I was in hell.

How can you be rude to a sixty-five-year-old lady who is feeling her oats. It was one more reason why I hated the damn truck. There I was, going round and round in a blinding storm getting molested by a not-so-sweet old lady. I've always thought the crew in the back knew what was going on and enjoyed it. I enjoyed that they were all wet.

Then there was Randall "Tex" Cobb. He was the motorcyclist from Hell in the movie *Raising Arizona*. He was also the transvestite who scared the hell out of Chevy Chase in *Fletch Lives*. He was big, ugly, and scary. Tex was the heavyweight boxer who got beat up so bad by Larry Holmes, the "Easton Assassin," that Howard Cosell said he would never announce a broadcast fight again. It was also the end of Cobb's fighting career, but the beginning of a new one in the movies and as a record promoter in Nashville.

The day we found Tex he was sitting on a bench with his son and dog in front of his house in a low-rent Nashville neighborhood.

When we were walking up to meet him we could hear him tell his son, "Here come the niggers." We were all thinking "Holy shit, what have we got ourselves into? The subject of our story is an out-and-out racist!"

As it turned out Tex was not such a racist, more an odd guy with a provocative sense of humor. He called everyone "nigger" except African Americans. To them, he was semi-deferential. Tex had become a fixture in Nashville, everyone knew him. His business as a record promoter seemed to be going quite well. After spending a couple days with him I could understand why.

We were there when he dropped in to see a singer-wannabe. Tex walked around behind the guy who was sitting in his office chair. The guy weighed well over 200 pounds. Tex grabbed him in a bear hug and started squeezing as he was asking the guy if he was going to agree to have Tex be his agent. Maybe it was set up for us, but I got the feeling the Tex manhandled everyone. I know he did me.

I remember in particular the interview with Tex in the pickup. We were in a thunderstorm just outside the approach runway for small, private aircraft at the Nashville Airport. I have spent too much time in small planes and I'm not a big fan of their safety record. They were landing and taking off directly over where we were parked in very low visibility. One small miscalculation and we would have been toast.

It was hot and humid. Again, because the pickup's windows had gels on them we couldn't open them and let in a little breeze. We had the klieg lights turned on for the interview, which added considerably to the heat.

The crew van was parked behind us where the soundman listened to the interview. Every minute or two Tex would reach over and grab me in a headlock and then give me a very vigorous head rub. It was not the kind of dignified position a network correspondent ought to be in. Every few minutes the soundman would come running up to see if I was okay. I was sure the crew was in the van laughing their heads off.

A postscript: "Tex" went back to school to get his degree. He graduated from Temple University magna cum laude. Not bad.

I may have mentioned that I hated the pickup. It hated me back. For me it became the "anti-Christ." On more than one occasion while I was at the wheel driving along a highway, straight as far as the eye could see, it suddenly veered off the road. I had to struggle with all my might to keep from turning over. This sort of thing happened all the time. The pickup became Stephen King's "Christine," the car.

One night I was driving back to the hotel on a dark night from a shoot near Helena, Montana, when the side rearview mirror started banging against the door. It was spooky. Finally I pulled off the side of the road to see if I could tighten the mirror. But it was as tight as could be. When I started driving the pickup again, the mirror starting banging against the door again. I was relieved when another car followed me into town.

Then there were the love letters. More than once, while the pickup was parked outside a café, I would return to find love letters on the windshield, but not for me. They were for the damn pickup. I remember once when we were parked outside a restaurant in Jackson Hole, Wyoming, the windshield got three love letters. Things like "you're so cute." I was not impressed.

It was only fitting that when we finally ended the series, with a bang, the soundman almost got flattened. The explosion was all done through the magic of a good director and digital technology.

The only thing we needed to add was actual parts and tires flying through the air. To accomplish that, Ned, the producer, who is larger than Tex Cobb, picked up a tire and tossed it in front of the camera. It bounced the wrong way and practically knocked out the soundman.

I'm not sure Ned ever fully realized how much I hated the pickup, although I told him enough. After *Today* cancelled our series, Ned bought the truck and drove it around Los Angeles. That gives you some idea of how crazy Ned was and remains.

A couple of years later he moved to Albuquerque and took the pickup with him. Every time I would drop in and see the truck parked out front of his home I'd get a sick feeling in my stomach. I have a big picture he sent me with him standing beside the pickup all decked out in Christmas lights. It's in the closet.

My producer Ned Judge checking out a shot in the monitor

The camera crew getting shots from the back of the pickup and recording my interview inside

Figuring out where we were going to go next with the damn pickup

BACK HOME AGAIN

I went back home for my fifty-fifth Hurricane High School senior class reunion. It was at the bottom of a mountain peak called Molly's Nipple, so named because it looks like Molly's Nipple. It was the first reunion since my twentieth.

When I stopped at a supermarket in Hurricane to get directions, the clerk said she knew there was a reunion in a clubhouse out of town. I said, "Clubhouse" Does that mean they serve alcohol?" She replied, "Do you know where you are? No." I'm not a big drinker but when I find I can't have a drink, it becomes an obsession.

I remember once when my producer Ned Judge and I found out we were in a dry county in Texas, we drove eighty miles to get a cold beer. I headed straight for the beer section of the market. I bought a tall can, parked under a tree and gulped it down. Then I chewed a package of gum.

I was reluctant to attend the reunion because I was afraid that when I looked at my classmates, I'd see how old I actually look. I'm pretty good at fooling myself. The person I see in the mirror is a much younger person than those I went to school with. Maybe everyone feels the same way. Almost all my old mates have retired and seem to enjoy it. I can't imagine. I've never thought about retirement, other than to tell myself that when I do, I'll die.

My wife tells me, and my three kids agree, that I have never grown up and I've managed to convince myself that I've not grown older. I have more aches for sure. But it's always a crushing setback when I realize I'm as old as that old guy over there. The last few years of my career, I would actually get excited when the interviewee was older than the interviewer, me.

The reunion wasn't as painful as I expected. Only two classmates were connected to oxygen. Most looked good for their age, probably better than me. It was actually a pleasant evening, good to see old friends, although there were far more that I barely knew. The majority of the fifty-seven seniors who still survived had spent their lives in Southern Utah or returned to retire. It has become a retirement mecca.

I still felt that I didn't belong, but I've come to realize that it may have more to do with me than them. My views have changed quite dramatically since I left high school. Even though I'd grown up in a conservative family, along the way I've become quite liberal. In fact I promised my kids I would not get more conservative as I got older. It's a promise I've kept. I also promised myself that I would not discuss religion or politics at the reunion. I knew I would be greatly outnumbered.

I no longer consider myself a Mormon and I'm sure that if they knew, my former classmates would think less of me. From what I could tell, virtually all my classmates had stayed in the bosom of the Church. They were married "for time and all eternity" in the temple, served missions, and proudly supported their children on missions.

There were only three or four who didn't mention church service in their yearbook biographies. Many said the Church had been the best part of their lives. I'm sure they would object to this characterization and it may be unfair, but it seemed that some wore their church-work like a badge of honor. I think in Southern Utah, and any place where one religion is so dominant, it becomes as much a lifestyle as a creed to live by.

I knew from their Facebook postings that they are Republicans. That comes as no surprise. I did a story about the trend years ago. Southern Utah, as with most of the Rocky Mountain West, is much more conservative today than it was when I lived there. Tens of thousands have immigrated from Orange County, California. They moved here because they knew it was Mormon and conservative. They moved "backwards to the future," to a place where gays, transgenders, and legal marijuana are still considered by many as products of a too-lenient society.

I knew also, from Facebook, that they voted for Donald Trump. They would post things like "Share if you love our president." It continues to baffle me that people of faith elected him president. I cannot find one moral value in Trump that can be found in the bible or Book of Mormon. When I asked why, the answer was, "Well, he's better than Hillary," which told me they watched Fox News almost exclusively.

I did an experiment during the 2016 campaign where I tuned into Fox News fifteen times over a two-day period. Fourteen of those times, the story was about Hillary Clinton's emails. One time the anchor raised his arms in the air and exclaimed, "I think we've really got her this time.!" If you watch Fox, you'll think that Trump is doing great. His supporters deride "fake news" but when I look at the websites they promote, they're almost all "fake news," sponsored by conservative organizations. Actually I don't remember the phrase "fake news' until the newly elected president came along. If we end up believing only the news we agree with, and that which we don't agree with is "fake," our democracy is in trouble.

Those I spoke with think the world was a much safer and better place when we were in high school. It didn't seem safer at the time.

I can remember hiding under the desk at school during those atomic bomb drills.

I don't think it was a better time back then, but I don't know. I grew up in blissful ignorance. I didn't know of any gay people when I was in high school, although chances are some of my classmates were gay and lived in fear that we might find out. I don't know whether I was a racist or not because I didn't know any African Americans. I didn't realize women were second class citizens, probably because my mom wasn't, but I rarely heard of women aspiring to become lawyers or doctors or professors.

The hot topic in Southern Utah is much the same as it was when I was growing up—the arrogant, overreaching federal government. In this case, the Bears Ears National Monument. Locals think it restricts access to public land, especially where they want to drive their four-wheelers. And they think it forecloses the possibility of new industry, especially mining.

There's no question the government can be arbitrary and arrogant, but if the local leaders in Southern Utah had their way, Southern Utah would be a different place. The state and counties have spent millions and millions of dollars over the years fighting federal regulations that prohibit power plants and coal and uranium mines.

I've never seen a mining operation that don't leave scars and a power plant that didn't emit pollution. And no matter what they say, Southern Utah is not farming or grazing country. I've seen the farms in Iowa and Nebraska, and the ranches in Texas and Montana. There's a reason why they haven't been selected as Wilderness Areas.

I still think that the feds can be heavy handed, that they've been guilty of overreach, but I'm convinced that if it hadn't been for the special protection they've bestowed on Southern Utah, it would not be nearly as spectacular and pristine as it is today. I imagine my view could cause me even more discomfort the next time I'm in Southern Utah. But you know, I'm old enough, I can make up my own mind.

I visited Virgin, which now has a population of 600. My aunt's home, which must be about a hundred years old, is for sale for $600,000. That may be more than the combined worth of Virgin when I lived there. There are new roads and street signs, a town park next to the new church. Amazingly to me, there are even plans to build a new motel.

Everything around Virgin seems prosperous. There's a new subdivision just outside of town, of million dollar homes with spectacular views. The old church where I was the pianist (we didn't have an organ) now has a new wooden façade and looks so much better than when I was there. The two-room school, where sixteen of us comprised the fourth, fifth and sixth grades, is in good repair. It's now the city office.

My mom and dad's business is now a used book store and post office. It seems an odd business to have on a highway leading to a national park. There are still no stop signs on the main road, so people don't have time to slow down before they've passed Virgin.

When I visited the bookstore, I found a picture of my dad standing in a good-sized room, knee-deep in books. I had completely forgotten his passion for reading. During much of my career I rarely read books, but about ten years ago I suddenly started reading as if there is no tomorrow. One rare, happy example where I became more like my father.

The Virgin cemetery has been upgraded. It no longer looks like a run-down boot hill. It looks like a spruced-up boot hill. I had a new headstone installed, made out of petrified red rock, along with a bench that says "In loving memory of Queenie and Dad." I wonder what they would think of me now and how I view my hometown. I'm sure mom would say, "Don't you dare say that."

Drinking kava with the prime minister in Vanuatu.

Vanuatu crew – Kathleen deLaski, me, soundwoman Kelly Watt, cameraman Jim Watt, producer Houston Simmons. Actually Kelly and Jim weren't quite married. They took care of that in Hawaii on their way home.

My mentor and all around brilliant producer, Ray Farkas. You can't
see them but he's wearing tennis shorts. It's about all he ever wore.
His way of saying "I do it my way."

My producer for many stories, home and abroad and my buddy,
Trent Harris

With Mr. Likey, the watch maker who transformed into the
conductor of the Marshall Missouri Philharmonic. The producer
taking the picture is Linda Ellman, one of the best. The story won
an Emmy.

With producer Tom Keenan and Mexican crew, chasing pollution in
Mexico City.

Shooting a rare on-camera standup in daylight. Most in Asia were shot at night because of the time difference with New York.

This was one ornery camel. I swear it tried to kill me.

With Chinese author and human rights activist Betty Bao Lord.

Paul Thiriot, The best cameraman I ever worked with and good friend. A Tom Brokaw favorite.

SCRIPTS

Writing for me is a pleasurable, painful experience. I dread it but I can hardly wait to sit down to it. The best scripts always take the least time. On average it takes me about an hour to write two minutes. It's not fun to be around me when I'm in the zone. When I come out of it, my producer and I go through the script and iron out our differences. I prefer to have the producer do the negotiating with the higher-ups because (I'm confessing here) I take it too personally. When I was in local news I would stand outside the control room even if it was after the last show of the day, to confront the show producer if my script had been changed and no one talked to me about it. The script is mine. I once had a producer in Boston who would send me a new script with her changes after I first sent her mine. Finally after nine different scripts I blew my top and never worked with her again, even though she was quite a good producer.

The scripts that follow are several years apart, and so the formats are not the same.

This was in 1986 for the NBC News magazine show called *1986*.

NO PLACE LIKE NOME   10:50

SEVERSON

This is a story about an Eskimo named Joe, a Millionaire named Jim, a governor named Bill, a newshound named Nancy, and a dog named Walter Cronkite. It's a story about where they live, a place called Nome, Alaska, which may be as much a state of mind as it is a small spot on the edge of the map.

Singer w/music over Nome scenics
"I'm living in Nome, Alaska because this is the last frontier"

SEVERSON
In case you haven't been to Nome, it's home to about 3700 people. None of them ended up here by accident. Nome is about as far West as West goes before it becomes East. You either come here on purpose or you had too much to drink at the last airport.

Drunken visitor:
"Nome is where the Nomers go. (laughs) Great town. Been one big party since we got here yesterday"

SEVERSON
There's a saying around here. If you don't believe hell freezes over, you've never been to Nome. January is like living on the dark side of the moon and you might as well be on the moon. There's a thousand miles of wilderness between Nome and the nearest city.

Nome gold panner: with cold winter scenes
"Winters are long but the summers are very intense."

SEVERSON

Truth is Nome is just about the end of the line. You can't drive there from here. Roads running out of town simply run out. If you go across the Bering Strait 137 miles you'll end up in Siberia. Rumor here is it's worse there. Communists are one thing you don't find in Nome. What you will find here are capitalists with a capital C as in Jim West.

JIM WEST

"What you first start out in life you get a rubber band. You don't buy it, you pick it up off the floor. You put that rubber band around your money and if you wake up in the morning, and there's no money in it you know you're broke. So you let that rubber band power your book keeping for you."

SEVERSON

Jim West is honest about his reason for living. It's to make money.

JIM WEST

"If I couldn't make money living in Nome, Alaska I'd just give up. It's so easy to make money I could fall out that door and make money."

SEVERSON

It's greed that motivates Jim West and he is highly motivated. For a start he owns the Board of Trade saloon, which is Nome's oldest and roughest bar.

Loud music with partying:

"Do you want me to take my pants off. No don't take your pants off."

JIM WEST

Lucky "We're renting our cars from you." JIM "You're renting your cars from me." Lucky "We're renting our apartments from you". "You're renting your apartment from me. "And if you go out on a boat you'll be renting the boat from me."

SEVERSON

If 'free enterprise' is the lifeblood of America it is the aphrodisiac of Nome. Always have been. It's why there is a Nome. Back at the turn of the century they discovered gold here.

JIM WEST

"Have a look at the little nuggets on that. That's what made Nome go completely wild, when they found that gold."

Scenes of gold mining

SEVERSON

At one point, there were 40,000 gold miners in Nome. Now 86 years later there are machines, big machines chewing up the permafrost. Last year this gold dredger near the heart of town dredged up about 6 million dollars in gold. But most operations around here are not nearly so ambitious. Take a walk along the Nome beach and you will see all sort of small time operators and big time dreamers.

Gold miner

"There's some pretty good size flakes, not big one but." Lucky "How long did it take you to get that much? The way we work probably 12 hours, something like that."

SEVERSON

So it took four men 12 hours each to earn a total of about 400 dollars. At that rate, if they save all their money, they'll be millionaires sometime around the end of the 21st century.

Unidentified man speaking Taiwanese

SEVERSON
Now Nome is discovering a new kind of gold, like the kind the tourists bring in. This tour from Taiwan can't quite get over these crazy Americans. Then after a while the craziness seems to be catching. It's not gold that brought Nancy McBride to Nome. She came 8 years ago and she has no intention of leaving.

NANCY MCBRIDE
This is probably one of the last outposts of the true spirit of the frontier. You gotta be pretty much independent.

SEVERSON
Nancy is publisher of the Nome Nugget, Alaska's oldest newspaper. It's not the New York Times nor is it the National Enquirer. Sometimes it's not too clear who is in charge here. Nancy, or her star reporter Walter Cronkite.

Walter leaving his mark

NANCY MCBRIDE
He gives his editorial opinion. Walter is our Nugget newshound. He's always on the trail of a good story. Lucky "I imagine there are a lot of good stories around here aren't there." Yes there are, especially around Iditarod. Actually he's interviewed the lead dog.

SEVERSON
As Walter will tell you, the Iditarod is the media event of the year. It is the grueling 1100 mile dogsled race that ends up like everything else, in Nome. Everybody who is anybody shows up for the Iditarod festivities.

Governor Sheffield hitting a gold ball on the ice

SEVERSON
Big wigs like Alaska governor Bill Sheffield. Politicians like to come to Nome because having fun here is serious business, like playing Ice Golf on the frozen Bering Sea. The governor was up for re-election.

Drunken Native: "I always remember you in my heart." Ok"

SEVERSON
The governor was also up for the 4th of July festivities (long pause) and for the egg run, which he lost. It turns out the governor may have spent too much time doing serious business in Nome. He also lost his bid for re-election.

Joe fishing through the ice

SEVERSON
For the past 75 years, Joe Kucherick has watched politicians and gold miners come and go. For him, nothing has changed. For him Nome is normal. He's never been anywhere else. Every year he chips through the ice on the Bering Sea, fishes for Tomcod and traps Alaskan King Crab. Considering that his mother always spoke one native language, 'Fish River', and his father another, 'Lower Yukon', Joe speaks pretty good English. And he remembers back in 1923 when he and his family saw their very first airplane.

JOE KUCHERICK
I looked at the airplane, and I looked at my mother. Her mouth was open, just completely open, looking at that airplane.

SEVERSON

It turned out the plane was out of gas, and it crash landed right in front of their tent. They saved the pilot's life.

JOE KUCHERICK

There was nothing wrong with that pilot. He didn't get hurt because that plane was so slow. The first ones to come along were real slow.

SEVERSON

Over the years Joe saw more and more planes land in Nome safely bringing Whiteman and their culture. But not all of what they brought has been good for the Eskimos.

Sad scenes of drunken natives

SEVERSON

This is not an unusual picture for Nome. You can find tales of drunkenness and craziness in every edition of the Nome Nugget.

SEVERSON STANDUP

Take the police report. July 2nd, police were notified that an intoxicated person was jumping out into the road at trucks and almost caused an accident. The news is not all humorous. Nome has a serious alcoholism problem.

SEVERSON

Under the glare of the midnight sun and during the long winter darkness, cops spend most of the time saving drunks from each other and from themselves. Nome has more than its' share of bars and one of the most notorious is Jim West's Board of Trade Saloon, which is conveniently right next door to his ivory shop.

Scenes inside saloon:

Eskimo lady blows a kiss at the camera and says "I love you."

SEVERSON

One Whiteman import that has been good for the Eskimo is the reindeer, like Sheldon, he was named after the government man who first introduced the reindeer to Alaska. Sheldon takes kids for rides. If Sheldon doesn't improve his attitude he may end up like these reindeer (pause) that are grown like cattle, (pause) rounded up (pause) and dehorned.

Koreans disembarking from plane

It's what's in the horns that bring Koreans to Nome. These two men come with anxious anticipation and about $40,000 dollars. They are reluctant to admit it but many of their countrymen believe that ground-up reindeer horns improve sexual activity.

Korean through interpreter says
"It's good for good health"

SEVERSON

Cliff Huawana owns the reindeer herd. He may not believe in horn dust the way the Koreans do, but at 30 dollars a pound he'll believe in almost anything.

CLIFF HUSWANA

After I get the money, I smile a little bit. Lucky: Do you think it works. Cliff: No it don't work. I've tried it.

Korean through an interpreter

Lucky: " Does it have anything to do with the sex life? Does it make their sex life more interesting?" Korean" "Maybe, I don't know, exactly."

CLIFF HUSWANA

Lucky: "It's part of their religion. It's not part of your religion?"
Cliff: "No, no, I'm a Lutheran."

SEVERSON

So if you're searching for something to believe in, or for gold or adventure, you're tired of being a number and you feel there's no place to go, there's no place like Nome. ls

For *Religion & Ethics Newsweekly* May 2011.

VOODOO

WALK TO THE CEMETERY

SEVERSON
It's about midnight, the first of November, known in the world of voodoo as 'The Day of the Dead' – a time to visit a cemetery and the spirits of those who have passed on. This is New Orleans, and the voodoo priestess leading the celebration is Sallie Anne Glassman.

SALLIE ANNE GLASSMAN Sound on tape SOT 02 59 15
We all have loved ones who have passed, and what a comfort to be able to visit with them, and to know that they are there with you and to be able to tell them that you love them and know that the message is received, and to just be in their presence again. It's a tremendous comfort.

SEVERSON
It had been a long evening, starting with the ritual dancing, the beat of the drums, Sallie Anne in her element. There are other Voodoo priestesses in New Orleans, but she is one of the most popular, one of the most unlikely – a Jewish girl from Maine, who says she knew as a child that there was something different about her.

SALLIE ANNE GLASSMAN SOT 02 39 10
I started to put things together and realized that particularly adults were a little taken aback by me and they really seemed a little afraid of me, and then I started realizing that I knew more about them than they were telling me…

SEVERSON

Those outside the Voodoo realm seem to have always been afraid of it. She thinks she knows why.

SALLIE ANNE GLASSMAN SOT AFTER 02 40 29

I think when you ask questions about why Voodoo is so vilified, the clearest answer that I can give you is that Voodoo recognizes an invisible world of great power and of spiritual power and that the surface reality is really just the surface of things. There is a vaster more beautiful world going on inside, throughout, above, beyond, within, all of that.

SEVERSON

There are several varieties of Voodoo that share some common characteristics, such as, a majority of the practitioners are women, and many are Catholic. Martha Ward, is a Professor of Anthropology at the University of New Orleans. She wrote a book on the queen priestess of them all, who was actually two women, a mother and daughter, each known as Marie Laveau.

MARTHA WARD SOT 02 17 20

The great voodoo practitioners and leaders of the 18th and 19th centuries came out of Catholicism. They were good Catholics. The Leveaus are a great example of this. They were married and buried within the Catholic traditions. They attended mass.

SEVERSON

And there are other similarities, she says.

MARTHA WARD SOT 02 18 15

The Catholics have a lot of saints....They lose something, they have a saint for losing things. They have a saint for battered women, Saint Freda, they have a saint for, you want your crops to flourish, you want your voyages to be safe, whatever you want, there's a saint that will specifically help you…

SEVERSON
In voodoo, they're called spirits, the spirits of ancestors.

SALLIE ANNE GLASSMAN SOT throughout 02 50 48
There are all these myriad spirits that are really intermediaries, and first I should say there is a supreme deity in voodoo; there is a God called Bonju. But in between God and humanity are these thousands of little spirits ….Maybe one time you're possessed by Ogoo, the warrior spirit….and another time you're possessed by Azilee Freda, and you see the world through rose colored glasses.

KAREN JEFFRIES SOT 1 53 53
When I look at voodoo, I see this is a group of spirits who are there to help us in everyday life.

SEVERSON
Karen Jefferies moved to New Orleans after divorcing her husband, a Lutheran minister. She says she grew up in a fundamentalist Christian home.

KAREN JEFFRIES SOT 1 53 53
Christ is still my foundation of spirituality, but then I find that voodoo acknowledges an additional spiritual realm.

SEVERSON
She now owns a bed and breakfast in the French Quarter.

KAREN JEFFRIES SOT 1 51 52
Shortly after I purchased this house I heard about a voodoo ceremony for the protection against hurricanes….so I went out of curiosity…. so I had like a traditional church, native American,

Pentecostalism. It was really fascinating to me and so I ended up going back to all the bigger ceremonies that Sallie Anne Glassman would hold.

SEVERSON
As the celebration of 'The Day of the Dead' danced on, there seemed to be a discernable change in Sallie Anne's countenance.

SALLIE ANNE GLASSMAN SOT 02 46 24
There are different levels of possession that a person can experience and when I go into that kind of a state I have no idea what's happened. I just know that when I come out of it people are looking at me funny and I'm in a different place than I was before.

SEVERSON
Sallie Anne says she has been accused of casting spells on people, something she says she wouldn't do even if she could. She says using black magic can be risky business. Professor Ward says cursing someone in voodoo, such as sticking pins in dolls, is not something to fool around with.

MARTHA WARD SOT 02 35 21
All religions are used that way, period, full stop. I've done it and you've done it. Have you ever cursed somebody?….We're all capable of bringing mild to big curses on others. In voodoo what goes around comes around, and if I curse you, I'll get fixed.

SEVERSON
She describes voodoo as a religion that can be shared with other religions. In New Orleans, back in the early 1800s, voodoo was the widely accepted religion among slaves, until it was seen as threatening.

SALLIE ANNE GLASSMAN SOT 02 41 38

If you were a slave living in captivity and hard labor and your prospects were certainly very limited, this belief in an invisible world of great spiritual power will certainly be empowering, and if you were a slave owner intent on keeping a people down, oppressing them, and this belief would be terrifying and disturbing and instead of saying the institution of slavery was this terrible evil, it was much easier to say these people are evil and we're just keeping them contained.

MARTHA WARD SOT 2 27 58
They said slave rebellions. Like the same way we say crime. They were terrified…..Voodoo was from, went from being an ordinary accepted thing, the way people now take Baptists, went from being that to a demonized, stigmatized, racialized, sexualized white ideology.

SEVERSON
Sallie Anne says she knows what it's like to be called evil

SALLIE ANNE GLASSMAN SOT 03 15 24
And I'll say to them how can you possibly think that it's alright to call me evil. How can you even think that? I've certainly been called a witch, sometimes a good witch, sometimes a bad witch. I'm not a witch. I'm just a person like anybody else.

SEVERSON
But she's not just anybody else when she walks through the neighborhood. Everyone seems to know and like her. Even the dog that growls at everyone, whimpers around Sallie Anne.

SALLIE ANNE GLASSMAN SOT 03 03 25
Being a priestess is a demanding job and I say job lightly because it doesn't pay.

…people come to me and need things, they need help…..I'll try to be an intermediary between these individuals and help them to…those crossroads where human prayer meets spiritual presence and do all kinds of healings.

SEVERSON
She says she experienced first hand the power of healing when she was diagnosed with cancer at 49. Her mom died of cancer when she was 49.

SALLIE ANNE GLASSMAN SOT 03 10 19
I focused on, this is my chance to absolutely prove to myself the power of healings, and healing belief, so I made it go away. I made the tumor go away in 4 days.

MARTHA WARD SOT after 02 18 11
Sally has worked tirelessly here in the community. She makes the streets safer because that's something the spirits can do if we ask them, make our streets and neighborhoods safe. Help people put on roofs after Katrina.

SEVERSON
The priestess says the spirits have always protected New Orleans from Hurricanes, and Katrina would have been worse if the spirits hadn't intervened.

SALLIE ANNE GLASSMAN SOT after 03 007 40
As it happened, Katrina did not hit us over the head, it did go over the East and it did downgrade from a category 5 to a, I think it was a category three or lower when it hit, and it wasn't the hurricane that kicked our butts.///after 03 05 33 You have to spend a little time taking care of your environment or you're going to get hurt…

SEVERSON

Since Katrina, she has been working on a huge healing center, which is about to open, and a new community center. Still, she says, there are people who say it's not a good idea to have a voodoo priestess involved in such a public project.

SALLIE ANNE GLASSMAN SOT 02 43 38

But I always say to myself, you know, voodoo's ancestors endured slavery and captivity and they kept their beliefs alive....who am I to be upset over having to defend a practice, who am I to say I can't handle this.

SEVERSON

It seems improbable that voodoo will ever be widely regarded as anything but scary and dark, and perhaps a little misunderstood. ls

Final Brownsville Script

BROWNSVILLE REVIVAL

Script 4 Tape 7 070808 1 love Jesus, praise G-d. Hold your nose Kristine, we baptize you in the name of the Father, the Son and the Holy ghost.

NARRATION: Its a Friday night ritual at the Brownsville assembly of god church in Pensacola, Florida. for five years, believers and skeptics have been coming here to witness what some say is now the longest running spiritual revival in the u.s. in the 20th century. **Visitor**: Tape 5 51351 It's amazing. I've never seen anything like it in my life. Nothing can compare to it.

SEVERSON STANDUPPER (inter-cut with scenes from 1995) Here's what happened Father's day 1995. A guest preacher named Steve Hill was at the podium. He was nobody in particular, a missionary who had just returned from Russia. He was reportedly giving a powerful sermon when, according to witnesses, the Brownsville church was suddenly filled with a rush of air. Tape 13

Pastor Steve Hill sound on tape SOT 041503 1 happened to be the vessel that was there on Father's day that seemed to open up the floodgate.

Pastor John Kilpatrick SOT 060600 It was awesome. I never dreamed that it was possible to feel the presence of God like that.

NARRATION: It was pastor john Kilpatrick's congregation. he says the spirit was so strong it knocked him to the floor. if you look carefully, you can see him in the church video.

Pastor Kilpatrick SOT 060509 It's something that you can't contrive. It's something you can't plan. You can't fake it. I mean it's either here or its not. If it's not you know it.

NARRATION: So now, its written in bold letters on the church marquee-and people still line up before the doors open - over three million altogether, from all over the world.

VISITOR OUTSIDE CHURCH 051148 What have you heard about it? That there's a revival going on and God is moving.

NARRATION: The dictionary defines revival this way - "recovery as from depression. „and that is almost precisely the way it is viewed here, according to Michael Browne, head of the Brownsville school of ministry.

PASTOR HILL SOT God Steps down from heaven// gets hold of his people, shakes them up, turns them upside down and sends them out to touch a dying world. Revival starts with the church, spreads out through the society.

NARRATION: Randall Balmer is a religion professor at columbia university. he characterizes revival this way.

PASTOR KILPATRICK SOT 010823 The general characteristic for someone looking from the outside would be that people are affected by the Holy spirit, according to the theology of those leading the revival. There's a lot of emotional outpouring, a lot of enthusiasm and also religious conversions of various kinds, depending on how they're defined within that particular tradition.
NARRATION: Brownsville is the most recent example of a revival in america - but this country has a long history of awakenings.

PASTOR HILL SOT 011259 The revival tradition in America dates back to at least to the 1690s.//The next major focus for the revival was the Atlantic colonies in the 1730s, 1740s, a phenomenon known as the Great Awakening, that really kind of united all the colonists behind this religious revival or enthusiasm. //the most important and influential revival in American history is what historians call the Second Great Awakening that took place roughly from the 1790 through the 1830s.

NARRATION: What is generally known as the third awakening or the azusa street revival grew out of a small house in los angeles at the beginning of the 20th century. it was the beginning of the modern pentecostal movement in the united states, which now claims about 20-million followers.

ORGAN MUSIC
NARRATION: It's difficult not to get into the spirit of things at brownsvlle. almost impossible to stand still. there is a minister of music here, lindell cooley, and he knows what connects people.

Lindell Cooley: SOT 061915 They're walking in// from different attitudes, different religious experiences, some without any religious experiences. And, the music is a kind of bridge. Its brings people from this point to this point.

Steve Hill preaching 130248 Religion will damn you friend. Religion is hanging around the cross. Christianity is getting on the cross.

NARRATION: After pastor hill, a self-proclaimed reformed drug pusher, gives one of his sermons, which can last an hour and a half, it's not easy to remain unmoved.

Pastor Kilpatrick SOT 061345 1 can tell you unequivocally that I would not, I would not sit here in this church and let a man get up and whip people in their emotions. I hate that. I won't do it myself and I'm not gonna let somebody else do it.

NARRATION: For those familiar with more restrained church worship, pentecostal services may seem a bit more exuberant.

Pastor Browne: Voice over VO 022000 People jumping, shouting, dancing, celebrating, that's who we are.

Pastor Hill: SOT TO VO 050402 1 don't focus in on those people. I just look at that and say, wow, that message really touched his heart. 050420 It's an awesome thing for a person to get on his knees and repent.

PEOPLE SPEAKING IN TONGUES

NARRATION: People speak in tongues, they sometimes can't understand themselves. for pentecostals, this is one of the most important signs of g-d's presence.

Kilpatrick: VO 060709 Speaking in tongues is an experience that you can trace all the way back to the book of Acts It's a glorious experience.

Pastor Hill: VO 130104 When I give this altar call, you're gonna come down here quick.

NARRATION: sinners are saved at the altar.

VO to SOT Pastor Hill They're prostrating themselves before G-d saying, G-d take my life// You've pretty much gotten rid of most of the pride in your life when you do that in front of thousands of people.

NARRATION: Along the way, the brownsville revival, has generated some controversy.

Pastor Browne: SOT Browne 020818 You can have controversy without revival, but you cannot have revival without controversy.

Pastor Hill: VO Walking 040126 This is just a place for me to come and get a grip, study the word, pray.

NARRATION: Pastors hill and kilpatrick have been criticized for moving their homes out of town to get away from the adoring crowds. and there have been some accusations that they have gotten rich from expanded church collections, and video and c-d sales. they deny the criticism and say their salaries have only increased slightly. the revival is now an approved member of the evangelical council for financial accountability.

Pastor Hill: SOT 040604 I've become accustomed to criticism. And, anytime you're gonna do anything you're gonna be criticized for it when it comes to evangelical preaching.

NARRATION: But the most criticism is about the nature of the revival itself -as in, how much good does it do in the long haul.

Pastor Hill: SOT 041708 You know what the critics say. A moment of emotionalism and then it goes away// Personally it doesn't make any difference if a person falls backwards, if he shakes, if he jumps up and down like he's on a pogo stick, or twirls like a top. I wanna know down the road has his life been changed.

Pastor Kilpatrick: SOT 061728 But the people of the world that's been living for the Devil, they see this and they come here and they say, My G-d, there's something there. And they start getting help. We started a bible school here. We've started discipleship classes. **Pastor Browne** riding in golf cart describing student body

394

NARRATION: They started an intensive revival school for missionaries in 1997 with about 120 students. today there are almost 1200 from all over the world.

Pastor Browne: SOT to VO 020502 1 think revival doesn't have to be happening in the church walls. It goes out into the streets and that's what we're seeing, with this school, especially.// Instead of keeping the revival in the church building, which is what we do, we're taking it out to the streets.

Student: SOT p7 What am I gonna do? I'm gonna be a missionary, but I don't know to which country yet.

NARRATION: But revivals have a way of coming and going, and there are signs that this one may be going.

LINES OUTSIDE CHURCH TWO YEARS AGO
NARRATION: A couple of years ago, people starting lining up for services the day before. today the auditorium built for the overflow crowd is usually empty.

Pastor Hill showing a tape of Awake America.

NARRATION: And evangelist hill is looking to move to a new location near an international airport to take his 'awake crusade' on the road.

Pastor Hill: SOT 042439 1 am leaving because God has spoken to me and said that my segment of time at this revival is over, that it's time for me to reach out and work with other churches.

NARRATION: THE PEOPLE ARE STILL COMING, TWO OR THREE THOUSAND A NIGHT, THREE NIGHTS A WEEK.

Pastor BrownE: SOT 020958 The phenomenon known as the Brownsville revival, which at its peak had people standing in line 12 hours to get in, some of that is certainly ebbing. The spiritual work within it is intensifying and growing and the fires of revival are getting hotter.

Baptism 071531 To me this is just the most awesome thing in the world, and I thank Him. (Three ministers watching and smiling)

NARRATION: The true test of a revival is the lasting effect it will have on the people who have experienced it - the lives it has changed. the people here, the believers, anyway, are convinced that the brownsville revival will stand the test of time. is

For *Religion & Ethics Newsweekly* 9/13/16 (FINAL).

NADIA BOLZ-WEBER SCRIPT

PASTOR NADIA BOLZ-WEBER (2012 ELCA Youth Gathering):
My name is Nadia Bolz-Weber. I am a pastor in the Evangelical Lutheran Church in America. Maybe you've heard of that?

LUCKY SEVERSON, Correspondent:
It's been said that this tattoo-adorned pastor is trying to reinvent the idea of church. She would argue that she has simply rediscovered it.

PASTOR NADIA BOLZ-WEBER:
So much of spirituality is about sort of sanding ourselves down, you know, smoothing ourselves out so that we're nice and shiny, but the fact is, is that I think the jagged edges of our humanity are what actually connect us to God and to one another.

SEVERSON:
Her church in Denver is called The House for All Sinners and Saints. Like its pastor, this is not a typical congregation. Take Stuart Sanks. He was one of the earliest members, a drag queen known here as The Minister of Fabulousness.

STUART SANKS, Congregant:
I don't have to check any piece of myself at the door, I can bring all of me, my wild socks and shoes, and you know, funny t-shirts, and earrings, and whatever. You know, I can bring all of that stuff with me. Just like people can bring their questions and their doubt and their unbelief.

SEVERSON:
Stuart left his old church because he felt marginalized by the members.

BOLZ-WEBER:
They want to be seen as accepting, so they're like 'We'll love anyone who comes to us' but then someone who's magnificent like Stuart shows up, and he's like 'Hey, I might want to help run the kids program.' They're like 'well we can't allow that.'

SEVERSON:
Carina DuHadway had been active in church for most of her life, until she felt like an outcast when she announced she was gay. And then she discovered The House.

CARINA DuHADWAY, Congregant:
Finding this church was pretty, um, I don't know, (*fortuitous?*) I guess fortuitous, yeah, I was in a really, kind of, place where I was very despondent and was ready to leave the church.

SEVERSON:
At first, Lorissa Brunk a working mom with three kids, felt very uncomfortable at The House.

LORISSA BRUNK, Congregant:
It blew me away. I just, I had just never experienced anything like it, the mix of the kind of the recovery, truth telling, honesty. I would look across the room and think 'God is looking at me' and it changed me.

(NATURAL SOUND: sound, Pastor Nadia Bolz-Weber: "The Lord be with you…")

SEVERSON:

Nadia Bolz-Weber has given speeches all over the world. Written two New York Times best-selling books. Her most recent is called *Accidental Saints, Finding God In All The Wrong People*. For thousands of fans, believers, the pastor has become a religious icon, but she says her parishioners are better Christians than she is.

BOLZ-WEBER:
You know, I do admit some fairly inelegant things about myself in my preaching and in my books. But for me, there's a purpose in it, and it's to sort of create a space around me that other people can step into to maybe safely consider that thing for themselves.

Church video: "My name's Badger…Bethany…Laurel. I'm Jim, and I am the church regardless of my sexuality…")

SEVERSON:
Approximately a third of her congregation of about 350 are in the LGBTQ community, but not all.

STEPHEN LUDWIG, Congregant:
The joke around the congregation is I'm the token straight white corporate guy.

SEVERSON:
Stephen Ludwig is a vice president of a Fortune 500 marketing firm. He was raised a Catholic, but says he found that his old attitudes about sin and imperfection have changed since he started coming to The House.

LUDWIG:
So one of the things Nadia is willing to do is go first, meaning, she'll tell one on herself. By your pastor saying 'I'm an imperfect person,' and it gives me a huge space to go, I'm an imperfect

person, oh, you have depression, guess what, oh I have depression too, your family is messed up, oh I have pain in that too…

VISITING AN AMUSEMENT PARK ROLLER COASTER

SEVERSON:
The pastor thinks religion should be about community and supporting one another. Once a month, she joins her unusual congregation for a bonding outing like this one at an old time Denver amusement park.

SEVERSON:
She has graduated from drugs to physical fitness, a recovering alcoholic who was once a pagan and, oh yes, she was a standup comedian.

BOLZ-WEBER:
I literally have no idea how anybody manages to be a preacher without being a stand-up comic first.

SINGING IN CHURCH

SEVERSON:
But as a pastor, she is dead serious.

BOLZ-WEBER:
I am actually a very Orthodox Lutheran Theologian.

SEVERSON:
She says her congregation is religious but not spiritual.

PASTOR NADIA BOLZ-WEBER (2015 Why Christian? Conference):

"At House for All Sinners & Saints, the absolution we often use goes like this… 'God, who is gracious and merciful and slow to anger and abounding in steadfast love, loves you as you are. As a called and ordained minister of the Church of Christ, and by his authority, I declare to you the entire forgiveness of all of your sins. (pause) No one says that shit to me in yoga class." (huge laughter, clapping)

SEVERSON:
She was ordained a pastor in the ELCA, the most liberal of Lutheran denominations. But she was raised in a fundamentalist church, where her family attended three times a week.

BOLZ-WEBER:
It was a sin management program basically. I mean this church was really about saying, 'You know you're Christian if you avoid doing these naughty things.' So there's the naughty list. If you're good at not doing these things, that means you're a good Christian.

SEVERSON:
As a child, she suffered from Graves' Disease, an auto-immune disorder that caused her eyes to bulge.

BOLZ-WEBER:
There wasn't a day that went by that I wasn't sort of, I didn't have a barrage of insults and name calling thrown my way.

SEVERSON:
She grew up angry and became addicted to drugs and booze when she was fifteen, flunked out of Pepperdine University. Then of course there are the tattoos. Mostly biblical figures…Lazarus, Mary Magdalene….

BOLZ-WEBER She's announcing the Resurrection. And I love that she has her finger up, like, literally, 'guys, guys, I gotta tell you something.' You know? I love this.

SINGING HYMN

SEVERSON:
She's married, with a daughter and son and very protective of their privacy, as she is her congregation, which is why there are so few pictures of an actual service at The House while we were there.

SEVERSON:
What nudged Nadia Bolz-Weber on the path to the pulpit was when she did a eulogy for a comedian friend, who committed suicide. That was the beginning. She started a study group in her home. Went to The Iliff School of Theology. The rest, as they say, is history.

She has admirers from across the religious spectrum, like Father Bob Hart, with the St. Thomas Episcopal Church in Denver where her congregation held its services until it found something bigger in a former synagogue.

REV. BOB HART, St. Thomas Episcopal Church:
I've worshipped with them, and they're actually…it's a really engaging and stimulating and interesting bunch of people. I'm sold on it. You get that sense that they, they want to worship together but they probably wouldn't be, uh, in church on Sunday morning in a more conventional setting.

BOLZ-WEBER:
My spirituality has definitely come from these encounters with people I would never choose out of a catalogue, who have, who change me on a regular basis.

SEVERSON:

Sarah Adam started coming to The House because she didn't have to get up early, the service is in the afternoon and they serve snacks. But that's not why she stays.

SARAH ADAM, Congregant:

The people here are incredibly authentic, and real, and willing to talk about issues of domestic violence, and mental health issues, and things that are not going well in their lives, and that is such a unique way to come and worship together, because it's about acknowledging our brokenness, instead of pretending that everything is fine.

SEVERSON:

In the beginning, there was so much brokenness in The House, the pastor didn't know what to do when seemingly normal people started showing up. Then a young member spoke up.

BOLZ-WEBER:

He's like 'Listen, you know, as the young transgender kid who was welcomed into this community, I just want to go on record as saying, I'm glad there are people who look like my parents here now, because they love me in a way my parents can't.'

SEVERSON:

Stephen Ludwig is one of the straight members.

LUDWIG:

I'm blessed. I feel like they let me come here. It's not the other way around, right? So they're doing me a favor by letting me come, and so this idea like 'oh you're a gay-friendly church' – nonsense. It's like this is the way it should be.

BOLZ-WEBER:

That's the thing that is so puzzling to me about conservative Christianity in America, is that what I read from Jesus, are things like that…the first shall be last and the last shall be first. Look at who he hung out with. Like he befriended tax collectors, and prostitutes, and he kissed lepers.

SEVERSON:

She is traveling Europe and the United States this fall, promoting her book, and preaching that we are all both sinners and saints.

For Religion & Ethics NewsWeekly, I'm Lucky Severson in Denver.

About the Author

Lucky Severson started out as a
reporter in local television in Salt Lake
City. He then went to work as a
correspondent for NBC News at home
and abroad. He hosted a popular
program on the Discovery Channel
called *Invention* before working 20
years as a correspondent for a program
on PBS called *Religion & Ethics
Newsweekly.* Severson earned a
bachelor's degree from the University
of Utah and a Masters of Studies in Law from the Yale Law School.
He is the recipient of numerous national awards including two
Emmys.